"This insightful boo[k] ... [a]nd courage of
women who ... [in]carceration. By
raising up the[ir] ... [str]uggles, this book
makes an imp[ortant] ... [t] to end prisons as
we know the[m]

— Michelle [Alexander], [s]cholar and author
of [The New Jim Crow: Mass Incarceration in the Ag]e of Colorblindness

"Too often we hear accounts of the atrocities that take place behind prison walls without also hearing about the acts of resistance that inevitably accompany them. Victoria Law's important book illuminates these under reported stories of individual and collective organizing by women in prison and encourages all of us to work in solidarity across prison walls to create a world that no longer includes the prison industrial complex."

— Angela Y. Davis, author of *Abolition Democracy: Beyond Prison, Torture, and Empire* and professor emerita of the History of Consciousness Department, UC Santa Cruz

"One of the ironies of the USA's failed experiment in mass incarceration is the relative invisibility of the more than 2.4 million kept behind bars. We sometimes catch fleeting glimpses of the statistics, or of skewed and sordid details via news or 'reality' crime shows, but rarely are the stories of the incarcerated truly told. Nowhere is this truer than with women. Though they remain a relatively small fraction of the incarcerated, the women's prison population has exploded in recent years, and the captured are— like their male counterparts—the young, the poor and people of color. And so too, further marginalized, hidden, and buried alive in the tombs that we call prisons.

Resistance Behind Bars illuminates the stories of the struggles of these women at last—of their efforts to not merely survive the violence and degradation of prison, but to organize at the intersections of race, class and gender, to build a community of resistance amidst the most alienating of circumstances. Victoria Law boldly shines the light and breaks the silence with her exhaustive research, her attention to both the personal and political, and yes, calls us—with the imprisoned women whose stories she shares, always with so much passion and respect—to 'a world without cages.'"

— Nancy A. Heitzeg, professor of sociology and critical studies of race and ethnicity at St. Catherine University and editor of Criminal Injustice at CriticalMassProgress.com

"A straightforward examination of the multiple harms that incarcerated women experience and the women's dynamic resistance to everyday systemic indifference and control. Law challenges both prison and patriarchy, each of which would erase women's agency. *Resistance Behind Bars* refuses to let women prisoners remain unseen and unheard. Instead, it encourages us to think deeply and critically about our own responsibility to redesign a social landscape on which coercion and confinement—and especially punishment for profit—will eventually fade away."

— Patricia O'Brien, associate professor, University of Chicago, and book editor of *Affilia: Journal of Women and Social Work*

"Organizing and community-building are not words one normally associates with women's prisons. *Resistance Behind Bars* will change that. A thorough and compelling work, *Resistance Behind Bars* weaves statistics and personal stories to portray the grim realities of life inside women's prisons. By providing examples of how incarcerated women work to change these conditions, it shatters myths of female passivity and preconceptions of what resistance looks like."

— Ayelet Waldman, editor of *Inside this Place, Not of It: Narratives from Women's Prisons*

"Victoria Law brings her characteristic—and remarkable—passion, personal experience, keen political analysis, courage, and great heart to this new edition of *Resistance Behind Bars*, an urgently needed and essential resource for all of us who want to learn more about and work to dismantle the structural evil of mass incarceration in the United States. Her intersectional approach, which clearly identifies the intersections of racism, gender violence, and heterosexism, informed by an unshakeable commitment to the human dignity and well-being of the prisoners who inspire her work, make this a unique and invaluable tool for crafting a politics rooted not only in resistance but relentlessly persistent visions of social and economic transformation. The focus on women and gender violence helps breathe new life into work and analysis around prisoner advocacy and prison abolition that too often has been framed through an exclusively male lens. We're all in this struggle together—but it is a struggle that demands close attention to the specificities of prisoner experience, rooted in those intersections of race, gender, gender identity/expression, sexuality, and class. Law's book is a brilliant and highly accessible contribution to the burgeoning movement that challenges and proposes to dismantle not only processes of criminalization but the bleak, inhumane nature of the prison industrial complex in its entirety."

— Kay Whitlock, coauthor of *Queer (In)Justice: The Criminalization of LGBT People in the United States*

"*Resistance* offers us a much-needed, much broader and nuanced definition of resistance—a woman's definition based on the real material conditions of women. I hope that when one reads about the experiences of women prisoners' organizing and resistance, the reader, both woman and man, will begin to glimpse the possibilities and necessity of such forms as we continue to struggle for a more just and equal world free from all forms of oppression. If women worldwide are unable to liberate themselves, human liberation will not be possible."

— Marilyn Buck, anti-imperialist political prisoner, activist, poet and artist

"Finally! A passionately and extensively researched book that recognizes the myriad ways in which women resist in prison, and the many particular obstacles that, at many points, hinder them from rebelling. Even after my own years inside, I learned from this book. Law breaks the AIDS barrier, recognizing and recording prisoner organizing on HIV as resistance against stigma and medical malpractice in the prison system."

— Laura Whitehorn, former political prisoner

"Constituting 6% of the U.S. prison and jail population, but over 130,000 in number, and growing, women are an all but invisible segment of the prison population. The issues unique to women, and their behind-bars struggle for justice and equality, are even more ignored by mainstream media than that of their male counterparts. *Resistance Behind Bars* is a long-needed and much awaited look at the struggles, protest and resistance waged by women prisoners. Excellently researched and well documented, this incisive book brings to light aspects of imprisonment unique to women, how the gender-common issues of captivity impact women and the response, protest and resistance to captivity by women. Highly recommended for anyone interested in the modern American gulag."

— Paul Wright, former prisoner, founder/editor of *Prison Legal News*, and coeditor of *The Celling of America: An Inside Look at the US Prison Industry, Prison Nation: The Warehousing of America's Poor* and *Prison Profiteers: Who Makes Money from Mass Incarceration*

"Repression tries not only to crush but to quiet. But as Vikki Law shows in this multifaceted book, all that is unseen is not absent. Guided by years of anti-prison organizing and a palpable feminist practice, Law documents the many ways women challenge the twin forces of prison and patriarchy, each trying to render women invisible. In the face of attempts at erasure, women prisoners resist to survive and survive to resist. We would do well to pay attention."

— Dan Berger, author of *Outlaws of America: The Weather Underground and the Politics of Solidarity*

"Written in regular English, rather than academese, yet full of fire, this is an impressive work of research and reportage. I hope you're able to get this to a greater audience, and that it sparks awareness and resistance. Well done!"

— Mumia Abu-Jamal, political prisoner and author of *Live From Death Row* and *We Want Freedom: A Life in the Black Panther Party*

"By documenting the myriad rebellions of the most despised and abused, Law has fulfilled a task long deferred by prison activists. A meditation on the 'weapons of the weak' that challenges dominant conceptions of what constitutes resistance and liberation, *Resistance Behind Bars* deserves a wide readership not only among those disturbed by mass incarceration, but by all students of the human spirit in the face of adversity."

— Daniel Burton-Rose, author, *Guerrillas in Our Midst: The George Jackson Brigade and the Anti-capitalist Underground of the 1970s*, coeditor, *The Celling of America: An Inside Look at the U.S. Prison Industry*

"Victoria Law's eight years of research and writing, inspired by her unflinching commitment to listen to and support women prisoners, have resulted in an illuminating effort to document the dynamic resistance of incarcerated women in the United States. Her work focuses not only on renowned political prisoners, but on the lives of ordinary women of all colors and ages, many being mothers separated from their children. Law makes clear that besides their myriad means of struggle and mutual assistance, they have one thing in common: they are poor and working- class, without the resources needed to achieve what passes for justice in the United States. A prison abolitionist herself, the author is well aware that in that long fight, women prisoners deserve support and honor in their daily efforts."

— Roxanne Dunbar-Ortiz, historian, feminist, indigenous rights activist, author, most recently of *Roots of Resistance: History of Land Tenure in New Mexico*

"There are too few books written about womyn in prison. Many focus on these womyn as victims only. It's a fact that a huge percentage have been abused as children or by husbands and certainly by the so-called justice system that overpunishes and neglects their every basic human need. But this book is different. Its focus is on the herstorical resistance of womyn prisoners! Not just resistance to their local jailers but often resistance to the prison-industrial complex and the 'masters of unreason' who own and profit from it. This is necessary information for all of us to have in our consciousness, especially our abolitionist consciousness."

— Bo (r.d.brown), former political prisoner, founding mother of Out of Control: Lesbian Committee to Support Women Political Prisoners and volunteer with the Prison Activist Resource Center

RESISTANCE
BEHIND BARS

THE STRUGGLES OF
INCARCERATED WOMEN

BY VICTORIA LAW

Second Edition

Resistance Behind Bars:
The Struggles of Incarcerated Women
By Victoria Law

ISBN: 978-1-60486-583-7
Library of Congress Control Number: 2012913619
Copyright © 2009 and 2012 Victoria Law
This edition copyright © 2012 PM Press
All Rights Reserved

PM Press
PO Box 23912
Oakland, CA 94623
www.pmpress.org

Illustrations by Rachel Galindo

Layout and design by Jason Justice:

www.justicedesign.com

Second Edition
10 9 8 7 6 5 4 3 2

Printed in the USA on recycled paper by the Employee
Owners of Thomson-Shore in Dexter, Michigan.
www.thomsonshore.com

Earlier portions of this work have been published in *Turning
the Tide*, *Women in Action* and on the website *Women and
Prison: A Site for Resistance*.

Earlier versions of "Unlikely Communities," "Barriers to Basic
Care," and "Women's Work" were originally published in
Clamor magazine; earlier versions of "Breaking the Silence"
were published in *Punk Planet* and *off our backs*.

Contents

Introduction[1]

I was arrested in Baltimore in May 1985 and spent the next nine months in the Baltimore City Jail.[2] The glass in most of the windows in the women's section had been broken long before, and, as the weather grew colder, the barred windows were covered over by taped-on garbage bags. Incoming prisoners got nothing more than a tiny bar of soap, a toothbrush and one raggedy housedress. It was not uncommon to see, in January, women still dressed in the hot pants and tank tops they'd been wearing when they were arrested months earlier.

I found myself living among the poorest of the poor: women, many of whom were unable to pay their small bails for minor charges such as petty theft, drug possession, sex work or simple assault. Most of the time I was the only white person in the women's jail—including every guard. Aside from me, only a few administrators, a nurse, and the nun who provided spiritual counseling were white.

Jail food was barely edible. Sometime in late August, when I was summoned back to court, I overheard the U.S. marshals—who hadn't

---

1 Susie Day provided extensive, invaluable editing and assistance in preparation of this introduction.

2 I was arrested in the "Resistance Conspiracy Case," in which six of us were charged with conspiracy to bomb several government buildings that were symbols of U.S. racism and imperialism, including the Capitol Building after the U.S. invasion of Grenada and shelling of Lebanon in 1983. I served a little over 14 years in prison as a result.

seen me since my arrest—gossiping, debating whether I was on hunger strike or had some rapidly progressing disease, so much weight had I lost. I was subsisting largely on apples (our fresh fruit) and pretzels (purchased from the commissary). Vegetables were virtually nonexistent; exotic delicacies such as tuna salad on lettuce appeared only once during my entire time there.

No surprise that every woman in that jail eagerly awaited Thanksgiving. "Turkey," we told each other, "they have to give us turkey!"

Dawned the day, and with it, the first disappointment: No coffee at breakfast. The coffee urns had been loaned, we were told, to the Salvation Army for their feed-the-poor Thanksgiving meal. When we grumbled, the guards told us we were stingy and ungrateful. Didn't we want to help the homeless?

Finally, came dinner, the big meal we'd been anticipating. Yes—turkey! Quickly, we formed an eager, obedient food line. And then we in the back started to hear loud thumps as the first women received their turkey. We quickly realized where the thumps were coming from: the food service workers were dumping on each passing metal tray one huge, gristly, stringy turkey leg. Dinosaur legs. Impenetrable. I have very strong teeth, but I was unable to bite into any part of the leg (of course, our utensils were plastic and never included knives). For many of the women who had few or no teeth at all, those turkey legs might as well have been rocks.

We were hungry, yes—but even more, we were crushed. We'd made the mistake prisoners should never make: hoping. Hope for decent treatment, for anything sensible or caring from a prison administration.

But six or seven of us had, some weeks earlier, already begun gathering to talk about whether we could do anything to improve our lot. And a few days later, this inmate council met. We griped, then discussed the disheartening prospect of the same kind of meal come Christmas. What should we do?

Always the hothead, I insisted we should all take our trays and, at a given signal, throw the rock-hard legs on the floor and march out chanting something defiant.

But the other women had a different idea. My plan, they told me, would get us all locked down for Christmas, so we couldn't have visits or make phone calls. And the guards would beat us up (another common occurrence in the jail, where there were rules for prisoners but not so much for "corrections officers"). Outvoted, I got with the program but privately bemoaned what I saw as their less-than-militant strategy: We would boycott the prison meal and have our own Christmas party.

Fast forward to Christmas day. Using our monthly food-package allotment of chips, pretzels, candy and crackers from our families; organizing donations from civilian workers (the medical staff, the traveling librarian, the nun) and some unusually friendly guards who had been neighbors of some of the prisoners, we arranged a calorie-heavy feast. Even better, someone from the civilian staff—I never found out who—made us some punch with an alcoholic kick. Another staff member brought in some leftover cold cuts and a boom box. And we partied.

I was amazed, not only by how much fun the party was, what a great a time we had, the upscale food (and drink!), but even more by the spirit among us. Not just festive; it was resilient, rebellious, proud. We realized in the days following that we had won a round: the prison administration was shaken by our ability to pull it off, and their realization that we didn't have to depend on them. We had, in my more political terms, "resisted." Wow.

This is what the book you're beginning is about: Resistance. Not necessarily the militant kind you might think of when you hear the word. Not so much the fist-in-the-air riots and strikes, but the simple, robust fabric of survival so often woven by women prisoners. In that fabric can be found rich, textured lessons about solidarity, social change, political evolution—about how human beings and society as a whole can transform.

•••

Over the past decade, the fight for prison justice has become integral to the more general movement for social justice. Every city, it seems, has seen the birth of not-for-profits offering support to prisoners, and proposals for reform of the criminal justice system. Books, magazines and online articles appear every day to discuss the subject. Most recently, I have been part of a broad and varied group of prison justice advocates, many of us formerly incarcerated, involved in the Occupy Wall Street movement. The size and enthusiasm of our group continues to exhilarate me.

Yet the prison statistics continue to grow depressingly familiar.

The United States, with 5% of the world's population, holds 25% of its prisons. There are more than seven million people under the jurisdiction of the U.S. courts or prison system, including 2.4 million people behind bars. There are at least eight times as many people in prison now as there were in 1970. There are 25,000 prisoners nationally in solitary confinement, held for years in conditions condemned as a human rights abuse under international law.

And the post-9/11 "war on terror" continues to terrorize Muslim communities, jailing many people for long terms, based on the word of a cynical informant or actions staged by a provocateur. The recent tides of anti-immigrant sentiment and the arrest, confinement and deportation of "illegal" immigrants who have already served jail time for minor, long-past offenses, have connected the prison justice activists to activists of immigrant communities, fighting for their human rights. And radicals working for the release of some one hundred U.S. political prisoners—former Black Panther Party members and others whose cases stem from their involvement in or solidarity with movements for Black, Puerto Rican, Mexicano and Native American liberation, or from the animal rights and environmentalist movements—have begun to link their efforts with those of millions of prisoners held for long sentences in despicable conditions.

But you don't have to be an activist in New York City and other urban areas, where police regularly stop and frisk young people of color, to have recognized a "pipeline" extending from inner city schools directly to jails and prisons, systematically funneling young people from oppressed communities into the prison system.

Michelle Alexander's book, *The New Jim Crow: Mass Incarceration in the Age of Colorblindness*, sums up many of these trends. Alexander compellingly argues that prisons and the government's "war on drugs" have provided a new way to disenfranchise Black communities. *The New Jim Crow* has helped make clear the central role that the prison system plays in maintaining white supremacy and racism. In doing so, it has helped the prison justice movement grow in size and focus.

Missing from Alexander's book, though, are women. It's true that, compared to the massive number of men behind bars, women prisoners constitute only a small segment —but this is a segment that has swelled exponentially in proportion to the numbers of men.

One reason why we, as women, are frequently missing from prison justice efforts, and from Alexander's book, is our comparatively small number. But in neglecting women in prison, we forfeit a closer look and more intimate understanding of the ways incarceration destroys human beings and communities. We also lose an understanding of how resistance can develop and grow, both inside the walls and out.

Where Alexander analyzes the ways in which mass incarceration criminalizes Black people and attempts to reestablish (both inside prisons and beyond) the disempowerment and disenfranchisement of Jim Crow, Victoria Law's *Resistance Behind Bars: The Struggles of Incarcerated Women* scrutinizes a system of incarceration designed to damage poor people by undermining the women of their communities.

•••

The first sections of Law's book, which you hold in your hands, describe the myriad everyday ways in which women prisoners are suppressed.

The threat—and reality—of sexual abuse by male guards, the lack of educational opportunities (even more extreme than in men's prisons), and the separation of mothers from their children, for example, result in damage not only to women and their children, but to their entire communities, as well. "Prison health care"—an oxymoron if ever there was one—endangers women prisoners' reproductive health—and often their psychological balance. At least thirty states, for instance, still insist on shackling women prisoners during childbirth.

For me, one of the most damaging and nearly invisible forms of sexual abuse was the daily pat-searches by male guards. On a regular basis in my years in federal prisons, I was forced to stand still and allow men to touch my body in ways that would have automatically provoked me to fight back if I had been outside of prison. But as long as I was labeled with that federal prison number, such self-defense would have gotten me an assault charge adding five years to my sentence. (Repeated legal challenges have proved unable to stop this practice in federal prisons.)

These means of control affect the women themselves, but almost as directly, they attack health of their families on the outside. When women are punished by incarceration, their family and children's lives receive the damage too.

The omnipresent threats by prison administrations to stop children from visiting their mothers in prison, or to cut off children's phone calls, can provide a potent tool to quash any objections women prisoners may feel empowered to express. Such threats are not only wielded by prison administrators whenever women confront them with demands for better conditions; they also hang unstated over any thought a woman might have of lodging a complaint about her treatment.

Because of the relatively small population of women in state and federal prison systems, women's prisons are few and—more significant—far between. Many women are already incarcerated miles from their families, making visits hard at best. Separating large numbers of Black women far from their families robs entire communities of mothers, disrupting the next generation and the hope of the future. When mass incarceration is able to tear apart populations of color in such truly elemental ways, the chances that this country might again see the massive uprisings of resistance that characterized the civil rights movement grow dim. And the long-lasting damage women carry after release—perhaps a result of the sexual degradation experienced behind bars—can deliver lasting damage to community efforts at advancement.

Another reason women prisoners are generally absent from discussions of prison justice is that our few efforts to fight back are less visible. The resistance of male prisoners —things like prison rebellions, strikes and takeovers—are usually newsworthy and recorded. The threat of resistance from male prisoners is often met with extreme and overwhelming physical brutality. In contrast, acts of resistance of women prisoners—and the system's reaction to such resistance— generally pass unnoticed. Less dramatic, less violent, less newsworthy.

•••

When Victoria Law, in her studies of prison rebellions, found a near-complete absence of any mention or discussion of the ways in which women fight back against their incarceration, she undertook the study that evolved into this book. The examples of resilience and survival in the following pages convincingly confute the belief that women prisoners don't question their incarceration. From learning and helping each other to file grievances, to refusing to allow another woman prisoner to be physically abused, the women in this book resist and survive. Examples of their defiance show us the essence of what resistance is—not only how it happens, but the lasting contribution each unique, ingenious act of standing up for one's own dignity can make to an entire tide of social upheaval.

Our Christmas rebellion at Baltimore City Jail, for example, expressed something profound about the ways in which women counter the conditions of imprisonment, and what can be learned from our resistance. That Christmas party was not a one-shot deal, a clever tactic.

It was part of a process, and it built a basis for community that changed the women's section of the Baltimore City Jail way beyond the twelve days of Christmas.

To pull off the party, we had to change. Accustomed to operating and surviving individually, we had to rise above our sense of self, becoming brighter, more connected beings. In our capitalist culture, competition is the default psychological mode for survival; and in prison, scarcity, the impulse to push ahead in line, grab and hoard—be the first or you end up with nothing—is even greater. But this time, generosity and cooperation overtook competition. Trust flowered to supplant suspicion. Sisterhood was not only powerful, it was transformative. Each of us found ourselves profoundly altered by the experience.

Women prisoners have little in the way of bargaining chips to use while incarcerated. We were generally far smaller and physically weaker than the male guards who watched us around the clock. We had to learn skills of communication and negotiation. We could not threaten to hurt them, nor to stage dangerous physical resistance. The two "riots" I experienced during my years in federal prison consisted of some faked fire alarms, including perhaps a few actual trashcan fires. Hardly threatening to the armed power of the prison guard.

We had only two things to wrest from our captors the few benefits we could win—things like having hot water restored, or getting our visitors approved; like being permitted to conduct educational sessions and counseling on HIV and hepatitis C, or limiting male guards' observation of women changing clothes or using the toilet. Those two things were our collective will to resist and our humane intelligence.

It's common to find women who have developed the ability to frame an argument for what they need, or the ability to represent articulately their own demands. They've done this during their years in prison. It's equally common to find women who have learned to read, write and interpret various aspects of the law during years inside, acquiring skills and confidence they lacked when they were arrested. Acquisition of these skills, it seems needless to say, happened not as a benefit of incarceration but in spite of it.

Men in prison certainly possess these powers as well, and it would be a misreading of this book to think that the processes and techniques Law describes apply exclusively to women behind bars. But, in the absence of the physical threat men are able to pose to their incarceration, women have developed and expanded these means of resistance. And from that, we can all benefit.

In the process of developing collective resistance, several things happen. One, of course, is the building of trust, of effective means of negotiation, and of robust relationships among individuals. Even more significant, I think—and the heart of the book you are about to read—is that, during the course of survival in prison, women change individually, transforming themselves from submissive victims to active, educated agents.

But the collective process that occurs is more than the sum of its individual parts. To have the shared strength to defy humiliation and injustice behind bars—without being obliterated in the attempt— women prisoners create bonds that result in a subversion of the very values that build prisons in the first place. They develop a culture that is fundamentally and thrillingly subversive. It is subversive not only to the prison system itself, which outlaws things like sharing (prisoners are regularly charged with possessing or giving something "of value" to another prisoner) and loving (touching is most often forbidden; in some situations even hugging another woman prisoner is an act of resistance, with possible consequences). It is also fundamentally anti-capitalist, rejecting individualism for the combined power of the group. This culture is often intensely democratic, challenging the model of organization based on a few leaders and many followers.

•••

During some of the hardest points of my own incarceration, I felt not only that the world at large did not know about the suffering of prisoners, but more painfully, that it did not care. No one knew when a guard withheld my food or access to a telephone for a critical phone call to my father when he was dying. No one knew that my cellmate and dear friend had been humiliated in the process of giving the regular urine samples we were required to supply to ensure the absence of drug use. She was made to strip naked, then stand on one leg, raise the other and pee into a cup. Like a dog.

The invisibility of such degradation makes it that much worse. We begin to think of ourselves as unworthy, deserving of such treatment. The suffering becomes internalized and harder to heal from.

So when I read this book, I nearly wept with relief. I felt that finally someone had seen what we endured. Equally important, someone saw and respected our myriad attempts to refuse our own degradation. I hope that as you read, you will want to participate in building the means to help further the battle prisoners wage for their own humanity. And for that of our entire society.

To be truly radical, to create that new world we hope is possible, we have to subvert the values of the world we inhabit now. That world, to limit the discussion for the moment to the United States, is characterized markedly by the prison system.

I find it hard to put this into words. So here's what I want you to do in order to understand what I'm trying to say. Read this book.

Laura Whitehorn edited *The War Before: The True Life Story of Becoming a Black Panther, Keeping the Faith in Prison, & Fighting for Those Left Behind*, by Safiya Bukhari (The Feminist Press, New York, 2010; feministpress.org). Since her release from prison in 1999, she has lived in New York City with her partner Susie Day. She is an editor at a magazine for people living with HIV/AIDS and works for the release of all U.S. held political prisoners.

Author's Introduction

When I was 15, my friends started going to jail. Chinatown's gangs were recruiting in the high schools in Queens and, faced with the choice of stultifying days learning nothing in overcrowded classrooms or easy money, many of my friends had dropped out to join a gang. One by one they landed in Rikers Island, an entire island in New York City devoted to pretrial detainment for those who cannot afford bail.

Each week I took the M101 bus from Queens Plaza to visit them. Sometimes I brought them the books that I had just finished reading.

When I was 16, I almost followed in their footsteps. The unspoken Chinatown rule was that boys held the guns and girls were simply girlfriends. Somehow I was allowed to be an exception.

My initiation—an armed robbery—turned into an arrest. I was sent to the Tombs, the holding area for those awaiting arraignment in Manhattan's criminal court. All of the adult women I met had been arrested for prostitution; the three other teenagers with whom I shared cells had been arrested for unarmed assault.[1]

Because it was my first arrest—and probably because 16-year-old Chinese girls who get straight As in school did not seem particularly menacing—I was eventually let off with probation.

That experience, coupled with the hours spent each week in the Rikers waiting room, pushed me to think about prison. Getting to know the wives, girlfriends, and mothers whom I saw visiting their menfolk each week pushed me to think about who goes to jail and why. Seeing how my friends devoured the reading material I brought in, got their GEDs and, until the 1994 Crime Bill cut Pell grants to prisoners, pursued a college education, pushed me to think about the circumstances that propelled my friends and others towards jail.

During this time, I also discovered radical politics. I discovered groups and literature espousing prison abolition. These analyses—coupled with what I had seen firsthand—made sense, steering me to work towards the dismantling, rather than the reform, of the prison system. At the same time, the countless hours spent first on Rikers Island and then in the upstate prison visiting rooms demonstrated the need to support those currently inside, even if the goal was the elimination of the system that caged them.

And so I helped start a program that sent free books to prisoners nationwide. I did support work for men organizing within their prisons. I co-curated a prisoner art show to draw attention to incarceration.

In college, I spent a semester researching current prisoner organizing and resistance. At the end of that semester, I looked at what I had gathered and realized that, with the exception of one story, everything was about men. Where were the women?

"Women don't organize," I was told again and again.

I refused to believe it. I began to search for stories—and women— who would disprove this assertion. I found mentions of lawsuits and, using the various state department of corrections' websites, looked up their addresses and wrote them letters asking if they would share their experiences with me. And—not wanting to take without giving back—I offered to send them books and to look up resources and legal cases for them.

Some of the women responded. They shared their stories, which were both painful and inspiring, but also contradicted the notion that women passively accept their conditions of confinement.

I wrote another paper. I realized that these stories—of both injustice and resistance—needed to be heard by more people, but the demands of a new baby, combined with a full-time job and the need to finally finish college, prevented me from acting upon that realization at the time. I handed in my paper and sent a copy to Anthony Rayson, a prison abolitionist and zinester whose prisoner zines had provided me with the addresses of some of the first women I had contacted. He, in turn, handed out copies at a talk he gave. Someone from the Austin, Texas chapter of the Anarchist Black Cross Network took a copy, turned it into a pamphlet and began distributing it.

In the meantime, one of the women I had been writing asked if I would help her. "I want to do a zine," she wrote. "I want people to read about the injustices here and our struggles. Will you help me put it out?"

How could I say no?

I collected stories from the women with whom I'd been in contact, typed their tales and spent hours laying out, copying and collating *Tenacious: Art and Writings from Women in Prison*.

My paper-turned-pamphlet made the rounds of Anarchist Black Cross chapters and other prison abolitionist groups. *Tenacious* hit infoshops and zine distributors. Both heightened awareness not only about incarcerated women's issues, but also women's actions to challenge and change the injustices they faced on a daily basis. Hoping to spread awareness outside prison activist circles, I fleshed out sections of my paper into articles for activist publications like *Clamor*, *Punk Planet*, and *off our backs*.

When Ramsey Kanaan and PM Press expressed interest in publishing this work as a book, I wrote to every woman who had ever shared her observations and stories with me and asked permission to include them in the book. To ensure that I was representing their struggles accurately and to give them the opportunity to add, update or delete any of the tales they did not want to share with the public, I sent each woman draft after draft of the chapters her voice and experience(s) appeared in. All had the option to ask me to omit certain anecdotes; none did, although some requested that I not use their real names.

This book is the result of seven and a half years of reading, writing, listening and supporting women in prison. Each of these chapters focuses on an issue that the women themselves have identified as important.

This book should not be mistaken for a call for more humane or "gender responsive" prisons. It is a long-overdue recognition of the actions that incarcerated women themselves have taken and are taking to challenge the injustices and abuses that accompany imprisonment.

Activist, advocate and former prisoner Angela Davis wrote, "As important as some reforms may be—the elimination of sexual abuse and medical neglect in women's prisons, for example—frameworks that rely exclusively on reforms help to produce the stultifying idea that nothing lies beyond the prison."[2]

However, while we strive for a better world—one in which prisons are obsolete—we must not forget about the more than two million people who are currently locked away. We need to acknowledge and address their daily realities, as well as recognize the dangers they face when they speak out about these realities, while also questioning **why** it is necessary to have this system.

As I struggle to articulate women prisoners' resistance and prison abolition, my seven-year-old daughter sits next to me folding a purple piece of paper for one of the women who has shared her stories with me.

"She can't get origami," I tell her.

"Why can't she get origami?" she asks, continuing to fold.

I'm stumped. I don't actually know how a child's paper swan threatens the safety and security of the prison.

"Why can't she get origami?" my daughter repeats.

"I dunno. 'Cuz it's prison," I mumble and turn back to my own paper.

Less than two minutes later, she has taped the edges of the paper together to form a pentagon. She has written a short note on the front. Proudly she hands it to me.

"I don't think she can get things that have tape," I say, handing it back to her. Her smile disappears and I contemplate including it anyway, even if it means the entire envelope will be returned.

My daughter finds scissors and cuts everything except the front of the pentagon, which she hands to me.

"There," she says.

Our five-minute exchange reminds me of why we need to aim for a world without prisons and its senseless rules and restrictions, a world in which no small child has to comprehend why she cannot send a simple folded giraffe to her mother's friend. Or why her own mother cannot receive her homemade Valentine's Day card because she drew it in crayon.[3] Or why her mother has to spend her birthday—and every other day—locked far away from her.

But while striving for that world, we need to also reach in, make contact with those who have been isolated by prison walls and societal indifference and listen to those who are speaking out, like many of the women who have shared their stories within this book. Because abolishing prisons will not happen tomorrow, next week or even next year, we need to break through these barriers, communicate, work with and support women who are in resistance today.

OVERVIEW

Although women in prison comprise nearly 7% of the U.S. prison population, their numbers are increasing more rapidly than those of their male counterparts: between 1990 and 2000, the number of women in prison rose 108%, from 44,065 to 93,234. The male prison population grew only 77% during that same time period.[4] As of June 30, 2009, there were 114,979 women behind bars.[5]

Many of these women defy commonly held stereotypes of prisoners as violent and predatory males:

▷ Women of color are overrepresented in the prison system:
The Bureau of Justice Statistics found that one in every 300 Black women, one in every 704 Latina women, and one in every 1,099 white women have been to prison. The incarceration rate for Black women was 3.7 times the rate of white women. The rate for Latinas was 1.5 times more than that of white women.[6]

▷ This overrepresentation is caused, in large part, by racial profiling, not by an increase in crime among low-income African Americans and Latinos: policing policies have disproportionately targeted inner-city African-American and Latino neighborhoods. Within the past decade, many police departments have increased the use of "stop and frisk" tactics, in which regular patrol or special tactical officers stop and question those they perceive as acting suspiciously and often pat down the person for weapons. These tactics often disproportionately target people of color. An April 2005 study by the U.S. Department of Justice found that African Americans and Latinos are three times as likely as whites to be searched, arrested, threatened or subdued with force when stopped by the police.[7]

▷ Class also impacts the likelihood of going to prison: only 40% of all incarcerated women had been employed full-time before incarceration. Of those, most had held low-paying jobs: a study of women under supervision (prison, jail, parole or probation) found that 2/3 had never held a job that paid more than $6.50 per hour.[8] Approximately 37% earned less than $600 per month.[9]

▷ Approximately 30% had been receiving public assistance before being arrested.[10]

▷ Only 40% had obtained their GED or high school diploma before arrest.[11]

▷ At least 65% report being mothers to children under the age of 18.[12]

▷ The majority of women in prison are convicted of nonviolent crimes, mostly property and drug offenses.[13] In 2007, the Bureau of Justice Statistics found that nearly 65% of women in state prisons are incarcerated for drug, property or public order offenses.[14]

▷ Unlike men's substance abuse, women's substance abuse is often tied into their past histories of trauma and abuse. (More than half of the women in state prisons and local jails report having been physically and/or sexually abused in the past).[15] The Bureau of Justice found that women were three times more likely than men to have been physically or sexually abused prior to incarceration.[16]

Overview

▷ In 1973, New York State passed the Rockefeller Drug Laws, which required a sentence of 15 years to life for anyone convicted of selling two ounces or possessing four ounces of a narcotic, regardless of circumstances or prior history.[17] That year, only 400 women were imprisoned in New York State. As of January 1, 2001, there were 3,133. Over 50% had been convicted of a drug offense and 20% were convicted solely of possession.[18] Other states passed similar laws, causing the number of women imprisoned nationwide for drug offenses to rise 888% from 1986 to 1996.[19]

▷ Unequal sentencing laws also play a role: Although crack and powder cocaine have the same active ingredient, crack is marketed in less expensive quantities and in lower-income communities. Until August 3, 2010, a person convicted of possessing 5 g of crack received a mandatory five-year sentence, the same penalty as a person possessing 500 g of cocaine. In 2010, the sentencing disparity was changed from 100:1 to 18:1.[20]

Prison scholars and activists have noted this dramatic increase, writing books and organizing conferences and symposia to examine the causes, conditions and consequences of female incarceration. However, ways in which incarcerated women have individually and collectively challenged these conditions have largely been omitted from the discourse.

This omission is not new. In the early 1970s, recognizing that prisoners were one of the most marginalized and voiceless populations in America, activists expanded their interests to include those of prisoners and their rights: new, critical analyses of prisons emerged, prisoners' rights organizations and unions were created, and new communications among prisoners, academics and community activists were established.[21] Activist academics also brought university courses inside prisons.[22] However, the focus largely remained on men and their issues.

Women prisoners' voices and concerns were overlooked not only by outside activists but also the politicized male inmates who benefited from the developing prisoner rights movement. While male prisoners gained political consciousness and enjoyed support from outside groups and individuals, these same groups and individuals ignored the female prison population with the exceptions of a few well-known political prisoners such as Angela Davis and Assata Shakur.

Although female incarceration has increased drastically during the past few decades, prevalent ideas of prisoners remain masculine: the term "prisoner" continues to conjure the image of a young, black man convicted of violent crimes such as rape or murder. Politicians seeking votes and media seeking sales play on this representation, whipping the public into hysteria to get tougher on crime and build more prisons. Obviously the public perception of the violent black male felon overlooks the growing number of women imprisoned under the various mandatory sentencing laws passed within the past few decades.[23] Because women do not fit this stereotype, the public, the politicians and the media often choose to overlook them rather than grapple with the seeming paradoxes inherent in women prisoners, who, by virtue of their incarceration, have somehow defied the societal norm of femininity.[24] Such neglect leads to the definition of prison issues as masculine and male-dominated, dismissing prison issues that are distinctly feminine (e.g., the scarcity of sanitary hygiene products, the lack of medical care specifically for women, especially prenatal care, and threats of sexual abuse by guards) and thus any actions that women take to address and overcome these concerns.

Today there is a renewal of interest in prisons and prisoner issues, with a growing body of literature examining female incarceration. However, the new literature largely ignores what the women themselves do to change or protest these circumstances, thus reinforcing the belief that incarcerated women do not organize. Karlene Faith, coordinator of the 1970s Santa Cruz Women's Prison Project, does not bring up examples of women's collective resistance until the second half of her book *Unruly Women*. In *In the Mix: Struggle and Survival in a Women's Prison*, Barbara Owen includes no instances of prisoner organizing despite the fact that her chosen prison, the Central California Women's Facility, had housed Charisse Shumate and many other women who organized to change the facility's appalling health care; their actions resulted in the *Shumate v. Wilson* class-action lawsuit which charged that the abysmal medical care amounted to cruel and unusual punishment.[25] More recently, Julia Sudbury's *Global Lockdown: Race, Gender and the Prison-Industrial Complex* recognized incarcerated women's agency and organizing in other countries, but failed to acknowledge efforts within U.S. prisons. The absence of these tales perpetuates the assumption that women imprisoned in the United States are not actively fighting to challenge or change these conditions.

There have been only two books about organizing among incarcerated women: Juanita Diaz-Cotto's *Gender, Ethnicity and the State* (1996) and the collectively written *Breaking the Walls of Silence: AIDS and Women in a New York State Maximum-Security Prison* (1998). Both focus on women's activism in Bedford Hills Correctional Facility, New York State's maximum-security prison for women. In *Gender, Ethnicity and the State*, Diaz-Cotto details organizing strategies among Latina prisoners between 1970 and 1987. *Breaking the Silence* follows the creation of the AIDS Counseling and Education (ACE) program. Written by many of the women involved in ACE, the book documents the organization's history and shares its curriculum with others seeking to create similar programs in other prisons. However, because many of its writers were still imprisoned at Bedford Hills and because they wanted to avoid jeopardizing the program, it does not frame the formation and continued existence of ACE as an act of collective resistance against existing prison conditions.

Since then, no other book-length work has focused on incarcerated women's activism and resistance.

Literature about women in prison that has emerged in this decade articulates how the needs of incarcerated women differ from those of their male counterparts. It does not, however, examine how these differences either act as obstacles to collective organizing or change the ways in which women organize. It also ignores how these differences prevent outside recognition of female agency. Women in prison face different circumstances during their incarceration and thus have different priorities—and different ways of challenging their conditions—than incarcerated men.[26]

Challenges in Organizing

Approximately half of all incarcerated women have suffered past physical or sexual abuse.[27] A 1999 study by the U.S. Department of Justice found that 57% of women entering state prison and 40% entering federal prison had been physically or sexually abused prior to incarceration. In contrast, only 6% of men entering state prison and 7% entering federal prison had suffered prior physical or sexual abuse.[28] Barrilee Bannister, a former prisoner in Oregon, pointed out, "A lot of women believe themselves to be helpless because of how they were raised, or perhaps because of childhood abuse. I see a lot of women with very low self-esteem and self-worth." Prisons further erode low self-esteem: a woman at the Central California Women's Facility stated, "It is easier for women to get bullied in here. If an officer raises his or her voice to you, some women are petrified. The fear from past abuse comes back and they are scared. Very scared."[29] As a woman incarcerated in Illinois put it, "Do you think women who are conditioned to be subservient to their men (and the world) are going to come to prison and suddenly just grow a backbone ?"[30]

Women prisoners also lack a commonly known history of resistance. While male prisoners can draw on the examples of George Jackson, the Attica uprising and other well-publicized cases of prisoner activism, incarcerated women remain unaware of precedents relevant to them. Virtually none know about the collective organizing that led to the 1974 August Rebellion at New York's Bedford Hills Correctional Facility or the 1975 riot at the North Carolina Correctional Center for Women.

Women who do challenge the system face extreme levels of administrative harassment. "Tricia," a woman in the federal prison system, incurred the wrath of a guard when she attempted to help another woman who had been unfairly sent to the Special Housing Unit (or SHU, a punitive form of segregation). Shortly after, the same guard sent Tricia to the SHU. She then searched her room to create a justification for her placement, throwing out many of her personal belongings, including photos of her children and other family members and items that Tricia had bought from the prison commissary. Although prison staff is not permitted to tamper with or destroy a prisoner's legal documents, the guard also threw away Tricia's papers for her appeal. The guard found files from the chapel that Tricia had been organizing for the chapel's sister. Although both the chaplain and the sister attested that they had authorized Tricia to take the documents, the prison administration refused to release her. After she had spent a month in SHU, the administration finally dropped the charges.[31]

Tricia's experience is not an anomaly. Solitary confinement—euphemistically called "Special Housing Unit" or "SHU", "control units", "administrative segregation" or even "therapeutic segregation", depending on the prison—is increasingly used to isolate and punish prisoners who challenge their conditions of confinement. In the 1960s, with the rise of prisoner organizing, prison officials used segregation or "the hole" to separate politically active prisoners, jailhouse lawyers, nationalists, communists and those they deemed threatening to the daily operations of the prison. George Jackson, for example, spent much time in San Quentin's Adjustment Center for his organizing efforts.

Most female facilities have some form of "the hole." At California's Valley State Prison for Women, the Special Housing Unit consists of eight-foot-by-six-foot cells with blacked-out windows where women are confined for 23 hours a day. Even in their cells, the women have no privacy—toilets are in full view of the cell door windows, guards can look through those windows at any time and male guards often watch the women in the showers. If the women complain, the guards turn off the water.[32] The federal prison at Lexington, Kentucky, opened a control unit specifically for women political prisoners in 1986. It was built underground and painted entirely white. Women were prohibited from hanging anything on the white walls, causing them to begin hallucinating black spots and strings on the walls and floors. Their sole contact with prison staff came in the form of voices addressing them over loudspeakers. Although the unit was shut down in 1988 following an outside campaign and a court decision that determined their placement unconstitutional, the practice of solitary confinement continues today, with jailhouse lawyers and other incarcerated activists often targeted.[33] Often this threat of staff retaliation dissuades others from acting. One woman stated that the level of harassment is "so great that most of your fellow prisoners think that you must be crazy for even attempting to challenge the prison system wrong doings."[34]

Lending to the silence around incarcerated women's resistance, those who do agitate or organize may also hesitate to write about their experiences. Barrilee Bannister in Oregon, Dawn Amos in Colorado, and a California prisoner who wished to remain anonymous have also stated that they are reluctant to write about certain aspects and instances because their letters can be read by prison officials. When Barrilee Bannister attempted to mail a drawing depicting a guard walking away from a prisoner who had obviously been sexually assaulted, the mailroom confiscated it. Bannister received a misconduct report. In the following three months, she was removed from the prison's minimum-security section, placed in medium-security and barred from attending a transition program for which she had previously been approved. She received two additional misconduct reports, one for allegedly making threats against another staff member during a phone conversation and the other for not saving receipts for items she had purchased between 1995 and 1999, years before the prison had been built.[35] Bannister's case, too, is not an anomaly. When "Tricia" attempted to use the Bureau of Prison's new e-mail system to describe certain conditions, prison authorities intercepted her e-mails, then closed her e-mail account. She was also threatened with placement in the SHU.[36]

Women also fear that speaking out or organizing will jeopardize their chances of an earlier release. "Often, you'll hear 'I would do something about it, but I come up for review in ____.' There is a prevalent fear that writing grievances, etc., directly has a negative effect on parole," wrote Dawn Reiser, a woman incarcerated in Texas.

Such fears are not always unfounded. "Having a major misconduct ticket could prevent an inmate from being eligible for a [parole] hearing and could mean she spends another year in prison," stated Deborah LaBelle, an attorney representing Michigan prisoners in a class-action lawsuit against the Michigan Department of Corrections.[37]

In 2001, the day after she testified against guards in a sexual abuse case, Michigan prisoner Robin McArdle received a misconduct ticket for not being on her bunk during count time. The officer who issued the ticket had testified in that same case on the guards' side.

McArdle, who had remained ticket-free during her first eight years in prison, received five misconduct tickets after testifying. These tickets extended her stay in prison by a week.[38]

Similarly, staff members at the Central California Women's Facility warned Marcia Bunney, a plaintiff in the *Shumate v. Wilson* lawsuit, that continuing her legal activities would cost her any chance of obtaining a parole date. "I have been told that I will never leave prison if I continue to fight the system," she wrote.[39]

Invisibility of Organizing

Women both inside and out are often perceived as passive. This perception leads to the dismissal of the fact that women can and do contribute to struggles for change. Just as the civil rights movement of the 1960s and 1970s downplayed the role of women in favor of highlighting male spokesmen and leaders, the prisoners' rights movement has focused and continues to focus on men to speak for the masses. "Something about women who protest bothers many people," observed lois landis, a prisoner at Taycheedah Correctional Institution in Fond du Lac, Wisconsin.[40] Additionally, incarcerated women who raise their voices face an additional burden: they have already defied societal norms by transgressing both laws and acceptable notions of feminine behavior and morality.

While prisons have always been a form of social control, they have also been used to control women's actions and freedom. The early 20th century saw the proliferation of reformatories for women. Women were sent to the reformatory for defying societally approved gender roles: being drunk, engaging in pre- and extramarital sex, contracting a venereal disease, or keeping bad company.[41] These women were seen as even worse than the men who committed the most heinous crimes and, until the advent of the reformatory, were seen as incorrigible.

The reformatory challenged the notion that "fallen women" were irredeemable. As its name indicates, its mission was to "reform" its wards—that is, to reinstill ladylike behavior, good moral character, and perfect domestic skills. Reformatories existed only for women; no such institutions existed for men, who remained unpenalized when they engaged in the same actions.[42]

Although the reformatory—and the ideas behind it—died by the mid 1930s, the moral condemnation of women sentenced to prison continues to influence public perception and policies. In 1994, a warden of an unnamed state prison for women summed up the prevailing attitude towards women prisoners:

> Poor men stick somebody up or sell drugs. To me, as strange as this may sound coming from a warden, that is understandable. I can see how you would make that choice. Women degrade themselves. Selling themselves, you should hear some of the stuff they do. There is no sense of self-respect, of dignity . . . There is something wrong on the inside that makes an individual take up those kinds of behavior and choices.[43]

Women who challenge or resist their conditions of confinement continue to defy proscribed gender roles, often leading to further disdain and dismissal. By protesting, they are further refusing to conform to society's expectation that they will passively accept the conditions of their punishment and refrain from stepping out of their prescribed gender roles again. "Women who protest are looked down upon, while male prisoners who protest are considered heroes by other inmates," stated lois landis.[44]

Researchers, scholars and activists often do not search for acts of defiance among the growing female prison population, often assuming that the silence around women prisoners' agency and activism signifies passive acceptance. "[W]omen inmates themselves have called very little attention to their own situations," wrote Virginia High Brislin in her research on incarcerated mothers during the 1980s. "They are hardly ever involved in violent encounters with officials (i.e. riots), nor do they initiate litigation as often as do males in prison."[45]

Statements such as these reinforce the invisibility of resistance among women prisoners. They also overlook the instances in which women **do** riot and initiate litigation.

In the 1970s, Carol Crooks, a prisoner at the maximum-security Bedford Hills Correctional Facility in New York, initiated a lawsuit against the prison, its warden and several staff members. She claimed that the prison's practice of placing women in segregation without a hearing and refusal to provide 24-hour notice of charges violated their constitutional rights. On July 2, 1974, a court agreed with Crooks, issuing a preliminary injunction, prohibiting the prison from placing women in segregation without 24-hour notice and a hearing of these charges.[46]

The next month five male guards beat Crooks and placed her in segregation. Her fellow prisoners protested by holding seven staff members hostage for two and a half hours. Male state troopers and (male) guards from men's prisons were called to suppress the uprising, resulting in 25 women being injured and 24 women being transferred to Matteawan Complex for the Criminally Insane without the required commitment hearings.[47] Only a long struggle and a lawsuit won their return to Bedford Hills. Because it lasted only two and a half hours and because no one was killed, the story was relegated to a paragraph buried in the back pages of the *New York Times*. Thus, although it occurred at a time when prison issues were still a hot topic for many on the left, the "August Rebellion" remains overlooked by those seeking information on prisoner protests and disruptions.

Similarly, women in a California prison held a "Christmas riot" in 1975: protesting the cancellation of family holiday visits and holiday packages, prisoners gathered in the yard, broke windows, made noise and burned Christmas trees in a "solidarity" bonfire.[48] However, because the impetus for the "riot" was women's lack of access to family during the holidays, an ostensibly "feminine" (and thus less important and less glamorous) concern, and because no one had threatened violence, this act of disruption is even more easily overlooked by those researching prison disturbances.

Women have also disrupted prison life in more recent years: on August 13, 1992, 90 women at the federal prison in Lexington, Kentucky, refused to leave the yard for the prison's afternoon count to protest a lieutenant's assault of a black prisoner the night before. "We sang Bob Marley's 'Stand Up for Your Rights,' and chanted 'Stop Police Brutality,' 'We Want Justice,' 'Let Them Out of Seg,' and 'Figueroa (the lieutenant) Must Go,'" recalled Laura Whitehorn, a political prisoner and participant in the stand-out. "While we demonstrated, we heard shouts of support from the windows of the housing units, and at least two 'all available officers' codes to different units—meaning that the women who had returned to the units for count were doing some kind of support actions too."

The women were handcuffed and taken to segregation. The next day, 12 were transferred to the new women's high-security unit at Marianna, Florida. Others were sent to FCI-Dublin in California. That afternoon, a smaller group of women repeated the stand-out, refusing to leave the yard for the four o'clock count. That night, other women protested by setting small fires in various housing units.[49]

In 1995, following rebellions at Talladega, Allenwood and other federal men's prisons, the federal women's prison in Dublin, California was placed under lockdown. Although there had been no disturbances at that particular prison, FCI Dublin remained under lockdown all weekend and women were forced to go to work that Monday under lockdown conditions. To voice their protest, women began staying away from meals and, that night, set simultaneous trashcan fires in all of the units. Approximately 70 women were sent to administrative segregation and charged with arson and "engaging in a group demonstration."[50]

By ignoring instances such as these, Brislin and others researching and writing about women prisoners' issues reinforce the idea that women do not organize, thus discouraging further research.

While Karlene Faith acknowledges that women have participated in resistance actions, she states that, in the 1970s, incarcerated women "were not as politicized as the men [prisoners], and they did not engage in the kinds of protest actions that aroused media attention." Her assertion dismisses the fact that women **did** engage in similar types of protest actions, which often garnered some media attention.[51] For instance, between 1969 and 1973, there were four "disturbances" at the women's prison in Milledgeville, Georgia.[52] In 1975, women at the North Carolina Correctional Center for Women held a sit-down demonstration to demand better medical care, improved counseling services and the closing of the prison laundry. When prison guards attempted to end the protest by herding the women into the gymnasium and beating them, the women fought back, using volleyball net poles, chunks of concrete and hoe handles to drive the guards out of the prison.[53] Over 100 guards from other prisons were summoned to quell the rebellion.[54] The demonstration also garnered media coverage from radical alternative news sources such as *off our backs* as well as mainstream newspapers such as the *New York Times*.

Instead of claiming that women in prison did not engage in riots and protest actions that captured media attention, scholars and researchers should examine why these acts of organizing fail to attract the same critical and scholarly attention as that given to similar male actions.

Juanita Diaz-Cotto, one of the few scholars to study women prisoners' activism, argues that books written in the past decade often "highlight the role played by women's prison family groups and kinship networks, almost to the complete exclusion of other types of prisoner organization."[55] The emphasis on prison families not only substitutes for research about resistance but also reinforces the stereotype that women's sole concern is to maintain their traditional gender roles.[56] Past research on women prisoners has overwhelmingly favored details of prison family and kinship networks over the more painstaking task of searching out and documenting the less visible instances of resistance. This becomes a self-perpetuating cycle: by highlighting the various family and kinship networks to the exclusion of other forms of organization, scholars have given the impression that this is the only form of organizing within women's prisons, not only silencing the voice of women prisoner activists but also paving the way for others to do the same.

Resistance

Despite fears of administrative reprisals and a lack of outside support, women in prison have found ways to individually and collectively challenge, resist and organize around their conditions of confinement. These ways are often not recognized by outside researchers and are sometimes belittled by other women in prison: "Women prisoners are notorious for complaining amongst themselves or for writing paper complaints to the administration," wrote lois landis, a Wisconsin prisoner, who dismissed such actions as "useless in getting changes within the prison system."[57] While the processes of both verbally complaining and filing grievances may have little effect in changing the conditions of confinement, the fact that women not only utilize them but are "notorious" for doing so indicates that women do not passively accept their circumstances, but attempt to change them in any way possible.

Women's resistance often lacks the glamour and excitement of the prison riots and work strikes for which male prisoners are known.

Overview

Some actions, such as introducing new methods of teaching literacy, can be seen as working with the prison system. A cursory dismissal of such actions overlooks the fact that seemingly non-threatening ideas are still met with suspicion and refusal by prison administrations. As Kathy Boudin, a former prisoner at Bedford Hills, pointed out, "I, like many other prisoners, wanted to be productive and to do something meaningful with my time in prison . . . Yet prison administrators usually limit the amount of responsibility and independence a prisoner can have."[58] The premise of prisons lies in obedience and control. Prisoner-generated programs, projects and groups challenge that premise. Conservative prison administrations do not allow any such initiatives on the part of their prisoners; even more liberal prison administrators, such as Elaine Lord, the former warden at Bedford Hills, remain suspicious, if not hostile, to the educational and group work of their prisoners and make every effort to suppress such initiatives. Incarcerated women have observed that lack of literacy plays a large role in women's lack of protest and resistance. Amos noted that most of the women around her "are very illiterate, they don't even have education to take a pre-GED test, let alone read a law book or even a newsletter about other prisoners and what they have been subjected to. They can hardly comprehend the rules that we have to live under let alone a way of comprehending a way to stand up for their rights."[59] "Elsie," a former prisoner in Illinois, agrees: "I know illiteracy is one of the hindrances to pursuing any relief. We need to educate women about how to write grievances and we need to have available people to help the illiterate and the mentally/emotionally ill prepare grievances regarding their rights."[60] Thus, a seemingly innocuous act, such as encouraging literacy and critical thinking among fellow prisoners, may lead to greater resistance and more widespread agitation against prison injustices.

Other actions are more gender-specific, focusing on issues that, until recently, were not recognized by prisoner rights activists. More than half of all prisoners have left minor children behind. However, maintaining relationships with their children is an obstacle faced more often by women than men. Ninety percent of the time, when a father is imprisoned, his children are cared for by their biological mother. Conversely when a mother goes to prison her children are more likely to be in the care of a grandparent, another non-parent relative or have no one to care for them. An incarcerated mother's children are five times more likely to enter the foster care system, thus increasing her chances of losing legal custody.[61] In addition, because they are fewer in number, women's prisons tend to be located farther from the urban areas where they had lived before their arrests. This distance often makes visits from children more difficult and infrequent. Incarcerated women have worked with prison administrations and outside groups, often churches and other religious institutions and individuals, to maintain contact and legal custody of their children. These actions are often overlooked by prisoner rights activists and scholars both because they are not visibly dramatic, and because the issue of mothers and children is often perceived as less pressing by those accustomed to dealing with male prisoner issues.

Actions such as organizing transportation for prisoners' children, assisting others with their legal work and visiting women in the intensive care unit disrupt prison realities, sometimes leading to more far-reaching change, such as the formation of AIDS counseling and education programs and support groups for domestic violence survivors.

Resistance Behind Bars will highlight issues confronting women in prison, including inadequate medical care, sexual abuse, separation from children, and the lack of educational and work opportunities. It will also show the ways in which the women themselves individually and collectively challenge these conditions. It will explore tactics traditionally employed by male prisoners, such as lawsuits and disruptions, and strategies that women have devised to challenge gender-specific injustices such as maintaining contact and custody of their children and combating sexual abuse.

In 1995, prisoner rights activist and scholar Nancy Kurshan, in her history of female imprisonment, provided a one-page overview of women's resistance from the Civil War until the 1970s. She acknowledged that this one page was not enough: "One topic that has not been adequately researched is the rebellion of women in prison. It is only with great difficulty that any information was found. We do not believe that is because resistance does not occur, but because those in charge of documenting history have a stake in burying herstory. Such a herstory would challenge the patriarchal ideology that insists that women are, by nature, passive and docile."[62]

Resistance Behind Bars expands herstory, challenging readers to re-conceptualize and reframe what is commonly thought of as resistance and emphasizing the voices and actions of the women fighting for change. *Resistance* will hopefully spark further discussion and research into incarcerated women's organizing as well as galvanize outside support for their struggles.

UNLIKELY COMMUNITIES

Breaking the Alienation of Incarceration

When Michigan prisoner Kebby Warner attempted to call her daughter on her fourth birthday, she discovered that the phone number, which she had been calling once a month, was restricted. The reason? Michigan Department of Corrections had started a new phone program with Sprint. Those on a prisoner's telephone list had to pay a minimum of $50 before they could receive a call from their incarcerated loved one. If the outside person was unable or unwilling to pay, Sprint and the prison kept the number restricted.[63] Wittingly or unwittingly, this new system reinforced the sense of isolation and alienation that prisons inflict upon their prisoners.

"Roberta," an incarcerated mother in California, learned of Warner's situation and offered to pay the $50 deposit from her own prison wages. (The pay scale at Roberta's facility ranges from eight to 32¢ per hour.) "I know how it is not to hear your child's voice," she wrote in her offer. "I've been there. And thank God for the kindness of strangers that I was able to talk to them [my children] a few times during the roughest times. I would give it [the deposit] to her [Warner], just let me know if I can and where to send it, okay?"[64]

Although women in prison often complain about the apathy among their peers, giving the impression that there is little to no unity in female facilities, these same women have also demonstrated a willingness to share and help each other in times of need.

Simple Actions

Some acts can be as simple as listening. Six years after Michigan prisoner Kebby Warner lost custody of her daughter, she met a prisoner returning from the hospital after giving birth to her first child. "She was distraught! I felt her pain deep in my soul!" Warner reminded the woman that her parole date was only a few months away, encouraged her to focus on that date and offered to listen if the new mother needed to talk about her feelings. Because they lived on different housing units, Warner made plans to meet her on the yard. "I know she's hurting and I want to be a shoulder that she can cry on," she wrote. [65]

When Oregon prisoner "Boo" was taken to a prison infirmary after turning yellow, Barrilee Bannister made a get-well card and had 80 women sign it.[66] After Boo was released from the infirmary, the women on her unit, seeing how much weight she had lost, shared their food from the canteen with her.[67]

While these actions do not overtly challenge or change Boo's medical condition, the inadequate health care system or a protocol that separates mothers from their newborns, they do break through the sense of isolation that prisons inflict upon their prisoners.

In Colorado's Clear Creek County Jail, women detained on immigration violations are housed with citizen women awaiting trial or sentencing. Although the jails receive money from INS to keep these women, no efforts are made to accommodate their needs, such as translation assistance. Sarah Daniel and RJ, two women awaiting sentencing at Clear Creek, remembered that other women often attempted to help monolingual detainees be understood. Women who spoke both languages, no matter how badly, acted as translators. Those who spoke no Spanish used a Spanish-English dictionary to try to help the Spanish-speaking detainees. RJ, who had taken three years of Spanish in high school, translated for one older Peruvian detainee. "We would also exchange English and Spanish by reading poetry books together," she recalled. While the citizen women's actions did not change the jail's lack of translation assistance, they did help alleviate the exacerbated fear and frustration the monolingual detainees must have felt at their inability to communicate. [68]

When Marcia Bunney first began her 25-to-life sentence in California, the prison routine disoriented her:

> Mealtimes were traumatic because I had somehow acquired the notion that prisoners were assigned to specific eating areas and that using the wrong door to the cafeteria would be cause for a disciplinary report. This fear caused me to avoid most meals for my first few days in the main population until I became acquainted with a woman on my housing unit who recognized my plight. She literally led me by the hand to the cafeteria, as one would a small child. For years afterward, we often went to meals together, sometimes hand in hand as a reminder of the way our friendship had begun.[69]

The action of that one woman helped Bunney begin to overcome not only her fear of prison, but also the effects of years of abuse she had suffered on the outside. Bunney later became a jailhouse lawyer (a prisoner who assists her peers with their legal cases and paperwork).

Larger Effects and Multiplying Resources

Other strategies have had even broader effects. After Kathy Boudin, a prisoner at New York's Bedford Hills Correctional Facility, began utilizing prisoners' interest and concern about AIDS to teach literacy in the Adult Basic Education (ABE) class, her students became aware of themselves as a community—first in the classroom and then in the larger setting of the prison. They not only began to help one another over the stumbling blocks towards literacy, but also used their new-found knowledge of the disease to support and comfort others.[70]

One student told Boudin that a woman on her unit had attempted suicide after learning that she had AIDS. "I'm the one person she told. I know why she tried. She came to me, I'm the person she talks to."

She was not alone—although HIV/AIDS had previously been a shameful and taboo subject, prisoners began to seek out ABE students on their housing units to talk about their concerns, fears and experiences.[71]

Sometimes women's acts of sharing have multiplied available resources, such as when women have assisted their peers with their legal work. After losing custody of her own daughter, Kebby Warner used the knowledge she had gained in the prison law library to assist another prisoner with the legal paperwork that kept her from losing her own child.[72] While in federal prison, Yraida Guanipa used her self-taught legal skills not only to advocate for herself but also to help the women around her with their appeals. "They don't speak the language, they don't see their children, so I have to file motions for them," she stated.[73] Colorado prisoner Dawn Amos, who financed her college education by finding scholarships, did not hoard that information: she helped three other women find and obtain scholarships.[74]

Similarly, "Marg" and "Elsie," in two different Illinois prisons, have assisted women around them with their legal work.[75] This sharing of resources is often reciprocated: when "Elsie" was placed on a suicide watch after engaging in a hunger strike against the unsanitary preparation of food, another woman lent her a pen and paper to write letters to outside supporters.[76] Similarly, when Kebby Warner filed a grievance against a male officer, the woman whom she had helped agreed to hold her paperwork so that prison officials would not "lose" or destroy it during a search or transfer.[77]

In Texas's Hobby Unit, the "old school" jailhouse lawyers took the time to teach new prisoner Helen Caples about the law. Caples used her newfound knowledge to file a lawsuit against the Texas Department of Criminal Justice, challenging its dangerously unsanitary conditions, including maggots in the shower, birds in the chow hall, rats throughout the facility and contaminated drinking water that caused widespread illness. [78]

Creating Programs

In the 1980s, prisoners at New York's maximum-security Bedford Hills Correctional Facility visited the patients with HIV and AIDS isolated at the prison's In-Patient Care Unit (ICU).[79] In doing so, they broke through the isolation and ostracization that ICU patients faced from both their fellow prisoners and their unit's medical staff, who often knew little about the disease and were afraid to have physical contact with their patients. In one instance, fear led to a woman dying alone at ICU with no nurse or guard willing to attend to her needs.[80] These women not only visited the ICU to provide contact and counseling, but also helped bathe and cooked for the patients.[81] These early efforts to combat the stigma and ignorance around HIV/AIDS led to the formation of ACE (AIDS Counseling and Education program). Women organizing around the issue began to feel a sense of responsibility to one another. Later, when the AIDS Institute provided the program with English-language educational materials and certification training, two bilingual prisoners voluntarily sat with ten monolingual Latina prisoners during the entire three-day training, translating eight hours each day.[82]

ACE's community-building is not an anomaly. AIDS peer education programs have often had the effect of creating community among women prisoners. Linda Evans, a political prisoner, used ACE as a model for PLACE, the Pleasanton AIDS Education and Counseling program at California's Federal Correctional Institution at Pleasanton. Her fellow prisoner (and PLACE organizer) Laura Whitehorn later recalled, "In every prison I've been in, when we start doing the AIDS work effectively, it's meant that everything improves. There's an overall direction that picks people up and lands them in the center of their own humanity. It's not something you can necessarily articulate. But it exists in the looks and the touches and the being together that we can give each other."[83]

Domestic violence survivors have also reached out to connect with others in similar situations. Bunney, who had been convicted of shooting her abuser, became one of several prisoners who formed self-help groups for battered women at both the California Institution for Women and the Central California Women's Facility. The groups were originally initiated by the prisoners themselves, then formally implemented through the prison's administrations. The programs use a one-to-one approach between prisoners, a method which Bunney characterizes as "a major strength and source of effectiveness for self-help groups, as it encourages a degree of sharing, frankness, and insight not generally achieved by more traditional methods and exercises."[84] At the Massachusetts Correctional Institution at Framingham, "Dolly," a grandmother and a domestic violence survivor convicted as an accessory to murder, did not allow her life sentence to keep her from helping others. She began a support group for other battered women in the facility.[85] Given that domestic violence survivors have often been isolated by their abusers and then further humiliated by court proceedings that refuse to understand the effects of battering and often blame the victim, the simple act of being among others who have had similar experiences is a breakthrough.

Becoming Political

In some cases, groups that were originally formed to support individual women on a path to recovery became more political as women realized that they had come to prison not simply because of their individual choices but because both society and the legal system were stacked against them. Such was the case with the LIFE (Looking Inward for Excellence) Group in Marysville, Ohio. The LIFE Group was originally formed as a support group for women serving life sentences.

> It was made up of all women that were doing life and it was sort of like a big support system within itself, because . . . when you're doing life, you had nothing there. All the programs are made up for people with short time. You know, it's about getting you educated or whatever 'cause you're moving on to society. And we were not going back . . . And so they needed something to kind of get through.[86]

As time went on, members began discussing how the institution was run and actions they could take to improve their conditions. Recognizing that many members had been sentenced to life imprisonment for killing their abusers, the group began working around issues of domestic violence, particularly petitioning for clemency for survivors of domestic violence. In 1990, the group met with Linda Ammons, aide to then-governor Richard Celeste, and Celeste's wife Dagmar. Their stories of abuse and imprisonment for self-defense moved both Ammons and Celeste, both of whom worked to organize a process in which women incarcerated for self-defense could request clemency.

LIFE members spoke with other prisoners and encouraged survivors of domestic violence to apply for clemency. In some instances, LIFE members helped women overcome denial about their abuse, understand that they had been abused, remember incidents of battering, and recall where documentation of their experiences might be found.[87] Their efforts led to 18 additional women to apply for gubernatorial clemency.

Members also began monitoring parole board hearings, timing the amount of time that each woman spent before the parole board: "We were sort of taking inventory about how many minutes did you stay in that [hearing] room when you went? Some women said three minutes, four minutes. Well, how could you tell a life story in three or four minutes?"[88]

They encouraged women to write follow-up letters to Governor Celeste about events they had forgotten in their applications or brief explanations to the parole board.[89]

These actions countered the usual way that prisons operated. According to one LIFE member (whose application for clemency had been successful):

> We were sending out for articles and . . . we would share it. When you're in the institution, you get to be kind of secret . . . But as we started to get information, we would put packets of stuff together, illegally Xerox stuff and kind of under the cover, 'Read this, you know, this is good reading.'[90]

In the end, 25 women were granted clemency.[91]

The actions of LIFE Group inspired women at the California Institution for Women to organize a clemency drive. Members of Convicted Women Against Abuse (CWAA), the support group that Marcia Bunney had helped form, wrote a letter to then-governor Pete Wilson asking him to consider commuting their sentences and inviting him to one of their weekly meetings so that he could understand how they had ended up in prison. Although the governor declined the invitation, the letter drew the attention of lawyers and advocates who offered to help the women draft arguments and gather evidence for clemency petitions.[92]

Wilson granted clemency to three, denied it to seven (including Brenda Clubine, a cofounder of CWAA serving fifteen-to-life for killing her abusive husband), and made no decision on 24 of the petitions.[93] This did not dissuade women from continuing to use CWAA meetings to share current news regarding domestic violence, homicide cases, and court rulings and their own experiences with the justice system. They also continue to discuss possible legal strategies, media stories about women who fight back and journalists with a focus on domestic violence.[94] The advocates and lawyers who originally helped CWAA members with their petitions did not disappear either. They formed the California Coalition for Battered Women in Prison and continued organizing and raising public awareness around the issue. Over 15 years later, the group, now called Free Battered Women, continues to advocate for the release of women imprisoned for self-defense.[95]

Both LIFE Group and Convicted Women Against Abuse began as domestic violence support groups operating with administrative approval. However, without the groups' work around educating their peers about domestic violence and empowering them to speak out about their experiences, the clemency process would not have occurred on the same scale. In addition, women who had suffered domestic violence—whether they were ultimately released or not—would have continued to feel alone in their experiences and ashamed to talk about them.

Sharing as a Threat to Security

Seemingly simple acts of sharing resources, comforting one another and supporting efforts to win clemency may not seem threatening to prison control and security. However, the potential power of women sharing and networking undermines the operations of a system that seeks to foster an atmosphere of alienation and isolation. Prison administrators recognize this and often impose seemingly arbitrary rules to prevent this threat: the Idaho Department of Corrections has an outright ban on its prisoners sharing resources or materials. Women who are caught either bartering or sharing items more than once are sent to "the hole" or segregation.[96] The administration at Bedford Hills scrapped Kathy Boudin's model of literacy teaching in favor of multiple choice questions about readings that had nothing to do with prisoners' experiences.[97] In the summer of 1988, less than six months after approving the formation of ACE, the prison superintendent, Elaine Lord, effectively shut the program down for six months. Years later, Lord identified the cooperation and self-reliance forming among prisoners as the administration's central concern: "How can you talk about community organizing in a prison when prison itself is a community paranoid by definition?"[98] The work of ACE—and individual prisoners—challenges this definition, threatening the system's complete control over its prisoners.

Because they pose a threat, women who reach out to their fellow prisoners risk repercussions. After nine years of assisting her fellow prisoners with their legal work, California prisoner Marcia Bunney was fired from her position as a law library clerk.[99] At the Central California Women's Facility (CCWF), women who demand medical attention for their fellow prisoners face reprisals: "Our administration has elected to punish us because our peers are dying," one prisoner reported. "A team [of guards] was assembled and trashed our cells within one to two hours of the last death . . . but not one inmate has been afforded grief counseling."[100]

Despite the risk of retaliation, women in prison continue to help each other. Women at CCWF continue to advocate for proper care of their sick peers as well as work to educate and empower them. "I believe that every person, Black, white, male or female, incarcerated or free, has a right to decent and responsible healthcare," stated CCWF prisoner Judy Ricci. "I collect information to share with other women here, so that hopefully with education will come empowerment."[101] At Oregon's Coffee Creek Correctional Facility, Barrilee Bannister reported that prisoners are usually the first to act when another prisoner is hurt or having a medical emergency. Realizing that staff members are slow or reluctant to respond to prisoners' health concerns, Bannister relied on a medical manual that she won several years ago and which she often lent to her fellow prisoners.[102]

Another woman circumvents her prison's no-sharing policy by donating her books to both an outside books-to-prisoners program and the facility's library so that other incarcerated women may also read and enjoy them. Others leave their books in the shower for their fellow prisoners to find and read. The more daring leave their paperback books face down and open to the center. "The girls 'fish' from room to room and, using string, can get it in their rooms," one woman recounted. "It's amazing to see the girls pass things."[103]

Occasionally even prison administrations recognize the benefit of prisoner cooperation and community-building: after years of hostility, the administration and medical director at Bedford Hills now ask ACE members to provide 24-hour care and companionship to prisoners with AIDS isolated in the ICU unit.[104]

BARRIERS TO BASIC CARE

In 1976, in *Estelle v. Gamble*, the Supreme Court ruled that deliberate indifference to a prisoner's serious medical needs violates the Eighth Amendment. Despite this ruling, prison health care continues to neglect, and even jeopardize, the health of its prisoners. Incarcerated women face the additional challenge of trying to obtain adequate care for specifically female health concerns within a system still designed with the violent male prisoner in mind.

Female Concerns

Pregnancy is one of the more common female health concerns. A 2006 report by the U.S. Department of Justice indicated that 5% of women in local jails, 4% of women in state prisons and 3% of women in federal prisons entered while pregnant.[105] However, despite these numbers, even prison wardens agree that several of the particular needs of pregnant women "have yet to be dealt with in any of the facilities." Most, if not all prisons, lack not only maternity clothing but also adequate resources to deal with false labors, premature births and miscarriages. In addition, many states require that pregnant prisoners wear belly chains when being transported to and from the hospital.[106]

A survey of women's prisons found that only 8 states provided prenatal medical exams, 19 provided proper prenatal nutrition and only 17 provided screenings and treatments for high-risk pregnancies.[107]

The lack of adequate prenatal treatment is even more alarming considering that many pregnant women have histories of inadequate health care, abuse and substance abuse, making their pregnancies high-risk.[108] Pregnant women are also not given the opportunity to exercise or taught breathing and birthing techniques.

In one instance, a 20-year-old woman who was almost five months pregnant began experiencing vaginal bleeding, cramping and severe pain. She requested medical assistance numerous times over a three-week period, but there was no obstetrician on contract with the prison. She was finally seen by the chief medical officer, an orthopedist, who diagnosed her without examining her physically or running any laboratory tests, and given Flagyl, a drug that can induce labor. The next day, the woman went into labor. Her son lived approximately two hours.[109]

In addition to inadequate prenatal treatment, pregnant women are often shackled during labor. In an interview with Amnesty International, one woman described giving birth while a prisoner in Chicago. Her legs had been shackled together during labor and, when she was ready to birth, "the doctor called for the officer, but the officer had gone down the hall. No one else could unlock the shackles, and my baby was coming but I couldn't open my legs."[110]

Dr. Patricia Garcia, an obstetrician and gynecologist at Northwestern University's Prentice Women's Hospital, has stated that shackling a laboring mother "compromises the ability to manipulate her legs into the proper position for necessary treatment. The mother and baby's health were put at risk if there were complications during delivery such as hemorrhage or decrease in fetal heart tones."[111] As of March 2012, only sixteen states and the Federal Bureau of Prisons have passed legislation that limit or ban the shackling of women in labor and delivery. The other states have no laws or formal policies.[112] Women returning to prison after giving birth are also subjected to vaginal exams in the name of security despite the risk of infection.[113] Women who have undergone Caesarean sections are routinely denied pain medication and antibiotics.[114]

Pregnancy is not the only specifically female medical concern ignored by prison officials. Prevention, screening, diagnosis, care, pain alleviation and rehabilitation for breast cancer are virtually nonexistent in prisons. In 1998, a study at an unnamed southern prison found that 70% of the women who should have had mammograms under standard medical protocol had not been tested. Although many of the women were at high risk because of family histories, they were not provided with a clinical breast exam, information or basic education on self-examination upon admittance.[115]

In 1991, Sherrie Chapman, a California prisoner with a family history of breast cancer, found a lump in her right breast. She waited two years for a mammogram. The radiologist found "extremely dense breast parenchyma" and recommended that a follow-up mammogram be done within one year. Chapman was unable to convince the prison's medical department that she needed another mammogram until late 1994. This time, the radiologist recommended immediate follow-up tests. The prison's doctor, however, refused to order a biopsy, ultrasound or fine-needle aspiration.

The next year, Chapman was seen by a different prison doctor, who immediately ordered a biopsy. By that time, the cancer had spread to both breasts and metastasized in her neck, forcing her to undergo two mastectomies. In addition, her uterus began to hemorrhage. Medical staff allowed her to bleed for 18 months before performing a hysterectomy.[116]

Similarly, cervical cancer and other female illnesses are commonly misdiagnosed and mistreated, sometimes with alarming consequences. At the Coffee Creek Correctional Facility in Oregon, Danielle Conatser's pap smear showed abnormalities. The prison's doctor informed her that she had cervical cancer. Conatser, who had had a baby six weeks earlier, requested a second opinion. She was told she would be put to sleep for a biopsy. When she awoke, she was told that the doctor who had originally diagnosed her had removed a good portion of her cervix, thus making it unlikely that she would be able to have children in the future. Conatser never received her second opinion, nor did she receive any follow-up care. She continues to live with the fear that she has cancer.[117]

General Medical Care

Not only are the particular health care needs of women ignored or dismissed, but medical care in general is often inadequate or life-threatening. This is all the more dangerous considering that women frequently enter prison in poor health already after years of poverty, poor nutrition, inadequate health care, and substance abuse. According to the U.S. Department of Justice, female prisoners also experience more severe health problems than their male counterparts.[118] However, the prison system does little, if anything, to meet their health needs.

This past year, officials in Oregon ignored Michelle Everett's repeated requests for medical care. She was given medical attention only after turning yellow. After both hepatitis and cirrhosis of the liver were ruled out, she was told that a bile duct was obstructed, but that the prison could do nothing about it. Like Conatser, she was not given a biopsy and has received no further medical care.[119]

In addition, illiteracy and poor literacy can be an obstacle to obtaining medical care. As Ellen Richardson, a prisoner at Valley State Prison for Women (VSPW) in California, testified, "The medical staff triage [is] based on how the patient states her symptoms on paper." This procedure ignores the fact that the average literacy level at VSPW is less than ninth grade, that over 700 women have a below sixth-grade reading level and that approximately 100 are illiterate or speak English as a second language. "A woman may have extreme stomach pain and cramping, but only have the literacy level to write, 'I have a tummy ache.' That is not enough for medical staff to let her see a doctor."[120]

This practice is not limited to California. Jerrye Broomhall, a prisoner at the Mabel Bassett Correctional Center in Oklahoma (MBCC), states that women unable to articulate their ailments are often denied medical attention: "If a woman is not literate or articulate enough to convince staff that she needs medical attention, she will be in a lot of trouble if she is quiet and/or friendless."[121]

Lack of funds may also prohibit a woman from seeking medical attention. At FMC Carswell, where the average wage ranges between 17¢ and 24¢ per hour, women are charged a three-dollar fee for each visit to the medical staff. "I do feel that the fee actually pushed away the people who really needed the health care," recalled Kirsten, a former prisoner who was released in 2007 shortly after the fee was implemented.[122]

The climate of medical neglect has sometimes led to preventable deaths. In February 2000, Wisconsin prisoner Michelle Greer suffered an asthma attack and asked to go to the Health Services Unit (HSU). When the guard and captain on duty contacted the nurse in charge, he did not look at Greer's medical file and simply instructed her to use her inhaler (which was not working). Half an hour later, Greer's second request to go to HSU was also ignored. After another half hour, Greer was told to walk to HSU but collapsed en route. The nurse arrived without a medical emergency box or oxygen. A second nurse arrived with the needed emergency box, but again with no oxygen. Forty-five minutes after her collapse (and less than two hours after her initial plea for medical help), Greer died.[123]

Greer's case is far from unique. At Central California Women's Facility, nine women died within eight weeks. In the case of Pamela Coffey, her fellow prisoners called for medical assistance. Not only did Coffey suffer from abdominal pain and numbness in her legs, but "her tongue was so swollen she could hardly speak." An MTA (or Medical Technical Assistant—a guard with low-level medical training) arrived and, according to Coffey's fellow prisoners, "he was laughing. He said 'I can't understand a word she's saying—you can do more for her than I can.'" Coffey died that same night. An outside medical investigation revealed that abnormal blood tests had never been followed up, and concluded that "there were significant problems with her medical care that might have contributed to her death."[124]

State prison systems have also begun contracting for-profit corporations to provide health care. These corporations promise quality care at a much lower cost than state governments can provide. What these corporations provide in actuality, however, is often little better and, because the main motive is profit rather than providing services, sometimes worse than prison-run health care.

Darlene Dixon recalled her visit to a private clinic contracted by the prison: "There was no disposable paper on the table to create a sanitary barrier between my body and the examination table. The room was basically in disarray; there were spilled liquids on the counter tops as well as debris on the floor." In the restroom was a sink filled with "soiled and bloody tubes, lids and bottles. Even more disturbing were the clean ones located on top of the toilet tank beside it. It rapidly became apparent to me that these items were being washed and reused."[125]

In New York State, Prison Health Services (PHS), a for-profit corporation won hundreds of millions of dollars of jail and prison contracts within the past decade. A yearlong investigation by the *New York Times* found that the care provided by PHS was often deficient, flawed and/or lethal. According to the *Times*, state investigators scrutinizing ten prisoner deaths came to the same conclusion after finding the same circumstances in each case: to cut expenses, PHS trimmed medical staffs, hired underqualified doctors, had nurses doing tasks beyond their training and withheld prescription drugs. The investigators also found that PHS allowed patient records to remain unread and employee misconduct to go unpunished.[126]

PHS is not alone. Correctional Medical Services (CMS) has been the nation's largest provider of prison health care, with nearly 300 sites in 19 states.[127] In 2007, the company garnered $750 million in annual revenue.[128]

Since 2003, the Michigan Department of Corrections has contracted with CMS to provide health care throughout its prisons.[129] Like PHS and other providers of prison health care, profit is the motivating force behind services, or lack thereof. An investigative article in *Harper's* revealed that CMS stymies those seeking treatment for hepatitis C, requiring them to fulfill a long list of conditions, known as "the protocol pathway," before they can receive any care.[130]

In 1999, CMS regional medical director Gary Campbell issued a memo to his fellow directors, stating, "I am not encouraging anyone to undergo therapy. However, if you have someone that is insistent, then this pathway is to be fulfilled."[131] Although the memo specifically referred to patients seeking treatment for hepatitis C, who make up approximately twenty to forty percent of the U.S. prison population, prisoners seeking care for other diseases, viruses and illnesses have also been frustrated when trying to receive care—or even information— about their medical conditions.[132]

In 2006, Stephanie Walters Searight entered the Scott Correctional Facility in Plymouth, Michigan. There she was tested and told that she had HIV. "The door [was] left wide open while I received the news. Prisoners walking by hearing the most devastating news of my life."

Lack of confidentiality was not all that Searight had to contend with: "I wait to see the doctor. I wait to ask questions. I wait to see if they will treat me. I start a medical journal to keep records of my health. I begin to request health care regarding my symptoms. I request mental health for counseling. I ask when I will see a doctor. They say don't worry. You will see him soon."

Searight waited three months before prison officials allowed her to see a doctor. However, once she arrived at the office, she found that her appointment was cancelled. "I still have questions that can't get answered. The nurses tell me that they don't specialize in HIV." When Searight finally did see the specialist, he prescribed her a multi-vitamin to boost her immune system. Upon her return to prison, Searight was told that the prison would not provide the vitamins free of charge; she needed to purchase them from the prison commissary.

In August 2007, Searight saw the doctor again. "I just saw the HIV specialist," she wrote. "I was just told that they will start medication in three to six weeks and that they want to run a few more tests first, but that is the same thing they told me six months ago."[133]

Organizing for Their Lives

Women have been active trying to change their sometimes life-threatening medical neglect. The most successful and well-known prisoner-initiated project organized around health care is ACE (AIDS Counseling and Education) at Bedford Hills. AIDS is the leading cause of death among U.S. prisoners, being five to ten times more prevalent in prison than in the outside society.[134] HIV has also become more prevalent among women than men in the prison system: the U.S. Department of Justice reported that the number of female prisoners with HIV increased 69% from 1991 to 1998 while the number of male prisoners with HIV decreased 22%.[135] A 2001 report found that women in prison are three times as likely as men in prison to be living with HIV or AIDS.[136] In 2005, 12.2% of women imprisoned in New York State were HIV-positive—a rate of infection more than double the rate of imprisoned men (6%) and 80 times higher than the rate of the general public (0.15%).[137]

This prevalence is not new: a 1988 study by the New York State Department of Health revealed that almost 20% of women entering the maximum-security Bedford Hills Correctional Center were HIV-positive.[138] By 1992, one of every five women entering the New York State prison system tested positive for the HIV virus. Despite these numbers, attitudes around HIV and AIDS were characterized by secrecy, denial, shame, ignorance and fear. Both prisoners and staff ostracized women who were believed to be HIV-positive.[139] In 1987, six women chose to act against the fear, ignorance and social ostracism around HIV and AIDS. They petitioned the administration to allow them to create a peer counseling and education group. ACE was the result.[140]

ACE founders recognized that changing attitudes toward the disease and those who had it required prisoners to play an active role in dealing with the crisis. Although representatives from the Department of Health and other state agencies did live presentations at Bedford, many women did not trust them because they were state officials. ACE founders hoped that having prisoners as peer educators would generate the cooperation, trust and support needed to change both attitudes toward and the care of women with HIV/AIDS.[141]

Although the prison superintendent Elaine Lord had originally approved the program, ACE continually faced staff harassment and administrative interference. For instance, because both Kathy Boudin and Judith Clark, alleged members of the Weather Underground, were active ACE members, the group was constantly monitored and sometimes prevented from officially meeting.[142] Fears that the one-to-one peer counseling sessions would lead to organizing around other issues as well as the staff's own ignorance and fear of HIV/AIDS, led to staff harassment and interference. Educators from the Montefiore Hospital holding training sessions were banned from the facility for suggesting that the Department of Correctional Services lift its ban on dental dams and condoms.[143] A year after its formation, ACE members were prohibited from meeting at its regular time, using its meeting room, giving educational presentations or referring to themselves as "counselors."[144]

Despite these setbacks, ACE members not only managed to implement and continue their program, they helped women prepare for their medical examinations by working with them to define and articulate their main questions. They also accompanied women to consultations and worked to improve communication between patients and medical staff. ACE members also presented educational seminars to women throughout the facility, often using role-playing to break through barriers, generate discussion and examine the issues—both inside and outside the prison—that surround the disease.[145] "If you hear stigma now, there are five people who immediately go, 'Why did you have to say that?' It's not okay anymore. And I know that is a direct result of ACE and the education process," reported Vinice Walker, a peer educator.[146]

The program was also awarded a $250,000 grant from the AIDS Institute that allowed it to create several paid staff positions for prisoners as well as hire an outside coordinator. In 1998, ACE members wrote and published *Breaking the Walls of Silence*, a book detailing the group's history and its positive impact on women with AIDS as a guide for other prison AIDS programs.

Other women political prisoners have focused on the AIDS crisis behind bars. Linda Evans, for example, started the Pleasanton AIDS Education and Counseling program.[147] During her 14-year incarceration, Laura Whitehorn set up AIDS peer education programs in every federal prison where she was housed.[148]

Women who were not politically active before incarceration have also created programs to challenge the prison's unresponsiveness to their health. HIV-positive prisoners at Central California Women's Facility began a peer-education program encompassing not only HIV and AIDS, but also other sexually transmitted diseases, tuberculosis and Hepatitis C.[149] The women went from prison yard to prison yard talking to their peers about these diseases: "There has been a great response from the population and HIV/AIDS testing requests have gone up tremendously," wrote Joann Walker, one of the peer educators.[150]

Not all of their efforts have been as successful. In late 2003, the women started PRIDE, a prisoner-run HIV support group. The group's desire for confidentiality clashed with the prison's security protocol: "We didn't want a CO [correctional officer or guard] sitting there listening to our medical information, so they shut us down after three weeks," recalled PRIDE cofounder Misty Rojo.[151]

However, with the exception of ACE at Bedford Hills, researchers and scholars have largely ignored these programs, overlooking the difficulties faced by those organizing around HIV/AIDS issues in prison. The reality of a prisoner-organized initiative, even one with the positive goal of educating women about HIV/AIDS, contradicts the concept of prison as a locale for punishment and control. "Once we, as prisoners, were given permission to become educated, to take initiative, and to organize our own community, many of us in ACE felt more motivated and empowered than we had ever before in our lives," wrote cofounders Kathy Boudin and Judith Clark.[152] Such empowerment runs counter to the premise of prisons and can be (and often is) seen as a threat to its security.

Women have also worked individually and without the auspices of administrative approval to change their health care, sometimes risking sanctions and retaliation. The California Department of Corrections and Rehabilitation (CDCR) expressly prohibits prisoner organizing, stating that all "inmate clubs, activity groups, associations, or other organizations within the facility are permissible only when specifically approved by the Warden."[153] Charisse Shumate, a prisoner at the Central California Women's Facility (CCWF), did not allow this policy to stop her from working with other women who had sickle-cell anemia. Until her death, she helped them understand the disease and the necessary treatments.[154] She also advocated the right to compassionate release for any prisoner with less than a year to live and was the lead plaintiff in *Shumate v. Wilson*, the class-action lawsuit filed by prisoners at CCWF and the California Institution for Women (CIW) against the state. Prisoners charged that those with cancer, heart disease and other serious illnesses were denied medical care and that the prisons' medical staff failed to protect the confidentiality of prisoners with HIV and AIDS. In 1997, the CDCR agreed to a settlement: untrained prison employees would be barred from making judgments about prisoners' medical care, prisons would ensure medicines without undue lapses or delays, and medical staff would offer preventive care, including pelvic and breast exams, pap smears and mammograms.[155]

Unfortunately Shumate herself died at CCWF. The Board of Prison Terms recommended clemency rather than compassionate release, which required the governor's approval. Because Shumate had been sentenced to life in prison for killing her abusive lover, then-governor Gray Davis refused to approve the Board's recommendation.[156] Shumate never expressed regret for her organizing work: "I took on [the battle] knowing the risk could mean my life in more ways than one . . . And yes, I would do it all over again. If I can save one life from the medical nightmare of CCWF Medical Department then it's well worth it."[157]

Shumate's work did not cease with her death. Women who had learned from her now continue the task of teaching others how "to understand their labwork and how to chart their results, keep a medical diary, hold 'these people' accountable to what they say and do to them."[158] Sherrie Chapman, one of the 26 women who testified in *Shumate v. Wilson*, became the primary plaintiff in a class-action suit over medical conditions in addition to filing a civil suit charging the CDC with cruel and unusual punishment after waiting over a decade for cancer treatment.[159]

Similarly, Judy Ricci, a prisoner with HIV and hepatitis C, taught herself about Hepatitis C and then passed her knowledge along to others at CCWF, many of whom called her Dr. Juju.[160]

In October 2000, women at CCWF, VSPW and CIW testified about the inadequacy of prison medical care at legislative hearings. The women's testimony drew public attention to the chronic neglect and malpractice that they experienced on a daily basis. Their stories highlighted prison policy of not informing women that they had tested positive for Hepatitis C; many women accidentally discovered their status years later. The women also described the lack of counseling and information provided to women with chronic illnesses and the steps they took to fill these gaps. They testified about the administration's retaliatory actions against the women who participated in *Shumate v. Wilson*.[161] These women did so knowing that after the hearings they would return to prison where, out of public sight, they risked retaliation for their outspokenness.

Women prisoners in California are not the only ones who have organized and acted surreptitiously around health care. Former Pennsylvania prisoner Waheedah Shabazz-El stated that when she worked in the prison's gym, women who were HIV-positive gathered as an informal support group. "We knew each other from [the] clinic," she recalled. "We'd talk about the meds, the side effects, the people in denial."[162]

Retaliation

Women in prison face not only medical neglect and malpractice, but also retaliation from the prison administration should they advocate for themselves and demand adequate treatment. Even after the *Shumate* settlement, those who speak out about the prison's medical practices have been subject to reprisals. At CCWF, prison officials have punished prisoners seeking medical attention by upending their cells, confiscating medications and threatening to break up the living arrangements of those who ask for help in the middle of the night.[163]

In December 2001, prisoner Delores (Dee) Garcia began speaking out against the physical abuse, medical neglect and staff callousness at the Skilled Nursing Facility at Central California Women's Facility (CCWF). Although the Skilled Nursing Facility (SNF) is the only licensed medical facility for California's women prisoners, the staff has continually displayed callousness, neglect and incompetence. "Getting the wrong medication is excused because the nurse got me 'mixed up' with another patient," Garcia wrote. "Medical staff also asks me to explain my condition . . . Needing my linens changed is called a 'comfort not a necessity' after a week."[164]

In response, staff members have threatened her, placing the entire facility on lockdown after Garcia and others filed grievances about conditions. In May 2002, she was moved from the Skilled Nursing Facility, the only facility able to treat her Chronic Obstructive Pulmonary Disease, sleep apnea, hepatitis C and arthritis, to Valley State Prison for Women, which has only an unlicensed infirmary with a part-time staff. After a month of advocacy by outside support groups, Garcia was returned to CCWF where staff warned her that if she continued to file grievances and speak to advocates, she would be returned to VSPW. Garcia immediately filed a grievance against the staff and, on July 12, 2002, was transferred to Valley State Prison, where medical staff admitted that they cannot adequately treat her illnesses.[165]

The actions and continued works of ACE members, Linda Evans, Charisse Shumate and many other lesser-known women address crucial issues facing women in prison. They also contradict the notion that women do not and cannot network and organize to change their conditions.

MOTHERS AND CHILDREN

In 2007, 65,600 women behind bars were mothers under the age of 18.[166] 62% of women in state prisons and 56% of women in federal prison reported being mothers to minor children.[167] While prisons do little to assist any parent, incarcerated mothers face greater challenges in remaining involved in and retaining legal custody of their children than their male counterparts.

Many mothers were single heads of household before coming to prison: in 2008, the U.S. Department of Justice reported that incarcerated mothers were three times more likely to be single parents than part of a two-parent household.[168] Only 37% of mothers behind bars reported that their children were living with their biological father. In contrast, 88% of incarcerated fathers stated that their children were living with their mothers.[169] Eleven percent of incarcerated mothers in contrast to two percent of incarcerated fathers stated that their children were living in a foster home, agency or institution.[170] Thus, mothers in prison are forced to navigate the legal maze of family law more often than their male counterparts in order to maintain contact with and retain legal custody of their children.

"Unfit Mothers"

Prisoner rights advocate Karlene Faith argues that the lack of support and assistance for incarcerated mothers stems from the notion that "no woman who has used drugs, worked as a prostitute or otherwise shown 'deviant' or criminal tendencies can be a 'good' mother."[171] The moral judgment surrounding women who go to prison extends to the perception of their capability as mothers: women prisoners are seen as incapable of being good mothers. In contrast, incarcerated fathers are rarely expected to share the responsibilities of childrearing before, during or after their imprisonment and usually escape similar judgments about their ability to parent.

The view of the imprisoned mother as unfit and unworthy has been used to legitimate prison and social services policies regarding the children of imprisoned parents. A 1978 directive of the Department of Social Services specified that it can refuse imprisoned parents visits with their children in foster care if it believes that visits will hurt the children.[172] In 1997, the federal Adoption and Safe Families Act (ASFA) was enacted, drastically reducing the time in which children may remain in foster care before parental rights are terminated. Under this act, if an incarcerated parent does not have contact with his or her child for six months, he or she can be charged with "abandonment" and lose parental rights. If the child is in foster care for 15 of the last 22 months, the child welfare agency is required to file a petition to terminate parental rights.[173] Once these rights are terminated, parents have no legal relationship with their children and are not permitted to have any contact with them.[174]

ASFA makes no exceptions for parents in state or federal prisons.[175] Many prisoners have sentences that run well over 22 months. Kebby Warner was sentenced to two to 14 years. She learned that she was pregnant one month after entering prison. Fortunately her parents agreed to care for her daughter Helen while she served her sentence. However, four months after the baby's birth, Warner's father died. Her mother, unwilling to care for the baby alone, gave Helen to the foster care system.

When Helen was two years old, a judge terminated Warner's parental rights, stating that the length of her incarceration constituted neglect and abuse. When Warner began to appeal this decision, her caseworker and the Family Independence Agency (Michigan's child welfare department) threatened to place Helen with a new foster family who would adopt her immediately, thus permanently sealing her file and preventing Warner from ever being able to find her. If Warner dropped her appeal, the agency promised that Helen would stay with her current family, a couple willing to allow Warner to remain in contact. Under this pressure, Warner signed an affidavit relinquishing her rights as a parent.[176]

Warner's story is only one example of ASFA's impact. Warner's sentence is also shorter than that of many of the women sentenced under the growing number of mandatory minimum laws. Under mandatory sentencing laws, many first-time offenses, even those that would have been treated as misdemeanors, mandated treatment or dismissed altogether, now warrant harsh sentences.

Given that approximately 65% of all incarcerated women are parents and that many had been raising their children on their own, ASFA's impact has been profound: a 2003 study found that termination proceedings involving incarcerated parents increased approximately 108% nationwide from 260 in 1997, the year of ASFA's enactment, to 909 in 2002. In contrast, in the five years before ASFA, the number of termination proceedings increased, from 113 in 1992 to 142 in 1996.[177]

Distancing Mothers from Children

A 2008 Bureau of Justice Statistics report found that 58% of mothers have never received a visit from their children since entering prison.[178] One major factor in this lack of visitation is distance: given that women in prison still make up less than 10% of the nation's prison population, most states have only one women's facility. These prisons are often located far from the urban areas where most prisoners lived prior to their arrests. In 2000, more than 60% of incarcerated mothers were housed more than 100 miles from their child's home. Less than 9% were within 20 miles of their child.[179]

Not only the physical distance, but the travel time and expenses make frequent visits less likely. For instance, federal prisoner Yraida Guanipa was housed 279 miles (or a five-hour drive) from her children in Miami. Oregon prisoner Barrilee Bannister's eight-year-old daughter lived with Bannister's mother in New York State.[180] "When I was arrested, she was four months shy of becoming three years old. I've missed the best years of her life. She'll be thirteen and a half when I get out."[181] However, throughout her incarceration, Bannister retained full custody of her daughter, a rarity among imprisoned mothers. One of Bannister's friends was not as fortunate: she lost custody of her four children "to their abusive father in Virginia. She's not seen them in over five years. She doesn't know what they look like."[182]

Women are often distanced from their families, weakening, if not severing, a woman's ties from her loved ones. Despite studies showing that maintaining family ties helps children process their mother's absence, eases family reunification, bolsters the children's well-being and development, and decreases the risk that the mother will return to prison, judicial opinion has remained unsympathetic: in 1987, *Pitts v. Meese* determined that prisoners have no right to be in any particular facility and may be transferred both within and out of state according to the institution's needs.[183]

Even when the facility is relatively near, the lack of transportation prevents many caretakers—especially those with meager resources—from bringing children to visit. Oregon's only female prison, Coffee Creek Correctional Facility, for instance, is less than twenty miles from the city of Portland. However, for those without a car, it may as well be twenty hours away. As of 2006, no public transportation to or from the prison was available. The nearest bus stops two miles away. From there, the prospective visitor would need to walk along the highway to reach his or her destination. For those bringing children, this is not an option.

If transportation is available, the travel time and related expense make frequent visits less likely. In addition, the unfriendly, if not hostile, treatment of visitors makes the prospect of an expensive and time-consuming trip all the less appealing. Kimberly, imprisoned in Texas, recounted that during her first (and only) visit with her seven-year-old son after three years of incarceration, the visiting room guard yelled at the boy not once, but twice: "I told you once already to stay in your seat and not get up, or I will end your visit and you won't be able to see your mom anymore!" The boy, who had flown from Utah with his grandmother for this special day, told his mother that he did not want to visit again.[184]

In California, women in segregation are restricted from any form of contact visiting. "I know of one situation where a client of mine was required to visit with her three-year-old daughter," reported Ellen Barry of Legal Services for Prisoners with Children. "They were separated by a wooden partition in county jail. The daughter did what any kid of that age would do, she reached up and went for her mother. The guard harshly reprimanded the child, not the mother. My client said to me, 'It wasn't her fault, it was mine. Why did [the guard] yell at my daughter?'"[185]

The Federal Correctional Center at Coleman, Florida, holds an annual Family Day, in which prisoners' families are allowed to spend time with their incarcerated loved ones inside the prison's dining hall, chapel, recreation and education areas instead of being confined to the visiting room.[186] Although Yraida Guanipa's family had traveled almost five hours from their home in Miami, they were denied entry for arriving five minutes late.[187]

Visitation, however—or the lack thereof—can be a deciding factor for prisoners with children in foster care. One of the exceptions to ASFA's stringent guidelines is that a foster care agency may delay filing for termination of parental rights if there is a strong parent-child bond —as demonstrated during visits and by other contact.[188] Given the expense, time and distance, as well as the often-degrading treatment of visitors, however, many mothers hold only a slim hope of a visit from their children.[189]

Prison policies also restrict visitation. In 1995, in response to an incident at a male prison, the Michigan Department of Corrections began limiting visitation rights in all of its prisons: all visitors, including minor children, had to be on an approved visiting list. Minors were only allowed to visit if accompanied by immediate family members or legal guardians. Prisoners with two violations for substance abuse were barred from receiving visits from anyone other than clergy or attorneys. Furthermore, if the prisoner's parental rights had been legally terminated, even if she had voluntarily given up those rights, she would not be allowed to receive visits from her child.

In June 2003, in *Overton v. Bazzetta*, the Supreme Court unanimously upheld Michigan Department of Corrections policies, citing that decreasing the number of children visiting benefited the safety and security of the institution. The Court acknowledged that letter writing is "inadequate for illiterate inmates and for communications with young children" and that phone calls are "brief and expensive," but stated that these "alternatives to visitation need not be ideal . . . they need only be available."[190] Nowhere in its decision did the Court acknowledge how the Department of Corrections' visiting policies affected a parent's chance to maintain legal custody under ASFA which by 2004 had been in effect for seven years.

Even without the threat of losing custody, the geographical distance, lack of visits and limited communication increase the gap between incarcerated mothers and children.

"Even though I consider myself close to my sons, I realized that I do not know much about them," observed Yraida Guanipa shortly after participating in FCC Coleman's Family Day. "I was afraid to ask, afraid to be wrong or to say something to prove that I am a mom that does not know her sons."

Like many mothers behind bars, Guanipa worked to stay in contact with her children and remain a presence in their lives. However, everything about the prison system, from its distance to the expense and time limitations of phone calls, discourages constant communication.[191] "My sons tell me over the phone what they do. Due to the time and financial limitations we do not get into details," Guanipa wrote. "For example if they tell me that they play baseball, that is all we have time to talk about. We cannot get into details such as what position they play."[192]

This, however, is an improvement from her sons' attitude at the beginning of her sentence a decade earlier. "My son Jeswil (the youngest one) was only thirteen months old," she recalled. "His father brought him to visit me at FDC [Federal Detention Center] Miami." During the family's third visit, Guanipa asked her husband what her sons had said when preparing for their visit. Her husband told her that Jeswil had said, "Oh I am going to get candies from the candy machine."[193]

One mother has been incarcerated in Colorado throughout her two daughters' adolescent and teenage years. Both girls have spent time in the foster care system. After disappearing for a period of time, her 14-year-old daughter resurfaced two-and-a-half months pregnant. Seven months after her daughter's baby was born, Social Services became involved. "I got a letter from the guardian ad litem," recounted her mother. "She said that J—was to be placed in one foster home and the baby in another. They opened a dependency and neglect case against J. So I don't know what's going on or where they are both at!!! I keep writing the guardian ad litem but so far I haven't heard anything back."[194]

Two years later, her daughter was still having problems with the foster care system and the child welfare system. "J—is not living with E— [her two-and-a-half-year-old son] anymore. She got a new caseworker and she's a bitch. She said J—wasn't being a good mom so she split them up. She gets to see him three hours a day and only lives down the street. She's jumping through the hoops to get him back AND she's pregnant again," her mother wrote. "The DHS people are threatening to take away the baby."[195]

The situation grew even more complicated when J's foster family offered to adopt her. Being adopted—as opposed to being in foster care—would remove Social Services from both J and her son's lives and so the girl welcomed the offer.[196] The adoption would also permanently terminate her mother's rights to both custody and communication. Fortunately for the mother, the prospective new parents changed their minds about the adoption.[197]

The younger girl has bounced from group home to group home, frequently running away, getting arrested and then being placed in another group home. "She ran away and was gone for three months," her mother wrote. "She didn't write this time. I was out of my mind with worry." When her daughter did surface, she was arrested and, after pleading guilty to violating her probation for running away previously, was sentenced to two years in the Department of Youth Corrections, a juvenile prison.[198] Although she was still a juvenile, the felony on her record caused problems: "Rules say no visits from felons until they've been off parole for three years," her mother stated.[199]

However, three years later, although the requisite amount of time had passed, the prison continued to prohibit the girl from visiting her mother.[200]

Another prisoner, "Roberta," did lose legal custody of her 14-year-old daughter. Despite this, she was still able to maintain contact via letters and phone calls. Then she learned that her daughter was pregnant. "I am even more worried about what will happen now," she wrote. "I am praying this is a false alarm because she has so much going on already and I can't be there to help her. It's driving me crazy."[201]

Roberta did not allow her incarceration and her distance from her daughter to stop her from doing her best to help the girl figure out what to do: "I gave her every one of her options in detail and she made her choice. I have never covered a subject more extensively but I wanted her to understand that she could only do what she could live with." Although Roberta wrote that she was fine with the girl's ultimate decision to have an abortion, one can imagine the pain and sense of helplessness she must have felt at being so far from her daughter during this time.[202]

While all mothers of teenagers worry about their children's escapades, incarcerated mothers' fears are often compounded by guilt as well. "I'm seeing my life played out again through my daughters," the mother in Colorado wrote five days after learning about her daughter's pregnancy. "And being in here makes it worse cause I can't help her. I feel very helpless and angry."[203]

Individual Resistance

Under such circumstances, mothers must struggle to maintain strong relationships with their children. Some women have refused to passively accept what they see as an overly harsh separation from their children. When Yraida Guanipa was sent to FCI Tallahassee, a federal prison in northern Florida, 481 miles from her two young sons in Miami, she pursued all administrative remedies to be transferred closer to home. Although English was her second language, she began a campaign for mothers in prison, writing to every U.S. congressperson and senator as well as prisoner-friendly organizations, universities and friends and family members of the women around her. Her first response came from a father on death row in Texas.

In 1999, after three years of unsuccessfully requesting a transfer, Guanipa staged a hunger strike, which lasted 17 days.[204] In response, prison officials placed her in a Special Housing Unit (SHU) cell where she continued her hunger strike. When her health failed, officials rushed her to the hospital, then returned her to SHU for 32 more days. Upon her release from SHU, Guanipa learned that the death row unit in Texas had been on a solidarity hunger strike with her.[205] The Bureau of Prisons (BOP) then transferred Guanipa to FCC Coleman, almost 300 miles from Miami. In response to her repeated requests, the Bureau of Prisons has told her that the federal facility in Miami had no room for her and that she would be ineligible for day furloughs until the last two years of her twelve-and-a-half-year sentence.[206]

Michigan prisoner Kebby Warner also used a hunger strike to keep her daughter longer.

Warner was one of the 5% of state prisoners who arrive pregnant each year.[207] She gave birth to her daughter in 1998 while still incarcerated.

Michigan prison policy separates an incarcerated mother from her newborn after only one day. Warner refused to accept this regulation and launched a hunger strike, winning two more days in the hospital with her child.[208]

Incarcerated mothers have used other tactics to maintain contact with their children: after arriving at the Edna Mahan Correctional Facility in New Jersey in June 2001, Marianne Brown began her efforts to secure an inter-institutional visit with her adult son (and codefendant) Michael. At first, the prison's social worker told her that there was no such possibility.[209] Brown refused to give up and, in January 2003, learned that inter-institutional visits are possible, although one had not occurred in two decades.[210]

Brown's request for a visit was denied. Instead, the prison social worker offered to arrange a video conference visit provided that New Jersey State Prison, where Brown's son was housed, agreed. "New Jersey State Prison then asked my son if he was interested in a visit. When he told them of course he was, they denied it, saying, 'This would be of no benefit to the inmate.'"[211]

Brown still did not give up. She began a letter-writing campaign, sending requests to the New Jersey State Prison's commissioner. When she received a negative response from the commissioner's assistant, she reached out to ministers and religious organizations asking them to write letters on their behalf. The pressure from her outside friends resulted in both prisons approving the state's first inter-institutional video conference visit.[212]

"So pen and paper made a big difference and gained a great victory to open a door for all imprisoned families," Brown wrote. "More prisoners need to write letters and more people from the outside need to care and help out too!"[213]

Although Brown's success did not immediately change conditions for the women around her, it set a precedent which other women can refer to in their own battles. "RJ" spent her entire pregnancy awaiting trial in a Colorado jail. Because both she and her boyfriend were facing lengthy sentences, she opted to place her baby for adoption. Although normal jail policy does not allow contact visits, RJ was granted two contact visits with her infant as part of the adoption counseling process.

Her visit prompted two other mothers to demand and win contact visits with their own children. One had not had physical contact with her baby since he was three months old. The other, awaiting deportation to South Korea, was allowed a contact visit with the 14-year-old twin daughters she was leaving behind.[214]

Organizing

Maintaining parental ties has not been won through prisoner boycotts, work stoppages or other disruptive behaviors, tools traditionally used by male prisoners to challenge their conditions.[215] Instead, women who want family maintenance programs have had to work with their prison administrators, a far less glamorous and visible path for those seeking information on prisoner organizing.

One example of such a program is the Children's Center at the Bedford Hills Correctional Facility in New York. The Center houses a nursery where incarcerated mothers and their babies are allowed to live together for the child's first year. It also offers a program helping the new parents "learn to be mothers." Although it is staffed by women prisoners, the Center is administered by the Brooklyn Diocese of Catholic Charities and funded by the state's Department of Correctional Services.[216] However, under the Center's auspices, prisoners, realizing the need for supportive programs for mothers, organized two parenting courses— one on infancy for new mothers and pregnant prisoners, and the other a ten-week course called Parenting Through Films, with each week devoted to a new subject on growth and care for children.[217] These were the facility's first courses both organized and taught exclusively by prisoners.

The Children's Center did not just benefit the mothers and babies who participated. "All people need to experience some sense of efficacy, individual potential, cooperative social activity," wrote Kathy Boudin and Roslyn Smith, two prisoners who worked with the Children's Center. Although the program had been implemented and managed by outside people, the women at Bedford did the day-to-day work. This responsibility enabled them to begin changing their self-perception from that of bad girls or victims to "women with real strengths who can make a difference."[218]

Out of the Children's Center also came more far-reaching change. Until 1983, children of prisoners placed in the New York State foster care system did not have the legal right to visit their parents in prison. Mothers at Bedford formed the Foster Care Committee which, with the help of outside advocates, led to new legislation not only giving prisoners with children in foster care the same rights and responsibilities as parents who are not incarcerated, but also the right to monthly visits provided that the prison was not too far away.[219] In addition, prisoners involved in the Children's Center published a foster care handbook for incarcerated mothers whose children had been placed in the foster care system.[220] The book galvanized advocates from two outside organizations, the Women's Prison Association and the Volunteers of Legal Services, to form the Incarcerated Mothers' Law Project, which provides educational workshops about family law, advocacy and legal counseling to mothers imprisoned in New York State.[221]

Many incarcerated mothers, however, lack the cooperation of prison administrators. In some cases they have had to work clandestinely to set up opportunities to maintain contact with their children. In 1997, Guanipa learned about a Lutheran church in West Virginia that provided free transportation for the children and families of the women incarcerated at Alderson Federal Prison Camp. "Nothing like that existed for Florida prisoners and their families. Then I decided that I was going to work tirelessly until I found a church or a sponsor that could provide free transportation for our children and families."[222]

Finding a sympathetic organization, however, was made even more difficult by prison rules. "As a prisoner, I *cannot* freely write to churches or organizations asking for free transportation for my sons, for fear of being indicted again for 'SOLICITING,'" Guanipa wrote. "As you may not be aware of, as a prisoner we can not 'Solicit' anything. Furthermore, I could not ask any of the church volunteers because as volunteers for the BOP [Bureau of Prisons] they cannot be involved with our families or with us outside of the specific volunteer job. With limited resources, limited budget and limited phone time I could not write or call everywhere or anybody until I found the right organization or church."[223]

Despite these limitations and the risk of being charged with "soliciting," which carries not only a penalty of losing phone and e-mail privileges but also an additional indictment and more prison time, Guanipa persevered.[224] In the fall of 2005, eight years after beginning her campaign, Guanipa found a church willing to pay for a bus so that forty-eight children, including Guanipa's two sons, could spend seven hours with their mothers at FCC Coleman.

"Even though I am getting released in eleven months I am happy that there will be children that will not suffer as mine did because they will be able to visit their mothers here at Coleman Camp."[225] Since that first church-sponsored bus, Guanipa has found two other churches that have paid for the transportation necessary for children to visit their mothers at FCC Coleman.[226]

Don't Rock the Boat

A mother's desire to spend (more) time with her child(ren) can be—and often is—used to dissuade her from challenging conditions and organizing for change.

Yraida Guanipa stated that while in the past she had "mass-produced cop-outs" (filed numerous formal complaints about prison conditions), she stopped once she became eligible for furloughs and release to halfway houses, opportunities that would allow her to spend more time with her sons.[227]

A woman incarcerated at Bedford Hills claimed that mothers who publicly criticize the prison's personnel are often denied entry into the facility's Family Reunion Program, which allows extended visits (usually 36 to 44 hours) by immediate family members in more residential settings than the prison visiting room.[228]

In addition, women impregnated by prison staff have also been denied participation in the Children's Center's nursery program. While interviewing women at Bedford Hills about sexual abuse, Human Rights Watch found that two women who had been impregnated by prison staff were denied entry.

> After her transfer to Bedford Hills, Iris R. stated that she applied to the nursery program, was initially accepted, and received a letter of acceptance. She later received a second letter withdrawing the offer when the institution realized that the father of her child was a corrections officer. A second woman impregnated by a corrections officer, who gave birth in 1993, was similarly denied entry into the nursery program.[229]

Human Rights Watch found that a third woman, who had been impregnated in 1995, had also been rejected from Bedford's nursery program.[230]

Prison administrators also use their control over visits to punish prisoners who challenge existing prison conditions. "They [the prison staff and administration] would attack people [advocating for reform] through their emotions," stated another prisoner at Bedford Hills. "Like the family would come in to visit somebody and they wouldn't find the inmate's chart and tell the family they weren't there and turn the family away at the gate."[231]

This practice is not limited to Bedford Hills or New York State. The Michigan Department of Corrections (MDOC) has also withheld visits to punish women who have challenged prison conditions: after Stacy Barker successfully sued MDOC for sexual abuse, guards targeted her cell and belongings for frequent searches. Each search yielded contraband, including a green leafy substance that the prison claimed was marijuana. In the eight months after MDOC adopted the policy banning visits for prisoners with repeated substance abuse violations, Barker, who had never tested positive for any drug during her eight years of incarceration, received four tickets for substance abuse. "I received two substance abuse tickets in one day," she recalled. "One was for borrowing Motrin (Ibuprofen) from a prisoner for cramps. I also had iron pills that had been prescribed to me that were a day over the expiration date."

In 1990, three years after entering the prison system, Barker had asked friends to adopt her seven-year-old daughter, providing the girl with a stable and secure home. "This was an open-adoption and they brought her to the prison every other week to visit and I phoned her weekly." Under MDOC's new visiting policy, because she had given up her parental rights, Barker was prohibited from receiving visits from her daughter.[232]

However, Barker did not allow the MDOC to deprive her of seeing her child. She signed onto *Bazzetta v. McGinnis*, a lawsuit launched by 11 women imprisoned in Michigan. The suit challenged MDOC's visiting policy, particularly the regulations limiting minor visitors to a prisoner's child, stepchild or grandchild, prohibiting prisoners from receiving visits from their children if their parental rights had been terminated, and banning all visits (except from recognized clergy and attorneys) for prisoners with two substance-abuse violations. Barker testified that exceptions should be made for parents who had voluntarily terminated their rights. The U.S. Court of Appeals found the new policy unconstitutional, stating, "Under our constitution, even those lawfully imprisoned for serious crimes retain some basic constitutional rights."[233] In May 2002, Barker was able to receive a visit from her daughter and meet her three-year-old grandson for the first time.

Even before the courts ruled against MDOC's policy, Barker fought for and won the right to visits: in 1998, Barker obtained a court order for a visit with her daughter, who was pregnant. In 2000, she obtained another court order, allowing her daughter to visit once a week.[234]

Although the Supreme Court upheld the MDOC's visiting policies in 2003, the suit launched by Barker and her fellow parents demonstrates that women are willing to—and do—challenge policies designed to keep them from their children. The silence from the larger prisoner rights movement reflects not only the idea that women do not organize, but also that issues of mothers and children are less important and thus merit less attention than issues raised by men in prison, if any at all.

SEXUAL ABUSE

At 4:30 every morning, "Gina" reported to work in the kitchen at Coffee Creek Correctional Facility in Oregon. For the first half hour, she was the only prisoner in the kitchen with the food coordinator, a male prison employee. The other women who worked as servers and dishwashers did not arrive until 5:00 a.m.

For the first several weeks, the food coordinator laughed and joked with Gina as they prepared breakfast for the women in the prison's minimum facility. On several occasions, he walked close to her and let his hand brush against her buttocks. He always apologized.

One day, however, he ordered her to drop her pants and bend over so that he could have sex with her.

Scared, Gina complied.

After the first time, sex became a daily routine. Gina did not know whether she liked it or not. She wasn't sure if it was rape. All she knew was that she felt alone, afraid and unsure of herself. She knew that she didn't want to do it, but she realized that she had no choice.

Gina decided not to report it to Internal Affairs. She remembered that after the last sex scandal hit the local media, the women involved were harassed and threatened by both prison officials and prisoners who had been trading sex for favors. She didn't want her time made harder. She only had a few months left in prison and did not want to risk being written up on a false misconduct report, thus losing her good time (credit for time served) and having to spend more time in prison.

Instead, Gina chose to keep quiet and endure what became a morning routine.[235]

"Gina's" story is far from rare. Sexual aggression and abuse by male prison staff is a far greater problem than most are willing to admit. In 1994, the U.S. Department of Justice launched an investigation of two women's prisons in Michigan and found that "nearly every woman . . . interviewed reported various sexually aggressive acts of guards."[236] These instances included not only rape and sexual assault, but the mistreatment of prisoners impregnated by guards, abusive pat frisks and other body searches and violations of privacy, including searches of the toilet and shower areas and surveillance during medical appointments. The evidence of widespread sexual abuse prompted the Justice Department to initiate legal action against the state of Michigan in 1997 under the Civil Rights of Institutionalized Persons Act (CRIPA). In its suit, the Justice Department claimed that the State of Michigan was "violating the constitutional rights of inmates incarcerated in Michigan women's prisons to be free from sexual misconduct and unlawful invasions of privacy."[237]

Extensive sexual abuse is not limited to Michigan: in 1996, Human Rights Watch released *All Too Familiar*, a report documenting sexual abuse of women prisoners throughout the United States. The report, reflecting the organization's two and a half years of research, found that sexual assaults, abuse and rape of women prisoners by male staff members were common and that women who complained incurred write-ups, loss of "good time" accrued toward an early parole and/or prolonged periods in disciplinary segregation.[238]

In addition, because at least 40–57% of women enter prison with extensive histories of previous abuse, they are more vulnerable to what the U.S. Department of Justice calls "inappropriate relationships" with prison staff.[239] Many women with histories of abuse are more likely to accept sexual abuse and misconduct from prison staff because they arrive in prison already conditioned to respond to coercion and threats by acquiescing to protect themselves from further violence.[240]

In both men's and women's prisons, prisoners are more likely to experience sexual violence at the hands of prison staff than from their fellow prisoners. Under Title VII of the Civil Rights Act of 1964, which prohibits gender discrimination in employment, both male and female guards have the right to gender-neutral employment in prisons housing prisoners of the opposite gender. Given that most states have only one to two female prisons but many more male prisons, this has usually been applied to female guards' right to employment in male facilities. However, Title VII also prohibits discriminating against male officers in female prisons.

In some instances, male staff members have been placed in female facilities with little to no training on cross-gender supervision and no procedures for investigating or disciplining staff sexual misconduct. In Michigan and other states, untrained male officers were assigned to positions in which they were able to walk, unannounced, into areas where women dress and undress, shower, and use the toilet. Male guards have also been given the task of performing body searches on prisoners, which includes patting down women's breasts and genital areas. They also transported women to medical care and were required to observe gynecological and other intimate medical procedures.[241]

The Official Response (or Lack Thereof)

Women who speak out about their abuse often find their complaints ignored. After being transferred to the honor unit at New York State's Bedford Hills Correctional Facility in 2001, Shenyell Smith was solicited by unit officer Delroy Thorpe. When she rejected his proposition, he raped her repeatedly.

Smith visited the prison medical center and reported vaginal and rectal pain from the repeated assaults. She also reported the rapes to the prison's superintendent, her counselor in the Family Violence program and the Inspector General.

She received no response.

Smith filed an official grievance with the state's Department of Correctional Services (DOCS), the governmental body responsible for all prisoners.

Her grievance was denied.

Despite other prisoners' complaints of sexual abuse and harassment filed with the Inspector General's office and despite the New York State Department of Correctional Services' "zero tolerance" policy regarding sexual assault, Thorpe continued to maintain his position in the honor unit.[242]

Bedford Hills is not the only institution to ignore or dismiss sexual abuse by its employees. Michigan has no laws criminalizing sexual activity between its prisoners and staff. Instead, it has Work Rule 24 that defines any employee-offender contact that falls outside official duties as an improper relationship. However, under Work Rule 24, a probation officer meeting with a parolee for coffee is subject to the same sanctions as a prison employee having sex with a prisoner.[243] In addition, Work Rule 24 is often not enforced: in 1997, officials at the Camp Brighton facility received an anonymous letter charging prison guard Edmond Hook with being a "sexual predator." Four months later, eighteen women complained that Hook groped them during pat-downs and leered at them while they showered.

Officials simply warned Hook to "exercise better judgment in dealing with females." No effort was made to monitor him more closely or to transfer him to a position away from female prisoners. Eight months later, Hook forced a prisoner to touch his genitals. The next month, he sexually assaulted and impregnated T'Nasa Harris. Only then was Hook arrested and charged.[244]

Sexual Abuse

Even when there is undeniable evidence of sexual misconduct, prison administrations and state justice systems often allow perpetrators to go unpunished. In December 1996, Heather Wells, a prisoner at Washington Corrections Center for Women, was raped and impregnated by a guard in the prison laundry room. She charged the guard with rape. Even after a paternity test proved her claim, the state of Washington did not file charges, allowing the guard to quit his job and move out of state.[245]

In 2003, 46-year-old prison guard Randy Easter impregnated Korinda Martin, a 25-year-old woman incarcerated at a Nevada prison run by the Corrections Corporation of America.[246] Easter was fired, but it was not until after the baby was born and DNA testing proved his paternity that the state charged him with a felony count of having sex with a prisoner. However, because Nevada law also penalizes the prisoner if she is perceived to have consented to sexual contact, Martin was charged with a misdemeanor count of conspiracy to commit a crime.[247] Although Martin argued that the inherent power and control that guards wield over prisoners makes refusing their sexual demands nearly impossible, the judge ruled that the two had had a consensual relationship and sentenced both to probation.[248]

Lack of Visible Coercion

As Martin has pointed out, prison sexual abuse is not always visibly coercive. When "Dee" was working at the law library at a prison in Colorado, another prisoner approached her and told her that a sergeant working in the kitchen liked her. Dee and the sergeant began passing notes and, with the other woman's help, had sex on two occasions in the kitchen. When the prison administration discovered the relationship, the sergeant was allowed to resign. Their relationship continued, with the ex-sergeant professing his love and moving Dee's belongings from the house of her former mother-in-law to his own house. "He said he wanted my stuff in 'our' house," Dee recalled. Then, with no warning or explanation, the sergeant ended the relationship.

Although Colorado corrections employees who have sex with prisoners face a Class Five felony, the District Attorney failed to file charges and years later the sergeant remains unreprimanded. "I got four years for a Class Five felony," Dee stated, referring to the charge that landed her in prison. "He'll probably get probation."[249] While the relationship may appear consensual and the break-up like a typical unfriendly split, the power that a prison official holds makes it impossible for prisoners to truly give consent. Had Dee been the one to end the affair, she might have suffered more than hurt feelings and the loss of her belongings, as Michigan prisoner Tanika Lynch learned.

On July 8, 1997, Lynch reported having a sexual relationship with then-corrections officer Phillip Lewis to prison authorities. Although Lynch had originally been willing to have sex with Lewis, when she tried to end their affair, Lewis became abusive.[250]

After reporting the affair, Lynch was targeted by both Lewis and other staff members. On July 9, 1997, Lewis issued Lynch a major misconduct ticket for stealing from the prison store. In the next four months, Lynch received 25 misconduct tickets. In the seven months before she had reported the affair, she had received only four. In September 1997, when Lynch asked a residential unit officer for permission to go to the bathroom, he not only denied her, but also stated, "Bitches like you get found in ditches."[251]

Lewis was found guilty of sexual misconduct, removed from his job and sentenced to two years' probation. Lynch is still harassed by guards and prison staff who blame her for Lewis losing his job.

Michigan prisoner Renee Williams encountered a similar problem with guard Rodney Madden. For a year, Madden gave her gifts, including a gold chain and money. "He called me his baby. When I wore the necklace with the cross, everybody knew he gave it to me," Williams recalled.

When the pair had a falling-out, Madden withheld her mail. Williams complained to the officer in charge of her unit. "She said, 'He might just be in love with you and don't know how to act.'"

Williams filed a complaint against Madden in June 2003. Madden claimed that Williams had been "acting strange" and was delusional. Her charges against him, he contended, were part of her sexual fantasies about him. He had her committed to the mental services unit.

After a prison psychologist determined that Williams was not mentally ill, she was transferred to another facility. She never learned the outcome of her complaint.[252]

The stories of both Lynch and Williams clearly demonstrate that there is no consensual relationship between prisoners and staff. "It's never over when the woman says it's over," stated former Michigan warden Tekla Miller. "Too many times their [the woman's] back is against the wall."[253]

In addition, women are often penalized heavily if they are discovered in relationships with staff. At the Gatesville Unit in Texas, a prisoner was caught having sex with the sergeant in charge of the Safe Prisons Program.[254] The sergeant was transferred to a male prison; the woman was placed in the Administrative Segregation unit at "a particularly tough unit," reported another woman at Gatesville. "I assume they wrote her a disciplinary case for 'establishing an inappropriate relationship with an officer.' I do not know if she was also written up for 'sexual misconduct,'" reported another woman on the unit.

Punishing the prisoner is standard: Dawn Reiser writes "When officers and inmates are found to be involved, the common court of action here is to move her to another facility. If she consented in any way, she will be placed in Ad Seg. Being moved with the jacket of a prior officer relationship can make time very difficult. And, if they found any reason to write the inmate a major case, it also costs her at least a one-year parole set-off. Being moved, time in isolation, a label and a set-off? Those are powerful motivations to keep a girl quiet."[255]

In addition to official sanctions, the woman is subject to informal retaliation by other staff members. "The officers on duty can choose whether or not to bring you supplies, exactly how nicely your food will be handed to you, when and if you get your mail, and on and on. If you are even suspected of being involved with an officer, your mail will be very carefully scrutinized—perhaps even by the warden. Your house [cell or room] will be shaken down thoroughly and often. You may be singled out more frequently for pat searches and strip searches. When you are patted or stripped, you are going to receive harsher treatment. When one official was mad at me, I suddenly could not squat low enough or cough deep enough to please her. I had to do it over and over again. All naked, of course. It's all about control and intimidation."[256]

Retaliation

Women raped by prison staff face not only a lack of justice, but also risk administrative harassment and retaliation for complaining. Dawn Amos stated that when two women were physically and sexually abused, they were transferred from the Colorado Women's Correctional Facility (CWCF) in Canon City to a prison in Denver while the offending officer remained, unreprimanded, on the job.[257] A prisoner at the Ohio Reformatory for Women (ORW) stated that, for prisoners who report sexual misconduct, staff make their lives "a living hell." Staff often strike back at these women by "tearing up your room" or arbitrarily "making restrictions."[258] Former ORW staff corroborated prisoners' testimonies, stating that women who reported sexual abuse were intimidated by staff members and subjected to lengthy periods of time in solitary confinement, where cells often had feces and blood smeared on the wall.[259]

Some women have faced more extreme retaliation. One prisoner at Ohio's Northeast Prerelease Center was transferred to the Ohio Reformatory for Women after she reported being raped by an officer. The ORW staff was informed of the reason for her transfer and, shortly after her arrival, seven to eight male officers entered her cell, held her down on the bed, choked her and spat in her face. After the assault, staff members continued to harass her—joking about the fact that she was afraid and that she had begged for her life while being attacked.[260]

In 1995, after Michigan prisoner Stacy Barker successfully sued the Michigan Department of Corrections (MDOC), prison staff began harassing her, calling her a "set-up queen." Guards subjected her cell and belongings to frequent searches. Although Barker had never tested positive for any controlled substances throughout her eight years of incarceration, each search turned up contraband, such as marijuana. Barker challenged these tickets, asking MDOC to allow her to submit a hair sample for testing and offering to pay the expense herself. MDOC not only denied her requests, but also prosecuted her in the (outside) Plymouth District Court for allegedly possessing 0.06 grams of marijuana. After Barker's attorney filed for discovery, the state entered a negotiated settlement in which the charges against Barker were dismissed and the state paid her court expenses.[261]

In January 1997, Barker was sexually assaulted by another officer, a defendant in the *Nunn* suit, a civil rights lawsuit filed by 31 women prisoners (including Barker) against the Department of Corrections for the widespread sexual abuse by prison guards. After a month of silence, Barker reported the repeated assaults to a prison psychiatrist. Barker was immediately placed in segregation and then transferred to Huron Valley Center, then a psychiatric hospital for prisoners, where hospital attendants verbally harassed her.[262]

In October 1997, Barker attempted suicide. In response, three male guards stripped her naked, placed her in five-point restraints (a procedure in which a prisoner is placed on her back in a spread-eagle position with her hands, feet and chest secured by straps) on a bed with no blanket and held for nine hours. She was then placed on suicide watch but received neither counseling nor psychiatric evaluation. One of the staffers monitoring her during her 29-day suicide watch repeatedly told her he would "bring her down a few rungs."[263]

Barker's experience illustrates the extent that prison staff will go to discourage prisoners from reporting official misconduct. Barker's case is far from unique: an investigation by the Department of Justice had found documentation of many instances of retaliation and a pervasive fear of reprisal among nearly all of the women interviewed. Despite this finding, however, the 1999 settlement agreement between the Department of Justice and MDOC allowed MDOC to issue major misconduct tickets to women whose claims of abuse are deemed "unfounded."[264]

"The reported number of rapes are down because these women do not want to deal with the retaliation they've seen me and others deal with," Stacy Barker observed in 2006. "The attacks still occur, but when a staff person is like 'do you want to tell or go home?' which would you choose?"[265]

The lack of support and the very real threat of retaliation, both officially and informally, are often compounded by the perception of prisoners as "bad girls"—because of both their crime backgrounds and the assumption that they have granted sexual access to men in the past. In addition, prison administrators often presume that incarcerated women are more likely to file false charges. At a New York City jail, officials prohibited a male outreach librarian from bringing books to the female housing unit. Although male guards work within that unit, administrators warned the librarian that, because of his gender, he ran the risk that a female inmate would falsely accuse him of sexual harassment or sexual assault.[266]

Technically, It's Illegal: Legislation Against Sexual Abuse

Criminalization has done little to ameliorate the problem of sexual abuse in women's facilities. In Ohio, sexual activity between prisoners and prison employees is considered sexual battery. Under Ohio state law, employees face a third-degree felony charge punishable with one to five years in prison and a $10,000 fine. The law has not deterred dozens of employees, who have been fired but not prosecuted for sexual activity with prisoners. In 1996, the New York State Legislature changed its Penal Law to make any sexual contact between a prisoner and prison employee non-consensual. Legislators cited Bedford Hills as only one example of "a state correctional facility for women, where female prisoners have been, and continue to be, impregnated by employees of such facilities." The state's Department of Correctional Services even advocated for this change because of the prevalence of sexual abuse by staff.[267] However, despite this criminalization, sexual abuse remains widespread enough that, in 2003, women in several New York State prisons, including Shenyell Smith, attempted to file a class-action lawsuit about the sexual harassment and assault they suffered at the hands of prison staff.[268]

In addition, legislation has not offered protection for women who do complain. When Oregon became the forty-ninth state to outlaw sex between prisoners and staff in 2005, prisoner Barrilee Bannister commented, "I think it's great DOC [Department of Corrections] supports stiffer penalties. But what good will it do if this stuff doesn't get reported?"[269]

In 2003, President Bush signed the Prison Rape Elimination Act (PREA) into law. The act, the federal government's first attempt to legally address prison rape, called for the gathering of national statistics about prison rape; the development of guidelines for states on how to address prisoner rape; the creation of a review panel to hold annual hearings; and the provision of grants to states to combat the problem.[270] In the first nationwide study conducted under the PREA, 152 male and female prisoners nationwide were interviewed. However, all of the case scenarios focused solely on prisoner-on-prisoner assaults in male prisons. The ensuing report did not even mention the existence of women in prison, much less sexual abuse by staff in female facilities.[271]

Not only does the PREA neglect the situation specific to women in prison, but it has also had adverse effects on women who attempt to alleviate the isolation of incarceration by forming intimate relationships with their fellow prisoners. Prison rules penalize women for any physical contact: "Keep in mind—even hand-holding is considered sexual contact here," reminded Dawn Reiser, a woman imprisoned in Texas. "It doesn't have to be a sexually intimate touch to get labelled as sex here."[272]

Dawn Amos has noted an increase in write-ups for sexual misconduct since the act was passed. "Women are more open with their relationships

than men are," she stated. "Now the DOC has changed sexual misconduct to sexual abuse because of the 'Prison Rape Elimination Act.'"[273]
While the PREA has the potential to reduce the prevalence of rape in
male facilities, it clearly did not take gender differences into account.
Thus, women are punished for consensual relationships with one
another, sometimes leading to devastating results.

One morning, while waiting on line for breakfast, RJ and her friend
forgot that rule. "I admit we acted totally stupid. We just weren't thinking
about where we are. She put her hands on me and the CO was out
there counting us. She saw it and took it to be sexual misconduct." Both
women were sent to segregation pending investigation; both received
write-ups for complicity in sexual abuse.

"My friend was set to leave on Friday [two days later] for treatment," RJ
recalled. "The write-up meant that she would not be leaving then." The
write-up would also affect RJ's chances of an early release in the future.

RJ's experience illuminates how easily a woman can be charged with
sexual abuse, often for actions that would warrant little to no attention
on the outside. Fortunately, because both women had exemplary
records and were liked by several staff members, the administration
dropped the charges.

"In the beginning, I was especially questioned as to whether I played a
consensual, willing role. I could have said that I was not willing and gotten
out of it altogether, which I would never consider," RJ remembered.
Had she done so, the charges against her friend would have been more
severe.[274] Unfortunately, when faced with the prospect of additional
charges, more time and a possible sex offender label, not every woman
is as principled: in March 2008, two women who had been involved in
a consensual relationship at the Denver Women's Correctional Facility
were sent to segregation for sexual misconduct. To avoid a charge of
sexual abuse and a lifetime sexual offender label, one of the women
claimed that the other raped her. When her girlfriend learned this, she
hung herself.

"Ever since the feds enacted that 'Prison Rape Elimination Act,' it has done nothing to help us [women]. Now someone is dead. With her girl crying rape to save herself from being convicted of a sexual abuse charge, it leaves Jamie with a sexual assault charge and having to register as a sex offender when she gets out and it'll be on her record, affecting her parole chances and chances of getting into a halfway house," wrote Dawn Amos, who had been a close friend of the woman who committed suicide. "That PREA law does nothing for women. I think it's good for men, but just the men."[275]

Protecting Themselves and Each Other

Male guards' pervasive presence and power over so many aspects of prisoners' lives makes it much more difficult for incarcerated women to form protective groups like their male counterparts who are primarily threatened by their fellow prisoners.

Despite these difficulties, they have, in some instances, managed to do so.

On August 24, 1974, Joan Little, a 21-year-old black woman and the only female prisoner in North Carolina's Beaufort County Jail, killed Clarence Alligood, a 62-year-old white male guard. Alligood had entered her cell, threatened her with an ice pick and forced her to perform oral sex. She fled after stabbing him, but turned herself in eight days later.[276]

Little was charged with first-degree murder that, in North Carolina, carried a mandatory death sentence.[277] Her case raised the question of whether a black woman had the right to defend herself against a white rapist in the American South, attracting the attention and support of African-American and feminist groups across the country.

During her trial, Little's defense exposed the chronic sexual abuse and harassment endured by women in the jail and prison system. Countering the prosecution's argument that Little had enticed Alligood into her cell with promises of sex, the defense team called on women who had previously been held at the jail. They testified that Alligood had a history of sexually abusing women in his custody: one woman stated that he had fondled her breasts while bringing her a late-night sandwich; another recalled that he had suggested that she had been in jail long enough to need a man.[278]

Little testified that Alligood had come to her cell three times that night. After she refused his advances twice, he returned with an ice pick. "By then, I had changed into my nightgown. He was telling me I really looked nice in my gown, and he wanted to have sex with me," she stated. "He said he had been nice to me, and it was time I was nice to him. I told him I didn't feel like I should be nice to him that way."[279]

Little was acquitted.[280]

Little's case garnered widespread attention and support from the women's movement and the African-American community. In contrast, most women who have suffered sexual abuse behind bars have received little to no attention, let alone support, from those on the outside. However, this has not stopped them from acting to protect each other.

One woman, incarcerated in Ohio during the early 1990s, recounted that a male officer constantly harassed her cellmate. "He'd make nasty insinuations about her breasts and what he would like to do to them and how he would like to do it and what he'd do to her."[281]

In addition to verbally harassing the prisoner, the guard threatened to place cocaine among their possessions if she or her friends reported his behavior. His threat worked; the women kept quiet about his harassment. One night, he assaulted his victim. Her cellmate and another prisoner heard her screams and found her with semen on her face. In spite of their fears, the three filed a complaint with prison officials and later testified before a grand jury, leading to the officer's arrest and conviction. Although the three women faced harassment from other prison officials as well as prisoners who had been trading sex for favors, their actions encouraged other women to resist male guards' abuse of power.

"We could never clean up the penitentiary or never change a lot of people's minds," the woman stated. "But you get rid of one nasty apple . . . It was a funny thing after that happened. A lot of the nastiness and that vulgarness . . . was seeming to cease a little bit and to ease up a little bit, because they began to get nervous. And more women stood up, and two other officers were escorted off because the women found enough courage to stand up."[282]

In Oregon, the passage of Measure 11 caused the rate of female incarceration to grow faster than the state could handle. In 1996, Barrilee Bannister and 77 other women were shipped to an all-male private prison in Arizona operated by the Corrections Corporation of America (CCA). Only weeks after the women's arrival, a captain visited several women in a cell and shared marijuana with them. He left the marijuana with them, then returned with other officers who announced that they were searching the cell for contraband. However, they promised that if the women performed a strip tease, they would not search the cell. "Two of the girls started stripping and the rest of us got pulled into it," Bannister recalled. "From that day on, the officers would bring marijuana in, or other stuff we were not suppose[d] to have, and the prisoners would perform [strip] dances." From there, the guards became more aggressive, raping several of the women. Bannister reported that she was placed in segregation and not given food until she agreed to perform oral sex on a guard.

Once out of segregation, Bannister called outside friends and told them her story. They, in turn, informed the media. The media attention led to the return of some of the women to Oregon, where they filed a federal suit, resulting in a public apology, a promise of stricter rules concerning sexual abuse, and the reimbursement of attorney's fees.[283] The negative publicity also led to the suspension and dismissal of several CCA staff members.[284]

Changing Conditions through the Courts

Women have filed lawsuits to stop conditions that allow staff to sexually abuse and prey upon them. While these suits have not stopped sexual abuse and exploitation altogether, they have established that staff sexual misconduct does occur and draws public attention to these realities.

In 1977, women at Bedford Hills filed *Forts v. Ward* to keep male staff members from being in areas where the women would be partially or fully exposed (e.g., sleeping and shower areas and the infirmary). In 1978, a judge ruled that women prisoners were entitled to protection from being viewed by male guards while partially or completely unclothed, receiving medical treatment at the prison hospital, showering, using toilet facilities, or sleeping in the housing units.[285] He ordered officers to give a five-minute warning each morning before entering the housing area. He also granted the women's request for an injunction against male guards working the night shifts. When the prison appealed the decision, the Second Circuit Court upheld the five-minute privacy warning. It also ruled that women could cover their cell windows for 15 minutes while undressing or using the bathroom.[286]

In 1992, without the aid of a lawyer, five women imprisoned in Washington State filed *Jordan v. Gardner*, a suit challenging the state's new policy allowing male officers to conduct pat searches on female prisoners. They won a temporary injunction: the court determined that, in light of many of the women's histories of abuse, pat searches by men could cause "severe psychological injury and emotional pain and suffering" and thus violated the Eighth Amendment's prohibition of cruel and unusual punishment.[287] The court's decision was the first in the country prohibiting men from searching women.[288]

In 1993, women in DC filed *Women Prisoners v. District of Columbia Department of Corrections*, a class-action suit against DC's Department of Corrections (DCDC) for sexual misconduct by guards. The next year, a judge ruled that the rapes, sexual assaults and degrading language in DCDC facilities violated the women's Eighth Amendment rights against cruel and unusual punishment. He also found that DCDC had not made adequate efforts to prevent and punish staff sexual misconduct.[289]

In August 1996, three women in California filed *Lucas v. White* against the Bureau of Prisons (BOP). They had been held at a male detention center where male prisoners had paid staff to grant them access to the women's cells to rape them. Two years later, the women settled their suit for $500,000. The settlement agreement also forced the BOP to make system-wide changes to its protocol for investigating claims of staff misconduct. Under the settlement, the BOP was ordered to set up a confidential hotline or other confidential reporting mechanism, provide medical and psychological treatment for women who had (or have) been abused and establish new training programs on sexual misconduct for both staff and prisoners.[290]

In 1996, women in Michigan filed two suits against MDOC for institutional sexual abuse. *Neal v. MDOC* is a class-action lawsuit against the MDOC. Approximately 440 women signed onto the suit, stating that they had suffered sexual assault, sexual harassment, invasions of privacy and retaliation for reporting staff misconduct.[291]

Thirty-one women in two prisons also filed *Nunn v. MDOC*, stating that they had been "subjected to various degrees of sexual assault, sexual harassment, violation of their privacy rights, physical threats and assaults on their persons and retaliation by male employees of the MDOC." The women also claimed that MDOC officials had been aware of the sexual misconduct and assaults, but had done little to either investigate or to discipline their employees.[292] In 1997, the district court heard the *Nunn* case and ruled that "a person's right to bodily integrity and privacy do survive incarceration, although such rights may be limited."[293] In 2000, the MDOC signed a settlement agreement limiting housing unit staff to female officers. It also banned cross-gender pat-down searches and limited the circumstances in which male officers can transport female prisoners or remain with them in medical examining rooms.[294]

Stacy Barker, one of the plaintiffs in the *Nunn* case, recalled that fighting against the prevalent sexual abuse pulled her out of her suicidal funk: "I overcame all that I was feeling by finally opening up and sharing my experiences with others," she recalled. Realizing that her fight against MDOC was inspiring other women to step forward renewed her spirit and determination: "I have to speak up! I speak for those who are too afraid to speak up! I speak for those who don't know how to speak up!"[295]

EDUCATION

W hile women prisoners face issues not pertinent to male prisoners, they also share issues. Education is one of these issues, yet it is often overlooked in the current literature on women's incarceration.

Imprisoned women and men have similar education rates: a 2003 report by the Bureau of Justice Statistics found that in state prisons 42% of women and 40% of men had neither high school diplomas or GEDs, only 36% of women and 32% of men had graduated from high school, and even fewer had attended a postsecondary institution prior to incarceration.[296] Despite these similarities, studies of the impact of education have traditionally focused on male prisoners. While education on any level is not a particularly masculine concern, the omission of women in these studies indicates that researchers do not perceive this as an important issue for women.[297]

It is unclear whether women have greater access to educational opportunities than their male counterparts. A 2005 exploratory study of higher education programs in state prisons found that 37% (or 37) of women's prisons, compared to 18% (or 133) of male state prisons, reported having an on-site college program.[298] However, the researchers, both of whom have founded higher education initiatives in women's prisons, remind the reader, "Given the number of state prisons for women averaged fewer than two per state (compared to over 14 male facilities per state), it is not surprising that 34% (17) of states reported an on-site college program for women in at least half the facilities, compared to only 12% (6) of the states reporting a program in at least half the facilities for men."[299] Whether women truly have greater access to higher education than their male counterparts, they have nonetheless demonstrated that they value education and have often struggled to retain or start educational programming.

In 1972, Karlene Faith and Jeanne Gallick, two professors from the University of California at Santa Cruz, taught a university course, Women in Society, to 50 prisoners at the California Institution for Women (CIW). Their students urged them to continue and expand the program, leading to the formation of the Santa Cruz Women's Prison Project (SCWPP), the first program to ever offer university courses in a women's prison.[300] Most of the original 50 students had not completed high school; Gallick tutored those who required specific academic skills.

In contrast to the prison's existing vocational programs, such as hairdressing, sewing and office work, and its high school equivalency program, the SCWPP offered courses that challenged students to analyze the social issues affecting their lives.[301] The women worked with outside volunteers to design the courses, which were held as a series of four-to twelve-hour workshops on the weekends so as not to interfere with prison work assignments. At any given time during the project's four-year existence, approximately 100 women were enrolled in the accredited courses, which included Women and the Law, Drug Use in U.S. Culture, Creative Arts, Radical Psychology and an ethnic studies course which focused on the historical and sociological perspective on women of color in the United States and which, because of the high number of women of color at CIW, was "exceptionally popular."[302] In addition, the SCWPP offered non-credit workshops for women who were not interested in taking classes for college credit. These workshops were generally one-time events, but attendees often gained enough confidence to enroll in the accredited college courses during subsequent terms.[303]

The women at CIW demonstrated their eagerness for higher education not only by participating in the classes and designing the curricula, but also by protesting any threats by the prison administration to the project. In 1972, when Karlene Faith was temporarily banned from the prison and the program suspended, prisoners organized a work strike and a sit-in before the warden's office.[304] Similarly, when the project was barred in 1973, the students circulated petitions, held work strikes and met with the administration to protest the project's removal.

An unexpected result of the SCWPP was the emergence of dialogue between groups of prisoners who might otherwise never speak to each other. During one of the periods in which the project was banned from CIW, a woman who had been at the prison for years observed:

> I witnessed something I would have believed [three years ago] was impossible. We had an [illegal] meeting where Black and White were united, under one common cause. There were women there who in the past would never have spoken to each other but here they were standing together, agreeing, touching shoulders. The tone of the meeting was not loud or wild. It was a confident approach to bringing back the workshops. It is something we all want. It was beautiful. We elected a six-woman committee to speak for the group. We are not afraid.[305]

The opportunity to critically examine issues affecting their lives and to challenge prevailing stereotypes built bridges between prisoners who had previously believed they had nothing in common. And, when this opportunity was threatened, these women already had the groundwork to set aside their differences and unite to pressure the prison to reinstate the program.

This is not the only case of direct action for education. In 1988, 28 women at the Oregon Women's Correctional Center (OWCC) staged a hunger strike and sit-in to protest the lack of educational programming for female prisoners, especially in comparison to the opportunities available at the neighboring men's prisons. The sit-down protest was the first in OWCC's history.[306] Although the women identified as the sit-in's leaders were sent to segregation, ten of the protesters were allowed to participate in the college courses that had previously been limited to men at the Oregon State Prison.[307]

Women have also used other opportunities to further their access to education: in 1981, after six years of ignoring the initial court decision, the administration at Bedford Hills finally agreed to observe *Powell v. Ward*, which stated that prisoners had a right to due process during disciplinary hearings. As part of the settlement agreement, the administration set up a $125,000 "settlement fund" to be spent by the prisoners for improvements at the prison. The women at Bedford Hills set up ad hoc committees (such as an Education Committee and a Recreation Committee) and utilized the existing prisoner groups to collectively discuss how the money should be spent. For the first time in the prison's history, attorneys were allowed to hold group meetings with women in the housing units so that no prisoner was left out of the decision-making process. The women collectively decided to spend the entire fund on educational materials, drawing up polls to decide which particular items they wanted purchased. They ultimately decided to expand the library collection; buy Spanish-language literature, books on African-American history, materials for the bilingual classrooms and computers for business classes; hire an educational consultant; and offer Spanish vocational classes.[308]

Michelle Fine, a professor at the Graduate Center of the City University of New York researching the effects of higher education on incarcerated students at Bedford Hills, observed that despite the conditions discouraging focused study, for many women "prison has become a place for intellectual, emotional and social growth . . . A space free of male-violence, drugs and overwhelming responsibilities, college-in-prison carves out a space which nurtures a kind of growth and maturity that would perhaps not have been realized on the outside."[309] While Fine does not delve deeply into this issue, it does suggest that women are often unable to focus on learning with the myriad of responsibilities and distractions of the outside world.

Jerrye Broomhall, a woman who finished her bachelor's and is now pursuing a master's degree while imprisoned in Oklahoma, agrees. She recalled that drugs and, later, the suicide of her boyfriend prevented her from seriously pursuing an education: "I was already dabbling in drugs in high school, but once I got to Norman [the University of Oklahoma] I started seriously using and selling drugs: marijuana, cocaine, and LSD. Public [high] school was so easy for me; I never did homework and skipped a lot of classes to get high. College was, of course, not so easy, but I still managed to stay afloat while partying all the time."[310]

Entering prison changed her outlook: "When I realized how much time I was facing it broke me down and the only way I could reconcile the loss of this huge chunk of my life was to somehow use the time to [my] advantage."[311]

Marcia Bunney, incarcerated in California, recounted, "Difficult experiences at school during my childhood and adolescence had left me with memories of loathing conventional education and everything connected with it."[312] The abuse that she had suffered in previous relationships had implanted the idea that she was not smart enough to attend college: "I was skeptical of the idea of returning to school, certain that college was beyond my ability, ready to give up before I had given myself a chance to start."[313]

However, without the continual discouragement of verbally abusive lovers and with the encouragement of her fellow prisoners and her prison work supervisor, Bunney overcame her doubts and fears about education, earning an associate's degree. That was not her only lesson: "Beyond the specific components of the curriculum, I learned many valuable lessons, the greatest of which was that I was *capable*. After a lifetime of seeing myself as a failure and as inferior, this represented a complete reversal, one that admittedly required effort to accept and absorb."[314]

These experiences and insights should not lead to the conclusion that prison, with its numerous disruptions and deplorable conditions, is an ideal educational setting. RJ, who is pursuing her associate degree at Colorado's La Vista Correctional Facility, states, "Prison *can* remove us from those [factors] to some extent." She goes on to note that prison relationships can also be violent and abusive and that, while not as prevalent on the outside, drugs of any type are still available to women who want them. She also states that while the absence of daily responsibilities in prison allows her more time to read and study, prison itself is an overwhelming environment and that "just as personal growth is possible, it is all too possible that we are stored, shelved in a prison warehouse, needing a new environment, experiences and sources for continued growth."[315]

Bringing Back College Programming

Since 1965, prisoners had been eligible for Pell Grants, noncompetitive, need-based federal funds available to all low-income people seeking to attend college. In 1994, then-president Clinton signed the Violent Crime Control and Law Enforcement Act, which included a provision denying Pell grants to prisoners. Although prison education accounted for 1/10 of 1% of the Pell grants' annual budget, Pell grants had supported most college-in-prison programs.[316] The act shut down all but eight of the 350 college programs in male and female prisons nationwide.[317] In New York State, TAP (Tuition Assistance Program) grants had supplemented Pell grants to pay for college-in-prison programs. In 1995, state legislation disqualified prisoners from receiving TAP.

At the Bedford Hills Correctional Facility in New York, these cuts ended the four-year college program that had enabled women to earn bachelor's degrees. However, the women did not passively accept this loss. In 1996, seven prisoners at Bedford Hills met with then-superintendent Elaine Lord and the deputy superintendent of programs to find a way to restore the prison's college program.

"We thought it would take about three years [of planning], and we'd have maybe a course," Lord later told the *New York Times*. "They [the women] did the whole thing in about eighteen months."[318]

The women worked with the prison administration and representatives from thirteen colleges and universities throughout New York State to restore higher education programs. By 1997, they succeeded in implementing College Bound, an undergraduate college program aimed toward a bachelor of arts in sociology. Students pay the equivalent of one month's wages (approximately $10 in 2001) to participate in either the college or pre-college program.[319]

In the first three years of the program's reestablishment in spring of 1997, 196 of Bedford's 650 women became college students. Most had past histories of academic failure: upon entering Bedford Hills, 43% had neither a high school diploma or GED; 21% had a GED and 22% a high school diploma; and only 14% had some college credit.[320]

Although College Bound is one of the better-known education programs, like other higher education initiatives, it is overlooked in discussions about prisoner resistance and organizing. Although women have demonstrated and participated in direct actions to protest the lack of educational opportunities or to preserve existing programs, the majority of actions are not as visible. In some cases, such as the College Bound program, women must work with prison administrators to develop and implement higher education opportunities. Although working with the prison to establish educational programs does not overtly challenge its daily operations and conditions, it does provide an opportunity that many of these same women lacked on the outside. A 2001 study conducted by Michelle Fine and a research team of Bedford prisoners found that "the very groups of women who are not well served by public education on the outside—young adults of poverty, disproportionately African American and Latina—are the very women, age 17 to 58, who are now pursuing rigorous college education behind bars at Bedford Hills Correctional Facility. African Americans represent 59% of the college students at Bedford Hills Correctional Facility, Whites 27%, Latinas 13% and 'other' 1%."[321]

The College Bound program is unique—and somewhat unreplicable— in several respects. Unlike the majority of women's prisons, Bedford

Hills Correctional Facility is in the affluent suburb of Westchester County whose residents, such as actress Glenn Close, place a high value on education. Other celebrities, including Eve Ensler, Ruby Dee and Ossie Davis, Paul Newman, Joanne Woodward and Camille Crosby, have also supported the program.[322] Multiple colleges and universities surround the prison, making it easy for staff to commute to the facility. In addition, Bedford Hills holds (and has held) several famous prisoners, including Pamela Smart, Kathy Boudin, Judith Clark and Caroline Warmus, whose notoriety and celebrity may have increased the public profile of the program. These factors make it difficult to replicate the program in other prisons.[323]

Women without the same level of institutional and public support have also organized to pressure the administration for educational opportunities. At the Edna Mahan Correctional Facility in New Jersey, women under the age of 26 with less than six months left on their sentence are eligible to take free college courses. However, women over 26 or with lengthy sentences remained ineligible. "We all put in written requests to Mr. Metzger [the prison's education supervisor]," recalled Marianne Brown, a 48-year-old serving a 21-year sentence. When they received no response, the women began a pressure campaign: "Every time Mr. Metzger would walk through the compound, we all would take turns stopping him and discussing the problems and asking for a solution. He heard the same complaints and questions from many of us over and over again (nagging) till he fought desperately for us in negotiations and got the administration and Union County College to agree along with the teachers to give us a course where we can obtain a small business certificate."[324] While the women's efforts did not result in free college courses for those over 26, the prison did agree to institute courses that cost $100 to $150 per session.

Women lacking institutional support have also found ways to obtain an education. Jerrye Broomhall's father, recognizing the value of a college education, agreed to pay her tuition costs. Dawn Amos found scholarships offered by the colleges whose courses she was taking. "It takes a little bit of persistence and a lot of letter writing and research," she wrote.[325] In addition, not many colleges offered scholarships to prisoners "and they only pay for one class at a time and I have to buy my books out of my own pocket."[326] Luckily Amos had friends and family members willing and able to help her pay for her course books.[327]

Ten other women at the Colorado Women's Correctional Facility also found ways to take college courses despite the lack of assistance from the prison administration. Some have family members willing to foot the bill; others, like Amos, have found scholarships and foundation grants.[328]

Effects of Higher Education

From 1997 to 2000, professor and researcher Michelle Fine with the aid of eight Bedford prisoners, conducted interviews with College Bound students, their children and correctional staff about the effects of having a higher education program in a women's prison.

She found that higher education helped women transform their self-perceptions from helpless victims of external forces into active agents of both self-and social change: "Linda," a 45-year-old former prisoner was first incarcerated at the age of 18. Over the next 21 years, she was in and out of prison, serving a total of 17 years. She credits the College Bound program with helping her develop the skills necessary to successfully stay out of prison: "I'm a thinker now. Before I was a reactor," she stated. "If you're educated and you are well informed about a lot of things, you have a tendency to look at life through a whole different perspective . . . It's like knowing that you're not stuck in the substance abuse world, that you do have a brain, and that brain tells you, 'Oh, you do have choices,' or, 'You are capable of having a job.'"[329]

This transformation has occurred in other prisons as well: "My education helps my self-esteem and self-image immensely," stated Oklahoma prisoner Jerrye Broomhall. "I am able to see myself as more than a failure and a 'slave of the state.'"[330]

In addition, women have sought to encourage others to pursue their own educations: "Shannon," a 21-year-old serving an eight-to-ten-year sentence, recalled that when she first arrived at Bedford Hills, she was taken aside by an older prisoner. "You're going to be here for at least eight years," the older woman told her. "Think of this [as] an opportunity you never had before. Go to college. We'll help."[331]

Basic Education

Eagerness to learn has not been limited to women seeking higher education. For two years during the 1980s, prisoner Kathy Boudin worked as a teacher's aide at Bedford Hills' Adult Basic Education (ABE) class. Students—who ranged from ages 17 to 70—typically read paragraphs or short passages on unrelated themes and then answered multiple-choice questions that focused on skills, such as finding the main idea, understanding a particular word, or locating a detail. There was no classroom instruction or discussion. "What mattered most was whether the students answered workbook quest-ions correctly. The answer key and the teacher were the only sources of knowledge."[332]

When the ABE teacher resigned, the educational supervisor asked Boudin to assume responsibility for teaching the class for four months until a new teacher could be hired.[333] In September 1987, Boudin and the ABE reading class watched a television show on the National AIDS Awareness Test. Noting the women's extreme interest, Boudin utilized their questions and concerns about AIDS, which still carried a stigma, to introduce critical thinking into the classroom:

> I prepared a vocabulary worksheet, an activity that was familiar to the women. While the words were typically drawn from a textbook list for children at different grade levels, the words on this list came from the AIDS show. The women studied avidly, learning words far above their difficulty level in their workbook lists. Some words were conceptually familiar but difficult to spell, such as transmit, doctor, disease, patient, and pneumonia; some led to learning new concepts, such as immune system, antibody, and hemophiliac.[334]

In addition, Boudin posed three questions to her class:

- *What are the pros and cons of taking the AIDS test and how do you feel about it?*

- *If you tested positive would/should you tell somebody and who would you tell?*

- *What do you think would be a good program for AIDS here at Bedford Hills?*

Although her previous attempts to engage the class in dialogue had failed and students had demonstrated an earlier reluctance to work together, Boudin's questions led to animated discussions. Women who had resisted Boudin's past writing exercises began writing about their personal experiences with AIDS. Boudin recalled that Juana, who was about to transfer to the prison's GED class, brought in a story she had written about two women in jail, one of whom had AIDS. "When she read it, the women listened intently as they felt their own lives being described by one of their class members, and clapped enthusiastically when it was over. Juana worked on it, learning the concept of paragraphs, struggling with sentence structure and spelling." Boudin developed a reading lesson from Juana's story. "The class felt proud that one of their members had written something that they were studying. This was the first of many times that the women's own writings became the reading materials for the class."[335]

"Once the women had experienced a literacy education that focused on issues of importance, they wanted it to continue," stated Boudin.[336] When the new teacher reintroduced the basic skills model of workbooks and multiple-choice questions, the students complained to both the teacher and the administration and asked for "a return to teaching in which their ideas and issues mattered."[337] This level of active interest in education was unprecedented by ABE students at Bedford Hills.[338] Their complaints—accompanied by their declining attendance—led the teacher to agree to allow Boudin to teach the class two out of five days. On those two days, Boudin and her students explored themes such as their relationships with their mothers and their own roles as mothers.[339]

After a year and a half, the prison allowed Boudin to begin developing a problem-posing educational curriculum, utilizing prisoners as peer educators. However, midway through the planning process, the administration withdrew its support, killing the proposed program.[340]

In Illinois, all incoming prisoners must take the Test of Basic Adult Education (TABE). If a woman's test results reveal that she has less than a sixth-grade level in math and reading, the prison requires her to attend ABE classes until she can pass the test.

Linda Caldwell has been in and out of prison since 1989. While incarcerated at Illinois's maximum-security Dwight Correctional Center, she worked as a teacher's aide for both ABE and GED classes. Unlike Boudin, Caldwell encountered a mixed reaction from her students: "Some would not accept my help because of their own prejudice and because I was not trying to help them cheat. But there was always a few who really wanted to learn and did not care where they received their help as long as they were learning."[341]

In 1999, after fighting back against prison staff's continual physical and verbal abuse, Caldwell was placed in a segregation unit across the street from Dwight's classroom facilities. "I can see from my roadside window the school lines that pass by. Some of those women in that ABE/GED line were in that line ten years ago," she wrote. "I am concerned that it is taking women such a long time to achieve their GED."[342]

The length of time does not diminish a woman's joy when she does pass the test. Caldwell recalled one prisoner, "Nicky," who began serving a 54-year sentence in the 1980s: "Upon Nicky's entrance into Dwight, she could not read or write a lick! I believe she told me some years back that she only went to the second grade."

In 2002, Caldwell saw Nicky from her window: "Nicky was asking another woman outside this building if the unit supervisor was here.

When the other woman told Nicky that the supervisor was in his office, she began to make an 'unauthorized' move by coming up the walk to enter into the building. This could have landed her in segregation and/or the loss of privileges for up to ninety days. I was glad to see that the supervisor came to the door to see what she wanted. I then heard her say, 'Guess what? I passed the TABE test!' She was high on her accomplishment."[343]

Nicky's excitement—and her willingness to risk administrative sanctions to share her enthusiasm—illustrates that women do view education as important, not only as tools to help upon their release but also, in the case of Nicky and others with lengthy sentences, as a personal accomplishment in and of itself.

Self-Education

At the Ohio Reformatory for Women in Marysville, Ohio, a woman who had participated in the facility's Tapestry Therapeutic Community, a residential drug and alcohol treatment program within the prison, recognized the need for education. "Many of the women here have not had a chance to get their education; due to their drug addiction," she wrote. "In fact, some of us can barley [sic] read." She proposed the idea of a book club "to instill the importance of Education, and the joy of reading, and sharing with others" to the Tapestry staff and, once her idea was approved, solicited book donations from various books-to-prisoners programs.[344]

This option is not open to all women. Dawn Amos recounted that in 2001, the Colorado Women's Correctional Facility changed its policy about books: "Now we have a new sergeant in property, and she's the one in charge of giving us our 'allowable' items that come through the mail and she started enforcing the policy of all books have to be sent directly from a publisher with a receipt that the book was paid for." For Amos, who had previously received books from programs that send free literature to prisoners, this was the end of her self-education efforts: "I just feel like 'they' didn't want us prisoners to have something that might teach, educate or entertain us."[345]

The Colorado Women's Correctional Facility is not alone in this policy: state prisons in Michigan also require that all books be sent directly from the publisher, thus eliminating the opportunity for self-education among most of their prisoners.[346]

Obstacles

In addition to the lack of funding, incarceration presents other challenges and obstacles to women's attempts to pursue an education. Jerrye Broomhall listed the daily difficulties that she and other students at MBCC face:

> Here at MBCC controlled movement and long counts sometimes makes getting to the college classroom extremely difficult. There is no access to computer equipment or typewriters in the housing unit. The housing units can be extremely chaotic and noisy, even the best units are a lot more chaotic than your average college dorm. Library and computer resources are limited at best . . . A lot of the women here have never had to do anything academically rigorous in their lives and even if they are bright they sometimes lack even the most rudimentary study skills like note-taking and effective reading comprehension.[347]

Prison regulations and policies often hinder, if not conflict with, participation in formal education programs. In 2007, the Michigan Department of Corrections passed a rule preventing prisoners with life sentences from obtaining their GEDs or attending school. "Priority goes to women who are doing short time," wrote Kebby Warner.[348]

Prison security measures also disrupt students' ability to learn. Dawn Amos stated that when a woman self-mutilates or attempts to hang herself, the entire prison is placed on lockdown, meaning that classes—along with every other activity requiring movement—are cancelled.[349]

In addition, in most states, prison policy allows women to be transferred to other facilities without warning or regard to their participation in educational (or other) programming. Thus, women who begin a course have no assurance that they will be able to complete it.[350]

At Colorado's La Vista Correctional Facility, as local farmers' demands for prisoner work crews have increased, the prison has begun placing work ahead of education. Women enrolled in college classes who also work on farm crews have repeatedly missed large portions of their classes because they are returned late to the prison. When they requested to be brought back earlier in the evening so that they could attend class on time, they were told that the farms take precedence.

In addition, during a critical time in the harvest season, prisoners have been pulled from their classes, including GED classes, to fill vacant slots on farm crews. Those who refused to work faced write-ups and disciplinary actions.

Not all women are eligible to work on the farms. To be eligible, a woman cannot have any medical restrictions and must be qualified for a gate pass (which is determined by the type of crime and the length of her sentence). To fill the increased demand, the Colorado Department of Corrections has also started transferring women between its four prisons to ensure that La Vista has enough women who are eligible to work on farms. Although past prison policy had stipulated that women enrolled in educational classes would not be transferred to a different facility, this practice has now been abandoned. Women who do not meet the criteria for a gate pass are at risk of being traded for women who do. "Already one woman who was in my graphic design class and [who] was not eligible for a gate pass has been traded to another facility."[351]

Even when students are not being pulled from class to harvest fruits and vegetables, the prison environment often hinders focused learning. During the Winter 2008 semester, materials needed for college classes at La Vista were delayed. "We haven't been able to receive paper for this course yet, which can be an issue because we have to buy it otherwise," RJ wrote.[352] Paper at La Vista costs between 67¢ to $1 per packet. For students who rely on poorly paying prison jobs to buy their necessities, the added cost can be prohibitive and they must risk a write-up to borrow, barter or ask another student for paper.[353] Students also had to wait for the prison to allow them to receive their textbooks, an occurrence that has happened several times in the past.[354]

Some women have found themselves discouraged by the very people who should be aiding them. Concerned by the low self-esteem of the women around her, Rhonda Leland, incarcerated at California's Valley State Prison for Women, has invited motivational speakers to promote self-esteem among her fellow prisoners. Her work on self-respect enabled Leland to move past her own humiliating public encounter with the person she had trusted to help her: after finishing a four-year course in air-conditioning repair, Leland participated in the graduation ceremony. "Only three people have graduated our class in the last three years. It is quite an accomplishment."[355] At the ceremony, although Leland had never been in any kind of trouble, her instructor publicly referred to her as "my punk student" and took credit for Leland's work around self-esteem issues.[356]

"I wanted to run out crying and had to hold it together for my own sake. The newspaper editor of the *Chowchilla News* was there to do an interview. She is the one who covers all of my achievements and speakers. Well, you can imagine how hard it was to smile for the photos for the paper," Leland recalled.[357]

Leland's humiliation lasted only through the ceremony. One week later, she was able to write, "Don't worry. Hard times only make me fight the battle harder! I am well motivated by people who don't believe I can do much."[358] However, she also acknowledged that not all women have the same level of self-confidence and that witnessing her treatment has deterred others from enrolling in the prison's vocational courses. "I did file a formal complaint, not so much for myself, but for the fact the next woman that is humiliated on her graduation day may not be as strong. So, this [complaint] is so it never gets done again."[359]

Leland did not allow her instructor's disparaging remarks to keep her from learning more and trying to create educational opportunities not only for herself, but also for her fellow students. She demanded a change in vocational courses and was switched to refrigerator work. "It's a leap, but you can never learn too much. I will keep learning all I can."[360]

Education and Resistance

Education not only boosts women's self-esteem and sense of self-worth, but often protects them from the full force of prison injustice. Jerrye Broomhall observed that her education has shielded her from capricious prison policy: "You are less likely to become a target if you appear able to defend yourself intellectually."[361]

In addition, women who have more education are often sought by their peers. Broomhall observed that less literate women rely on others to write their requests to staff members. "They are simply incapable of clear expression," she noted.[362] Dawn, a woman incarcerated in Texas, observed the same thing: "Frequently, I will hear women ask someone to help them write a grievance." She also notes that when a woman writes a grievance about a condition affecting all or most of the women on her unit, others will copy her complaint. "They believe that there is some right or wrong way to fill these [grievance forms] out and that somehow they are not qualified to write on this 'official form,'" she noted. "It's very daunting to some of them."[363]

Women's education has also led them to challenge systemic abuses: both the writing skills and the self-confidence that Marcia Bunney gained during her college classes led her to learn to use the prison grievance system to dispute prison injustices. Prison officials transferred her to the Central California Women's Facility where she took advantage of her job as a library assistant and taught herself law. She joined the National Lawyers' Guild, becoming one of five prisoner representatives of the National Steering Committee of the Guild's Prison Law Project.[364]

She also initiated contact with an attorney known to be interested in litigating to change prison conditions: "Soon I was organizing the active acquisition of information to support claims of systematically inferior medical care, including the names and particulars of prisoners willing to come forward to be interviewed."[365] In addition, Bunney began educating herself about civil litigation, again drawing on the skills she learned through her college classes: "My strong composition skills were an asset, and I grew adept at drafting clear, concise declarations as a means of documenting the serious medical problems of many women, including several who proceeded to file individual actions for damage."[366]

Sometimes, the changes that education brings are less obvious: the combined focus on critical thinking and HIV/AIDS in Kathy Boudin's ABE class contributed to a growing awareness and understanding of the disease among the women at Bedford Hills. During that time period, both prison staff and prisoners had been afraid of HIV/AIDS, stigmatizing and ostracizing women who were HIV-positive. In one instance, prisoners petitioned the administration to remove a woman whom they assumed was HIV-positive from their housing unit. The woman was eventually pressured into moving.[367] Learning that the ABE class was openly discussing the disease, other women began to approach the students to share their own concerns and fears.[368]

Students developed a play about the issue, performing it six times before their peers at Bedford Hills. "After several performances, we held discussions with the audiences about what could be done to deal with the crisis of AIDS here at Bedford Hills. The audience asked for support groups and a program to be built like the one depicted in the play."[369]

The class's focus and public discussions about HIV/AIDS reduced the stigma and shame associated with the disease and opened discussions among the women at Bedford Hills, who identified the need for an AIDS counseling and support group.[370]

In addition, the class's shift from multiple-choice testing to developing literacy and writing skills led to another project: during one six-month period, women in the ABE class devoted two days a week to writing a handbook for new arrivals.[371] *Experiences of Life: Surviving at Bedford Hills* covered many issues that the students had faced and wanted to share with incoming prisoners; chapters included "Coming from Another Country," "Being Pregnant at Bedford Hills," "Mothers and Children," and "Advice for How to Survive in Prison."[372]

Regardless of how they ultimately utilize it, women value the opportunity to further their education. Cheryl, who was sentenced to 96 years in prison as a 16-year-old, noted that, when she first entered prison, "The *last* thing on my mind was a college education!" Taking advantage of the prison's college program for women under the age of 25, she took occasional classes, culminating in an associate's degree. She decided to pursue first a bachelor's degree and then a master's degree, and came to a realization that echoes so many other women's reflections about education:

> As time went on, I realized that I wasn't pursuing a degree simply because it'd look good. My education meant so much more. I wanted so badly to turn things around and create something positive out of my situation. College classes helped to shape me into the person I am today. My education has aided me in building my character. I realize that, as terrible as my past mistakes are, they don't have to define who I am.

WOMEN'S WORK

Gender and Labor in the
Prison-Industrial Complex

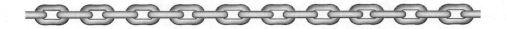

"A woman's labor, with few exceptions, is extremely alienated, exploited, and grossly underpaid," wrote Marilyn Buck, a prisoner at the Federal Correctional Institution in Dublin, California.[373] This reality does not end at the prison gates: for many women prisoners, the few jobs available are those that have traditionally been considered "feminine," such as cooking, cleaning, clerking or teaching. While these jobs keep the daily operation of the prison running smoothly, they provide little to no opportunity for women to learn job skills that can be used upon release.

With the explosion of critical literature about the prison-industrial complex in the mid-1990s came a rising outcry about the use of prisoner labor.[374] However, like many other debates about prison and prisoners, the lack of jobs and job choice as well as poor working conditions in female facilities have yet to garner much attention.

Women in prison, however, have not let the silence deter them and have been speaking out about the gender-based economic inequality within the prison system. They state that there are few job opportunities available to them. They believe that male prisoners have access to more and better jobs and higher wages, in some cases actually receiving minimum wage for their efforts.

Such beliefs are not entirely unfounded.[375] A 2000 study of the educational and vocational programs offered to incarcerated men and women found that programs offered to women tended to prepare them for underpaid, feminized, overcrowded jobs: women's facilities were 604% more likely to offer technical and sales trainings (e.g., sales associate, clerical staff, health assistant), 208% more likely to offer training in service jobs (e.g., food service or cleaning), and 100% more likely to offer training in operator/fabricator/labor jobs (e.g., sewing).[376] In comparison, male prisons are more likely to offer training in more lucrative jobs such as farming, fishing and trades such as masonry, building and automotive repair.[377]

Male prisoners often do have more job choice. In Oregon, where Measure 17 mandates that all prisoners work, men have access to jobs which provide them with skills such as small-engine repair, cabinetry, welding, furniture making, plumbing and computer programming.[378]

Until 1996, the Women's Correctional Center in Salem, Oregon, offered its prisoners the opportunity to work in its corporate division. Women answered phone calls from people on the outside requesting business information. However, in 1996, the division was transferred to one of the state's male facilities, leaving only kitchen work, cleaning and being orderlies, jobs that pay $8 to $84 per month.[379]

Private Work Programs

For the past 11 years, prisoners at the Central California Women's Facility (CCWF) have had the opportunity to work assembly-line jobs for Joint Venture Electronics. They are paid $7 to $8 an hour to solder circuit boards, inventory orders and inspect finished products. However, the California Department of Corrections deducts 80% of their wages for taxes, room and board, victim restitution, savings for release and family support. Even with these deductions, the pay is considered high, especially when compared to the eight to 37¢ hourly wage at most other prison jobs. Workers praised the Joint Venture program to the *Los Angeles Times* for enabling them to both learn a trade still relevant in the outside world and send money home to their families.[380]

The women were interviewed, however, at the assembly line, presumably within earshot of the prison guards. What they would have said about the program without fear of write-ups, pay docks or being fired may have been different. One woman has stated privately that because it is the best paying job at CCWF, Joint Venture has the ability to refuse to hire women with disabilities.[381]

Corporate jobs remain the most highly sought-after in prison, especially among women who do not receive financial support from the outside and rely on their prison wages to buy necessities, such as toothpaste, shampoo and menstrual products. These wages, however meager, become all the more important for basic survival. Marianne Brown recalled working for New Jersey's Office of Travel and Tourism (T-n-T) when DeptCor, the New Jersey Department of Corrections' employment industry, had a contract to provide workers. "When I started, we made great money: 58 cents an hour!" By working seven and a half hours a day every day, plus overtime (workers were still paid 58¢ per hour for overtime), Brown earned $130 to $145 per month. Prisoners answered calls about tourism, providing phone numbers and addresses for popular sites such as Great Adventure, parks, other recreational activities and accommodations. They also did data entry and filled requests for New Jersey travel guides.[382]

Those in the federal prison system have the option of working for UNICOR, a government corporation that ostensibly provides job-skills training to prisoners. UNICOR workers produce goods such as office furniture, electronics and vehicle parts for the federal government. They also provide services such as handling customer-service calls for private-sector firms.[383] At FMC Carswell, women can earn up to $2 per hour at the UNICOR-run call center.[384] While this hourly wage seems low, especially in comparison to jobs such as Joint Venture Electronics, UNICOR is the best-paying job that a federal prisoner can have and the low hourly pay adds up: by working overtime, women at FMC Carswell can earn up to $300 a month.[385] In contrast, other jobs, such as laundry, kitchen, floors, maintenance and orderly work, pay only 12¢ per hour. Women who have held these jobs for a long time may receive a pay raise to 17¢ or 24¢ per hour, but even that is uncertain. "Each department is only allowed so many slots with that pay range," recalled Kirsten, a former prisoner at FMC Carswell. "For example: The maintenance crews have ten positions. One [position] would be at twenty-four [cents], two at seventeen [cents], and the rest [at] twelve cents."[386] Thus, a long-time worker's likelihood of earning more depends not on her job performance but on the seniority of her fellow crew members.

Given the wages of these other jobs, it is little wonder that women cherish UNICOR jobs, no matter how monotonous, repetitive or intense they may be. "There is always a waiting list to get into UNICOR," recounted Yraida Guanipa.[387]

"[It] has been a blessing for me," wrote one woman who has spent more than a decade in the federal prison system. "Speaking as an inmate who didn't get much outside support, it was a help to have that two hundred to three hundred dollars coming to you every month (that's with a promotion up to Grade One) so that you can rest a lot easier know-ing that you will have money to buy your personal hygiene items and a little more."[388]

Although these are the top-paying jobs, these programs are not meant to benefit prisoners; they garner profits for corporations, who save money on overhead, taxes, vacation, sick leave, medical benefits, worker's compensation and unemployment. They also serve as a control mechanism, keeping prisoners from other activities, such as organ-izing against and/or disrupting the day-to-day operations of the prison.

Purchasing Power

At the Colorado Women's Correctional Facility, all prisoners are required to either work or attend school. Until February 2002, the daily pay rates ranged from 63¢ to $2.53 for jobs such as kitchen, laundry, housekeeping, maintenance, and library work, secretary and GED teacher.[389] Dawn Amos earned 63¢ for each of the four days she worked scrubbing and buffing the floors. In March 2002, the prison administration lowered wages even further. "I guess we were over budget or something," Amos speculated. "I'm sure that's a lie too cause the cops didn't get a pay cut."[390]

Prices in the prison's canteen do not reflect the women's income and purchasing power. One capsule of Tylenol costs 40¢, a stick of generic deodorant costs 96¢, and the cheapest soap available can be the equivalent of a day's earnings—63¢. Specific feminine items, such as tampons, cost $3.60 and must be saved for, even by those with the highest wage. There are no free items: "[They] don't give indigent people things cause technically there aren't any indigent inmates that's why they pay us."[391]

Even the "great" wages paid to women working for New Jersey's Office of Travel and Tourism Board barely cover their basic needs: "Fifty-eight cents an hour was the TOP pay and we never got a raise the whole four-and-a-half years I worked there. None of the jobs here have had any pay increases since I've been here! But commissary prices have went up about a dozen times."[392]

Job Mobility

Unlike women on the outside, women in prison have virtually no job mobility. Amos stated that at the Colorado Women's Correctional Facility, "if you want to leave a job for another one, it doesn't mean you can, it all depends on if your boss wants to let you go or not."[393] Women often are denied transfers from jobs such as maintenance and kitchen work: "It's like once they get you they never want to let you go."[394]

Women can also be forced off the better jobs. After working as the inmate representative at Denver Women's Correctional Facility for little over one year, Amos was told that because she had the position for so long, she was being returned to her previous job buffing the floors. "I was mad and shocked," Amos recalled. "I left in tears and wasn't sure I would come back to work."[395] Although she was assured that the change was routine and temporary, two years later Amos still has not been able to regain her position.

At Scott Correctional Facility in Michigan, once a woman is assigned a job, she must work at least 90 days. If she is fired or quits before then, she is forced to stay in her cell for 30 days and risks being ticketed for "Disobeying a Direct Order" or "Out of Place."[396] Although the prison offers "indigent loans" to women without jobs or outside support, those who lose their jobs are deemed ineligible. After losing her job as a relief porter, Kebby Warner applied for an indigent loan. "It was denied because I lost my job," she stated. "Now I have to wait until I get another job before I can apply again."[397] In the meantime, Warner ironed other women's clothes in exchange for soap, stamps and other items she was unable to buy at the prison's commissary.

At Scott, once a woman loses her job, her chances of being assigned another are slim: although Warner's unit houses 96 women, only 15 jobs are available to them. Those scheduled to appear before the parole board learn that, despite this shortage, the board holds lack of employment against applicants. Warner appeared before the parole board twice during the four and a half years she waited for a job. Each time, her lack of job was cited as a reason for being denied parole.

Hazardous Working Conditions

In some prisons, work environments resemble sweatshops, complete with the heightened risk of injury. At the Dwight Correctional Center in Illinois, the average monthly pay is $15 to $20 for 40 hours of work per week.[398] Women working as seamstresses are paid "literally pennies by the piecework." Supervising staff members are paid in proportion to their workers' output: "Women rushing to make the cut-off day have injured themselves on sewing machines—sewing their fingers."[399]

Some jobs hold even more risk of injury. At the Central California Women's Facility, a woman from Los Angeles was assigned to work on its farm. Despite the fact that she had never been on a farm, she received no training for her job. Shortly after she began, another prisoner, who had also never received any training, ran over her head with a tractor. She survived. Both women were disciplined.[400]

In California, women who are ill or have disabilities are still required to work unless the California Department of Corrections determines otherwise. California advocacy group Justice Now regularly receives complaints from women who had been designated as disabled by the Social Security Administration, but who are told by prison officials that they must work. Women who refuse to do so are punished by having their good time credits (time off sentencing) taken away. In California, a woman's sentence is reduced by one day for each day she works: thus, sick or disabled women may serve sentences twice as long as those who are able to work.[101]

Because of this policy, women push themselves to work despite illness, disability and resulting pain. In doing so, they risk further illness, disability, disfigurement or even premature death. One woman broke her foot in several places. Unwilling to give up her chance of an earlier release, she continued working a job that required her to stand for an entire shift, resulting in an ulcer on her other foot. Because she was a diabetic, the ulcer did not heal and soon, she was barely able to walk or stand. Despite this, the prison refused to recognize her medically compromised status, gave her virtually no medical assistance and continued to require her to work. Realizing that she would not receive adequate care in prison, the woman continued to work, hoping for a quicker release. One year later, she remained in prison. Her ulcer still had not healed; a bone protrudes from her foot and she may need to undergo amputation.[402]

Satisfaction

Some women still manage to derive satisfaction and meaning from their work. At the Central California Women's Facility, of 3,353 women, the prison's peer health education program has only four paid positions. The educators, who are paid 32¢ per hour, give daily presentations about harm reduction, transmission and prevention at the prison's various job sites.[403]

At the Edna Mahan Correctional Facility in New Jersey, women have the opportunity to work for Optical, an eyeglasses recycling program sponsored by the Lions Club. They sort, wash and log the prescriptions of hundreds of eyeglasses. They then repackage these glasses, label each box with the correct prescription and send them to the Lions Club, which redistributes them to those who cannot afford to buy new glasses.[404] Although she only earns $3 per day, Marianne Brown stated, "I love my job at Optical for it is a way to give back."[405]

At Scott Correctional Facility, Kebby Warner was assigned a job as a tutor for one of the prison's GED classes. Although she earned only 64¢ a day, she describes it as "a rewarding job." Most of her students have a fifth-grade literacy level but, "when they learn something new and [are] able to move forward, it's rewarding to see their happiness."[406]

Similarly, when Linda Caldwell was a teaching assistant at the ABE and GED classes at Dwight Correctional Center, she took pride in her work. "[Just] because I was in prison did not mean I should take my job less seriously. I liked what I was doing. I liked helping others learn."[407]

After being transferred to the Denver Women's Correctional Facility (DWCF), Dawn Amos was assigned to the job of inmate representative. "Basically I am an advocate for inmates who get a write-up," she stated shortly after starting. Amos not only worked with the women from DWCF, but also with prisoners at the neighboring men's prisons. "My main job is to make sure the paperwork (due process) is done correctly and the inmate was served on time."[408] Amos also advocated for mitigated sanctions for those who pled or were found guilty of the charges.[409]

Despite earning only 60¢ a day, Amos stated that she loved her job. "It's the best one I've ever had in and out of prison," she wrote ten months after starting.[410]

"Women work not to go crazy, not to have time to think about the world and life from which they were removed," stated Marilyn Buck, who has been incarcerated since 1985. "Working allows one to escape from thinking about the full extent of the punishment, not only to oneself, but also to family, children, friends, and former coworkers."[411]

For women in the newly instituted chain gangs, this has certainly been true. In 2006, while awaiting sentencing at the Clear Creek County Jail in Colorado, RJ was assigned a job on the jail's new female chain gang. Women on the chain gang do not get paid. Instead, they earn "good time" or time off their sentences.

RJ, who had recently given her newborn son up for adoption, stated that she was happy to be on the chain gang. She was not an anomaly among the jail's inmates: contrary to public expectation, the women at Clear Creek want to be on the chain gang. Although the job is tiring, backbreaking work in the hot sun, it is also the first chance they've been given to get out of their cells, be outdoors and accrue "good time." (The jail's male inmates have had the chain gang and other work opportunities for a while. They also have other chances to earn "good time.") "It helps me so much mentally and physically to be able to get fresh air, sunshine, exercise and to be able to interact with different people than usual," wrote RJ.[412]

The Clear Creek County Jail is not the only penal institution with a female chain gang. The Estrella Jail in Phoenix, Arizona, has had one since 1996. At six each morning, women are padlocked together by the ankle and taken to the county cemetery in the desert. There they bury the corpses of those without money or family members to pay for a funeral. The women, who are serving sentences of less than one year or are awaiting trial because they could not afford bail, volunteer for the chain gang to escape being locked in 8-by-12 foot cells for 23 hours a day. After 30 days on the chain gang, they are allowed to move from their cells to tents outside which, under the Arizona sun, exposes them to temperatures of 100 to 120 degrees Fahrenheit.[413]

In 2007, Colorado State Representative Dorothy Butcher proposed using prisoners to replace the migrant farm workers avoiding the state's new immigration laws. Ten women from the medium-security La Vista Correctional Facility were given the opportunity to earn $4 a day hoeing and thinning vegetables on five Colorado farms.[414]

One farm worker praised the program to the local paper the *Pueblo Chieftain*: "It's hard on your back, your arms and shoulders, the back of your legs," stated Lisa Richards, who relies on the $4 a day to buy the toiletries and other goods she needs from the prison commissary. "Add the temperature and wind, and some days it's pretty rough. But I'd much rather be out here than my last job in the kitchen at the facility."[415] Her job in the prison kitchen paid 60¢ per day.

Keeping Prisoners in Check

Like placement in family programs, prison officials have used job placements to prevent or punish women who complain or file grievances. In 2002, Kebby Warner filed a grievance against a male officer. Shortly after, another prisoner assaulted her at her job in the library. Prison officials used the assault as a pretext for removing her from the position "for the safety and security of the institution."[416]

Similarly, Barrilee Bannister was fired from her job as the visiting room photographer after reporting a male officer's sexual harassment. Despite receiving praise from officers with whom she had had problems in the past, her job was changed from full-time to part-time, then terminated altogether.[417]

The New Jersey prison system also uses job placement to control prisoner behavior: "A lot of women would apply for T-n-T and Optical [the DEPTCOR job that replaced T-n-T] because those jobs are considered 'a privilege.' You have to not be a troublemaker to get them," stated Marianne Brown.[418]

Similarly, unfair rules and restrictions that would immediately be challenged by workers on the outside are often instituted and enforced in prison: after authorities at the Federal Correctional Center in Coleman (FCC Coleman) learned that a 24-year-old prisoner had been impregnated during a seven-day furlough, they removed her from her position at UNICOR. "The Unit Manager gave us a speech to justify the authorities' actions," recalled Yraida Guanipa, who was imprisoned at FCC Coleman at the time. "He said that it is irresponsible to get pregnant while on a furlough because that is considered unplanned family."[419]

This is not the only instance in which employment has been used against women who defied institutional rules: when prison authorities at FCC Coleman discovered that another woman was having sex with an outside contractor, she was fired from her job at the prison's commissary, which paid over $100 per month.[420]

Fear of losing a higher-paying job keeps many women in line, especially given that the other jobs at FCC Coleman pay only $5, $16, $20 or $36 per month.[421]

Instances of Resistance

Those studying and organizing around labor issues have by and large neglected the female prison population. This is not to say, however, that women have never protested their working conditions—in 1975, prisoners at the North Carolina Correctional Center for Women staged a five-day demonstration, specifically citing "oppressive working atmospheres" as one of their concerns.[422] More recently, a woman in Texas, a state that requires all prisoners to work without pay, stated, "I refuse to work. I have sat down and quit doing prison altogether."[423]

Women have also organized to voice their discontent about the impact of prison work policies. Within a year of implementing the new farm program, the Colorado DOC began transferring women in and out of La Vista based solely on whether they qualified to work on the farm crew. Farm crews also took precedence over educational programs, causing women to either miss large segments of their classes or be pulled from class altogether.

In 2008, to accommodate the growing number of farm workers, prison administrators began planning to convert one of the two incentive units—dorm-like units with additional privileges for women who "behaved" themselves—to farm and kitchen-worker housing. The proposal caused a stir among prisoners: "This is a pretty big deal to everyone because it's going to cause major changes to people who are already in incentive, people who are in incentive as well as being farm workers, and future farm workers," reported RJ, who lived in an incentive unit but did not qualify for a farm crew. "Everyone here, especially those of us who are either in incentive, farm workers, [or] kitchen workers, are really riled up over all of this. In fact, this is the first time that I have seen this degree of organization between the women to do something about a concerning issue."[424]

After sending numerous written complaints to the prison administration and individually lobbying officers to oppose the plan, the women drafted a proposal outlining both their concerns and suggestions. They elected three representatives who met with prison officials who then took their proposal to a larger administrative meeting. "Staff members have said that what we came up with has had a big effect on everything," recalled RJ, one of the three prisoner representatives. "They think [that] if we hadn't said or done anything about it, the move would be underway."[425]

While the women's collective organizing did not entirely halt the prison's plan, it did force administrators to consider the women's needs: "They were rushing to get the changes done soon, but now we have been told that they want to wait four to six more months. I think they still have a lot to go over."[426]

Women working at prison jobs have also protested and blown the whistle on what they perceive as invasive or incorrect job policies. In 2004, Oregon prisoner Laura Maca not only quit her job as visiting-room photographer, but also wrote an exposé about a controversial prison policy which allowed not only prison employees, but also state employees, law enforcement officials and other government agencies to track prisoners, family members and friends through photos taken during prison visits.[427]

Women have also used work to express their dissatisfaction with other prison conditions. In 1971, women at Alderson Prison staged a four-day work stoppage to express solidarity with the (male) uprising at Attica.[428] In 1973, 90% of the women incarcerated in Clinton, New Jersey, participated in a three-day work stoppage to protest the prison's poor mail distribution, food and medical care.[429]

Work in women's prisons has garnered little to no attention from outside groups and organizations, perhaps because women's work (whether inside or out) is still largely invisible and perhaps because women's relationships to work complicate the existing discussions among those researching and organizing around prison labor. This silence and lack of outside support have not deterred women, such as RJ and others at La Vista Correctional Facility in Colorado, from speaking out and organizing against prison labor practices. Hopefully as interest in incarcerated women's issues continues to grow, others will begin to examine how labor and gender intersect behind prison walls and see the actions that the women have been taking to address them.

GRIEVANCES, LAWSUITS AND THE POWER OF THE MEDIA

L ike male prisoners, women struggle to change their conditions by filing grievances and lawsuits. These actions are rarely visible to the outside observer: grievances remain hidden behind prison walls and, unless some aspect of the case catches the attention of the media, most prisoner lawsuits also remain hidden. In addition, class-action lawsuits filed on behalf of (male) prisoners sometimes fail to recognize and address the concerns of women prisoners. For example, in the original settlement agreement for *Plata v. Davis*, a class-action lawsuit demanding improved health care for California prisoners, the CDCR sought to exclude incarcerated women on the grounds that no woman had been named as plaintiff. After a legal battle between prisoner advocates and the CDCR, the final settlement agreement included all women's medical issues and all women's prisons in California. In 2002, a settlement agreement was reached with the state of California. However, no woman had been named as a plaintiff and the health concerns of incarcerated women, including provisions for pregnancy-related care and breast and cervical cancer, had not been included in the agreement.[430] While the act of filing grievances and lawsuits has remained mostly unnoticed by both the general public and many outside activists, women have also reached out to the media in attempts to both expose and change their conditions of confinement.

Grievances

Women can—and often do—file official complaints or grievances about their conditions of confinement, including the abuse and neglect by the prison administration.

Many, however, have become disillusioned and/or fearful of this process. One woman prisoner interviewed by Human Rights Watch stated that the corrections officers "will tear it up and throw it in the garbage . . . or [they] will say, 'Go ahead and 602 [file an official complaint] me because I know it won't go nowhere.' Most 602s get thrown in the garbage before you go away. It's a joke to them."[431]

If the grievance does not go into the garbage, the prisoner faces a largely unsympathetic review board that often values the word of a staff member more than that of a prisoner. According to a former counselor at a Georgia prison, officials expect impunity for their actions because of the pervading belief that "inmates are criminals . . . their credibility is going to be in question from the very beginning."[432] Responding to the rash of sexual misconduct in Washington prisons, prison superintendent Kay Walter stated, "We will never take an inmate's word against staff— they're not in prison because they're honest people."[433]

As late as 1995, the Michigan Department of Corrections policy allowed an employee to participate in investigating a grievance against him or her. The accused employee often made the response to the complaint as well.[434] Although policy changes in 1995 removed the accused employee's participation in the investigation, he or she is still informed of the complainant's name and identification number at the onset of the investigation.[435] At the Colorado Women's Correctional Facility, the accused employee is still the one to address the prisoner's formal grievances, making it inevitable that the grievance will be denied. Dawn Amos observed that during her two years at that particular prison, she has "*never, ever* seen anyone win a grievance."[436] In California, any prisoner filing a grievance for sexual abuse must first speak to the perpetrator.[437]

"Most women know the grievance process is futile, unfair, and not complied with so they *won't* use it," stated a woman in Illinois. She, however, files grievances because, under the Prison Litigation Reform Act, a prisoner must exhaust the facility's grievance system before seeking court intervention.[438]

Not every woman views the grievance process as futile. Marcie Monroe, a prisoner at the Central California Women's Facility, points out that using the grievance procedure forces the California Department of Corrections (CDC) to comply with the court's orders to improve medical care. Monroe, whose back condition made her unable to work in the prison's kitchen, has filed numerous grievances against the prison for ignoring her medical condition and issuing disciplinary reports for her failure to work. These reports postponed her release date by six months. "I'm using my appeal and grievance procedure and I'm fighting these injustices," she wrote. She acknowledged that she may not win the battle for her original release date, "but at least I know that I did everything I could within my power to shed light on the hideous indiscretions we women are constantly subjected to while we are incarcerated."[439]

In December 2004, the Michigan Department of Corrections moved 817 women from the Western Wayne Correctional Facility to the Huron Valley Women's Prison, a facility that had previously been used as a 400 bed psychiatric hospital. Within four months, the women had already filed hundreds of grievances about their living conditions, including overcrowding, a shortage of toilets, inadequate medical care, and a lack of hot water for showers and heat.[440]

Their grievances had some effect: less than a year later, the prison had some heat (although, according to one woman's mother, the heat remained unreliable, going on and off without cause) and was seeking bids to begin construction on a cafeteria, which the facility had been lacking.[441]

Women at Huron Valley have not been the only ones to file grievances en masse to attempt to effect change. Yraida Guanipa recalled that at FCC Coleman, "mass-producing cop-outs" (filing complaints) has led to small changes. "However keep in mind that little things in prison means a lot," she stated.[442]

In November 2005, the women at FCC Coleman filed over 300 complaints against the facility's food. Their actions gained them a small victory: one evening, after a "town hall meeting" (the prison's term for a meeting in which staff lecture all of the prisoners in a given unit) in which the unit manager demanded that the women stop mass-producing cop-outs and reminded them that such an act was considered "inciting a riot," the prison cafeteria served shrimp for dinner. The following day, it served shrimp and rice soup.

"You may ask why I was so excited about these microscopic shrimp," Guanipa wrote. "We sometimes take small things in life for granted. Before coming to prison, shrimp did not mean anything to me, but after ten grim years of incarceration, I do not take anything for granted anymore."[443]

In December 2007, women at the Gatesville Unit in Texas used the grievance system not only to change conditions but also expose the cover-ups of prison officials. The women had asked outside family members to call the prison warden about the lack of heat. "Every time the wardens would call the lieutenant to verify [this] she would lie and tell them that the heaters were working in [housing units] 1B and 3B," recounted Dawn R. "Our dorm (1B) finally got together and wrote lots of grievances. We were able to get half the dorm to submit a grievance about the heater." Women who were more confident about their writing abilities helped those who were not. As a result, the women each received a second blanket and the wardens themselves visited the housing units instead of relying on the lieutenant's report. "The situation was so bad that the wardens made the call to evacuate women from 3B before the cold front came in. Sent them to other dorms or to other satellites. Obviously, we had been telling the truth." In addition, the lieutenant was placed under investigation.[444]

At other times, filing a grievance prompts prison officials to change policy before a court or outside agency can order them to do so. "Let me share this," stated "Elsie," a woman imprisoned in Illinois. "I've filed grievances. They've denied them in writing. However, they changed the practice or policy." She recounts one instance in which she filed a grievance challenging the prison's confiscation of self-addressed return envelopes from her correspondence bible studies courses. "In writing, each level [of administration] denied my grievance. However, they've stopped confiscating the envelopes." The change is a limited victory: because the prison had officially denied her grievance, it could begin confiscating the envelopes again at any time.[445]

However, while women have used the grievance system to obtain small changes, many do not. Marianne Sadelmyer, a former New York State prisoner whose sexual abuse case helped result in a law criminalizing sex between a prisoner and a guard, sees the grievance system as underutilized. "If every inmate that could file a valid claim against their state would, it would cripple corrections. Sadly, most women either don't know their rights, are unable to obtain counsel, or are just flat afraid of the repercussions that will surely come."[446]

Fortunately, not every woman allows fear to dictate her actions (or inactions): Marcie Monroe urged even "short termers" (women with relatively short sentences) at the Central California Women's Facility to utilize the prison's grievance process. "We may be going home in a few months or years, but what happens to those who are serving long terms or life? What if you were to come back? Or your mother, sister, aunt, daughter or friend find themselves in prison and they aren't getting the necessary medical treatment they need, and they die? Who will you blame? C.D.C. is only doing what we, the society, have allowed them to get away with."[447]

Lawsuits

Women have also gone to the judicial system to challenge conditions. They have filed class-action suits not only for themselves, but on behalf of **all** women imprisoned in their state.

In 1973, Michigan was one of several states that provided basic education programs in male but not female prisons.[448] In 1977, women imprisoned in Michigan's Huron Valley State Prison filed *Glover v. Johnson,* a class-action suit claiming that prison officials violated incarcerated women's rights under the Equal Protection Clause of the

Fourteenth Amendment by denying them access to the vocational and educational programs that were available to their male counterparts. In 1979, the court ruled in their favor and ordered the state to establish a general education program for women that was the equivalent to the one offered men.[449]

Interestingly, the court also ordered that the prison offer a course on legal skills to the women "because skilled women inmates are needed to provide access to the courts." In the court's opinion, although the Huron Valley law library met constitutional standards, its prisoners lacked the access to the courts guaranteed by the Fourteenth Amendment's due process clause. Male prisoners had a tradition of jailhouse lawyering and thus had developed expertise in utilizing legal resources, but "the women do not have a history of self-help in the legal field; the evidence tends to show that until recently they have had little access to adequate resources."[450]

In 1977, women at Bedford Hills Correctional Facility in New York filed suit against the prison system for an unconstitutionally defective medical care system. In *Todaro v. Ward*, the women charged the prison with failing to provide gynecological and general physical exams upon a prisoner's arrival, inadequate follow-up care and deficient recordkeeping. The Second Circuit Court of Appeals found that "interminable delays and outright denial of medical care" violated the women's constitutional rights and appointed an outside monitor to ensure that the prison complied with the court-ordered improvements. *Todaro* had long-lasting effects: 18 years later, in 2005, the Correctional Association of New York, an independent prison-monitoring agency, inspected Bedford Hills, interviewing prisoners about the facility's grievance procedure, medical care and programs. Most of the women had very positive comments about the quality of the gynecological care. Pap smears and mammograms were performed annually and the women received their test results in a timely manner.[451]

In 1995, women at Central California Women's Facility at Chowchilla and at the California Institution for Women at Frontera filed *Shumate v. Wilson*, a class-action suit against the state demanding an immediate improvement to the life-threatening medical care given to all women prisoners of the state.[452]

In March 1996, women incarcerated in Michigan filed *Nunn v. MDOC*, a federal lawsuit alleging staff sexual misconduct and sexual harassment. "The first time I sued the MDOC by myself (*Barker v. MDOC*). So, the second time I knew I had to get help," recalled Stacy Barker, one of the original plaintiffs. "It was happening to so many of us. I was the one who put my foot down and told them that it was going to keep on happening to us and others unless we did something about it." Because Barker had succeeded in her previous lawsuit against the prison for sexual assault, 30 other women agreed to sign onto the suit.[453]

That same month, women prisoners in Michigan also filed *Neal v. MDOC*, a class-action lawsuit on behalf of *all* women incarcerated in Michigan, charging the state's Department of Corrections with sexual assault, sexual harassment, violations of privacy, and physical threats and assaults.[454] These suits—and the embarrassing publicity that ensued—caused Michigan lawmakers to consider harsher penalties against DOC workers.

Lawsuits, however, can drag on with few, if any, visible changes before they are decided. Legislation on both the state and federal level has also limited prisoners' abilities to seek court intervention. In 1995, then-president Clinton signed the Prison Litigation Reform Act (PLRA), severely limiting prisoners' ability to legally challenge abysmal conditions. Supposedly passed to avoid frivolous lawsuits by prisoners, the PLRA requires would-be litigants to exhaust every administrative remedy offered by the prison before filing a lawsuit in civil court.[455] It also required that prisoners suing in federal court prove a lasting physical injury to collect for any mental or emotional harm wrought by prison staff or policy.[456]

Individual states have interpreted the PLRA differently. In New York State, a complainant is required not only to report the problem but also identify the means and procedures to remedy it. Thus, women seeking redress for sexual assault are not only required to file a grievance reporting the attack (an action which many women are hesitant to do for fear of reprisals) but also recommend reforms that the prison should enact to change the situation.[457] "The state is arguing that in order to have their day in court, women need to be able to articulate the failings of the policies and procedures which allowed the problem to occur," stated Legal Aid Society attorney Dori Lewis.[458] The state's argument ignores its own findings that nearly 60% of women imprisoned in New York State lack a high school diploma and that 40% read at an eighth-grade level or below.[459]

In 2003, 15 women imprisoned in New York State filed *Amador v. DOCS* to curb the widespread sexual abuse, harassment and assault by prison staff. Recognizing that their experiences were widespread, they sought class-action status in order to include all abused women incarcerated throughout the state. However, since many of the plaintiffs named in the suit had never filed grievances or official written complaints, the state's Department of Correctional Services has argued that they are ineligible to file a class-action lawsuit.[460]

States have passed additional legislation limiting or preventing prisoner lawsuits. In 1999, Michigan legislators approved HB4475 and HB4476, removing prisoners' rights to sue under the state's civil rights act. Legislators also changed the law: prisoners seeking monetary damages for assault now must prove lasting physical injury.[461] In 2005, the Michigan Court of Appeals upheld the legislature's changes; women who claim abuse after March 2000 are not covered by the state's civil rights act.[462] This requirement eliminated women's ability to seek monetary damages for most sexual abuse, including rape.

If a lawsuit is decided in favor of the prisoner plaintiffs, prisons are often slow to comply with a court's decisions and, in some cases, sign settlement agreements with limited monitoring periods rather than risk a court-ordered decision. The 1995 *Shumate v. Wilson* was settled in 1997. Just before the case was to go to court, a settlement agreement was reached with the State of California agreeing to change the way it provided medical care to women at the Central California Women's Facility (CCWF) and the California Institution for Women (CIW) and to submit to court-ordered monitoring. Valley State Prison for Women, another large prison across the street from CCWF, was excluded from the settlement agreement.

Under the settlement agreement, untrained prison employees would be banned from making judgments about prisoners' medical care, prisons would ensure medicines without undue lapses or delays and medical staff would offer preventive care, including pelvic and breast exams, pap smears and mammograms.[463]

The first court-ordered assessment occurred a year later and showed that the prisons were out of compliance in 11 of the 57 key areas. The second assessment found near-compliance. However, after interviewing nearly 200 prisoners and reviewing over 75 medical charts, advocacy group Legal Services for Prisoners with Children found evidence that medical files had been tampered with and prisoners who had received fraudulent lab results were never retested.[464]

In addition, despite the settlement agreement to improve medical care, women continued to experience delays in treatment and shoddy medical care, sometimes leading to preventable deaths. When Carolina Paredes entered CCWF in August 1999, she requested medical attention for abdominal pains that had plagued her all year. She was given a pelvic exam shortly thereafter, but not diagnosed with uterine cancer until October. The six cycles of chemotherapy that were to be immediately provided were continually interrupted when prison staff failed to transfer the required bloodwork or chemotherapy drugs with Paredes during her chemotherapy visits. In May 2000, she was given a terminal diagnosis of six months or less. She died alone on December 14, 2000, little over a year after entering prison.[465] The neglect leading to her death was not uncommon: in 1999, nine women died at CCWF. In 2000, 16 women at CCWF died. The prisoners' attorneys submitted a motion to the court to reopen discovery. The motion was denied and

Shumate v. Wilson was closed in August 2000.[466] Although the suit itself did not force the prisons to improve medical care, it nonetheless had an unexpected, far-reaching effect: outside activists formed the California Coalition for Women Prisoners (CCWP) to build support for the *Shumate* suit. The organization did not end with the lawsuit: CCWP continued and expanded its work, regularly visiting and corresponding with women at CCWF and CIW, advocating for compassionate release for women with terminal illnesses, and raising public awareness about issues facing women in prison.[467]

Despite their limitations, lawsuits have also provoked systemic change. The 1993 *Women Prisoners of District of Columbia Department of Corrections v. District of Columbia* forced the DC Department of Corrections to stop shackling—or otherwise physically restraining—pregnant women in labor.[468]

In 2006, Arkansas prisoner Shawanna Nelson, who had been shackled throughout her labor, filed a private suit against prison officials and private health care provider Correctional Medical Services. *Nelson v Norris* sought to ban the use of restraints on prisoners during labor and delivery. In response, the Arkansas Department of Corrections offered a compromise: women who met certain behavioral criteria would remain unrestrained while prisoners who were considered security risks would be restrained with nylon restraints instead of metal shackles and an 18" chain.[469]

As with prison grievances, when faced with a lawsuit, prison administrations have also changed conditions before a court could order them to do so. In 1973, women held at the Sybil Brand Institute, the Los Angeles women's jail, filed *Inmates of SBI v. The County of Los Angeles*, challenging the jail's refusal to allow children to visit their mothers, their lack of direct access to the general library, limited access to the law library, limited recreation time and restrictions on receiving magazines. In response to the filing of the suit, the administration changed its visiting policy to allow children. It also instituted two one-hour outdoor recreation periods each week.[470]

Grievances, Lawsuits and the Power of the Media

In response to the 1996 *Nunn v. MDOC*, the MDOC initiated several changes before it agreed to a court-ordered settlement. These changes included more extensive screening and increased training of both new hires and employees transferring to a women's prison, revised protocol for investigating complaints about sexual misconduct and training for prisoners about sexual misconduct.[471]

The MDOC also reached a settlement agreement in 2000 which limited housing unit staff to female officers, banned cross-gender patdown searches during an evaluation period, and limited the circumstances under which male officers can transport women or remain with them in medical examining rooms. The agreement also mandated that MDOC improve its procedures for reporting and investigating sexual misconduct and for controlling acts of retaliation against women who report misconduct.[472]

In 1999, after prosecutors refused to charge prison guard Michael Stevens for sexually assaulting and impregnating Washington State prisoner Heather Wells, Wells filed a $5,000,000 lawsuit against the state. The state settled with Wells for $150,000, the largest prisoner settlement in its history.[473] The year before, another prisoner impregnated by a prison employee sued the state and was awarded $110,000. A second prisoner, who had been fondled by the same employee, was awarded $3,500.[474]

The cost and publicity of these lawsuits led to state legislative support for a bill criminalizing staff-prisoner sex. In February 1998, a bill proposing making sex with a prisoner a felony lacked the support to bring it to a vote.[475] The next year, however, after the state had settled with Wells, the House unanimously approved SB5234, which criminalized all sex between prison staff and prisoners.[476]

Media

Gaining media attention often gains quicker results than filing lawsuits. After their abuse caught the media's attention, Barrilee Bannister and the other 77 women who had been transferred to Arizona from Oregon were removed from the abusive all-male prison. Prior to that, those who complained about the guards' attacks had been placed in segregation units, had good time taken away and were sometimes monetarily fined while their assailants suffered no consequences.[477] In 1996, after a highly publicized case in which a guard at Bedford Hills plea-bargained to sodomizing a prisoner, New York State enacted a law making it a felony for prison guards to have sex with prisoners.[478]

The power of the media became evident when, in 1999, national television journalist Geraldo Rivera's report on official sexual misconduct in prison was cited several times during a House debate about prison-related legislation.[479] In response, the MDOC adopted a new rule the following year: "a news media representative shall not be allowed to use or possess a camera or other audio or visual recording device while on a visit with a prisoner." The rule applies only to individual prisoners. The rule allows media representatives to interview prisoners by telephone or on a visit, but telephone conversations can (and will) be monitored and recorded. In addition, prison rules only allow prisoners to call the 20 phone numbers on their approved telephone access list. Phone numbers can only be added or deleted every six months. MDOC rules also limit a person to being on a visitor list of only one prisoner to whom she is not closely related. Again, list changes are only allowed once every six months.[480]

In 1999, *Nightline* aired a six-part series on conditions at California's Valley State Prison for Women. After prisoner after prisoner told *Nightline* anchor Ted Koppel about being given a pelvic exam as "part of the treatment" for any ailment, including stomach problems or diabetes, Koppel asked the prison's chief medical officer, Dr. Anthony DiDomenico, for an explanation.

"I've heard inmates tell me they would deliberately like to be examined. It's the only male contact they get," DiDomenico answered in front of the cameras. That DiDomenico made such a statement on network television demonstrates the belief that, no matter how egregious their actions, prison officials will not be held accountable. When a local

TV news program aired DiDomenico's statement, however, he was reassigned to a desk job in Sacramento and an investigation was begun.[481] Without media coverage of this sexual misconduct, DiDomenico most likely would have stayed at his position. Prisoner advocacy organization Legal Services for Prisoners with Children had been reporting the prisoners' complaints about medical staff's sexual misconduct to the CDC for four years with no result. After the *Nightline* series aired, not only was DiDomenico reassigned, but a second doctor was relieved of his duties six months later. As of 2001, both doctors had been criminally indicted.[482]

But while prison abuse remains behind closed doors and out of the public eye, policy makers, legislators and the courts remain reluctant to interfere in the daily operations and conditions of prisons.

Another example of the power of the media occurred in 2001. An anonymous female prisoner telephoned the *Milwaukee Journal Sentinel* to report staff medical neglect which had led to the death of prisoner Michelle Greer. This one phone call prompted *Sentinel* reporter Mary Zahn to begin investigating. Two weeks after Greer's unnecessary death, Zahn had not only publicized the story, but also turned her death into a "minor sensation." The publicity led the Wisconsin Department of Corrections to investigate the incident and suspend the two nurses who initially ignored Greer's requests for medical assistance, then bungled their eventual response, leaving her to die. The article also prompted the State's Assembly's Corrections and Courts Committee to hold investigative hearings into the incident.[483]

This one story led to the paper's own investigation as to whether the neglect causing Greer's death was an isolated incident. For the following eight months, Zahn and a fellow journalist Jessica McBride investigated every prisoner death since 1994, revealing "a dysfunctional health care system in which gravely ill prisoners, often while literally begging for medical treatment, are ignored—and sometimes even disciplined for being 'aggressive' or 'disruptive.'"[484] Their findings led to a series of articles about the inadequate and often times life-threatening medical care in Wisconsin prisons, prompting the state's lawmakers to introduce legislation requiring better-trained medical staff, improved medical record-keeping, and the creation of an independent panel of outside medical experts to review prison deaths.[485]

Had that one phone call not been made, the deaths of Greer and other Wisconsin prisoners, both male and female, would have remained swept under the rug. This anonymous woman prisoner protested the conditions of the prison-industrial complex by attracting media attention to the issue.

Official Retaliation

Fear of reprisals is not unfounded. Those who file grievances and lawsuits are often subject to administrative retaliation. A woman at the Colorado Women's Correctional Facility who participated in a class-action lawsuit received two disciplinary tickets and was transferred to a prison in Denver. "That may not seem harsh to you or others," explained Dawn Amos, "but the women in here over time find security and stability, with friends, lovers, or their jobs and the fear of being uprooted and moved to another city really scares them."[486] In retaliation for her involvement in *Glover v. Johnson*, officers issued major misconduct tickets to lead plaintiff Mary Glover at every opportunity, even when the charge was absurd. "I got tickets for things like not having a pass to a tree," Glover recalled. "I was standing under a tree. I had a pass to be in the yard, but they [prison staff] wrote me a major misconduct out-of-place ticket for not having a pass to the tree." The tickets resulted in repeated trips to segregation and, ultimately, seven additional years in prison.[487] Barrilee Bannister and the other women transferred from the CCA-run prison in Florence, Arizona are now viewed as "troublesome prisoners" and have been labeled as "Security Threat Groups," a classification used for street and prison gangs, anti-government groups, hate groups, environmental terrorists and motorcycle gangs.[488] New York State prisoner Marianne Sadelmyer was classified as a "maximum status" prisoner, transferred to various facilities throughout the state and denied work release.[489] Michigan prisoner Stacy Barker was assaulted by prison staff, issued bogus substance abuse tickets and denied visits with her daughter and grandchildren.[490]

Prison officials are even willing to jeopardize a prisoner's health in retaliation for filing a lawsuit. At Huron Valley, prison officials promised women serving life sentences that they would recommend them for parole if they intimidated Glover into transferring out of the prison. As a result, some of the women threatened to slash Glover's face. Glover brought the threats up in court and was subsequently transferred to Florence Crane Correctional Facility.[491] Because she was the lead plaintiff in *Shumate v. Wilson*, Charisse Shumate only received the blood transfusions necessary for those with sickle-cell anemia once every three months.[492] That such practices are allowed to continue signifies the extent that prison authorities have kept public scrutiny, and thus outrage, from their walls and can therefore conduct daily operations as they see fit. Since 1995, for example, California prison policy bans the media from talking to specific inmates.[493] This prevents prisoners from drawing more widespread attention to the abuse and neglect behind bars, reinforcing the invisibility of prisoners and any struggles to challenge and change their conditions. In 2002, the California Department of Corrections proposed restricting legal visits to attorneys, licensed investigators and professional paralegals, thus preventing many prisoner rights groups, who rely on interns, volunteers and law students, from assisting prisoners with their legal work. Another proposed change bars attorneys from inquiring about or investigating prison conditions. The amended rule would require that the visiting attorney be the prisoner's lawyer of record, be fulfilling a judicial request, be representing the prisoner in a legal proceeding or be consulting for possible future representation.[494]

Even those who file grievances risk reprisals: Vickie Hoskins, one of the 817 women housed at Huron Valley, told *Metro Times*, "I know I'm going to be retaliated against for speaking out." She understood that, by filing grievances and speaking to the media, she had opened herself up to arbitrary shake-downs (searches in which a prisoner's cell is ripped apart under the pretense of looking for contraband) and increased scrutiny by guards seeking to write more disciplinary tickets for her.[495] Hoskins' fears are not unfounded: Yraida Guanipa states that she had mass-produced cop-outs for the first few years of her 12-year sentence. "I suffered a lot for it," she recounted. "I was sent to solitary confinement; I was placed in the worst job in prison; my cubicle and my work place was shaken-down over and over again."[496]

Despite the lack of public attention and the threat of administrative retaliation, women continue to file grievances and lawsuits. Realizing that carrying a pad of paper made her actions more visible, Mary Glover, who went on to participate in eleven other civil rights cases against MDOC, used the prison's discarded cement bags to record legal information. She then passed these bags to her lawyers during her legal visits and, in at least one case, later had the bags introduced into evidence in court. "It was the only way we could prepare for court without getting knocked off," she laughed years later.[497] Although Guanipa no longer files grievances for fear of losing her eligibility for furloughs and the possibility of transferring to a halfway house, she stated that other women at FCC Coleman continue to do so. "I must confess that I truly enjoy watching the process," Guanipa wrote. "The seeds were well planted."[498]

Another woman who single-handedly files grievances and civil suits in an attempt to improve her surroundings stated: "If I give up I may as well lay down and die."[499]

BREAKING THE SILENCE

Incarcerated Women's Media

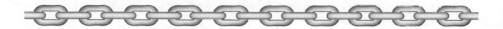

D uring her ten and a half years behind bars, Yriada L. Guanipa wrote to every mainstream newspaper and media source in the nation to draw attention to the plight of incarcerated women. The only response she ever received was a form letter from Donald E. Graham, the board chair of the *Washington Post*: "Thank you for your recent submission. Unfortunately, this is not the sort of work that *The Washington Post* is in a position to publish. I appreciate your interest and wish you the best in finding another outlet for your work." From other media, including National Public Radio, Guanipa received nothing.[500]

Guanipa's experience is not uncommon. Although the number of women behind bars nearly doubled from 68,468 to 104,848 between 1995 and 2004, their voices and stories still remain unheard by both mainstream and activist-oriented media.[501] Articles about both prison conditions and prisoners often portray the male prison experience, ignoring the different issues facing women in prison. While an occasional article spotlights the sexual abuse in female facilities, less-headline-grabbing concerns have largely remained unnoticed. "We do not hear from the media how many prisoners are killed every day inside our prisons, how many die for lack of proper or timely medical care, how many prisoners are raped inside our prison's walls, how many children are born inside prison walls, how many female prisoners are forced into abortion after becoming pregnant from a staff member, how many of us do not see our children for years, how many of us are just left behind these prison walls for years," stated Guanipa.[502]

Many activist-oriented publications mirror the mainstream media's masculinization of prisons and prisoners, contributing to the invisibility of women behind bars. Because they receive much less attention than their male counterparts, women in prison receive much less support from both individual activists and prisoner rights groups.

However, a growing segment of incarcerated women are recognizing the need to make their voices heard. Instead of waiting passively for others to take note of and report their concerns, women in prison are telling their own stories: some have used pre-existing alternative media, whether radical feminist journals or prison publications, while others have created their own outlets. Women's acts of writing—and publishing—often serve a dual purpose: they challenge existing stereotypes and distortions of prisoners and prison life, framing and correcting prevailing (mis)perceptions. They also boost women's sense of self-worth and agency in a system designed to not only isolate and alienate its prisoners but also erase all traces of individuality.

Utilizing Radical Feminist Media

While many independent magazines and newsletters receive and sometimes publish contributions from prisoners, the majority of the printed letters, essays, articles and columns are from men in prison. While the number of incarcerated men is still more than ten times their female counterparts, the lack of stories by and about women in prison reinforces the assumption that the prison experience is universally male. By focusing solely on the stories and experiences of men in prison, independent magazines and newsletters, such as *Maximum Rocknroll* and *Green Anarchy*, perpetuate the silencing of women's voices and concerns.

Radical feminist media, on the other hand, have been more receptive to the specific voices and concerns of women in prison.

Breaking the Silence

From July 1999 until its closing in late 2002, every issue of the feminist magazine *Sojourner: A Women's Forum* devoted at least one page not only to the unique issues facing women in prison, but also to the voices of the women themselves. The section, entitled Inside/Outside, sought to provide prisoners with "a forum within our pages so that their ideas and personal and collective battles could be better heard and included within national women's organizing."[503]

Most women entering the prison system do so with low self-esteem, often after years of repeatedly being made to feel as if their words, thoughts and actions are meaningless. For these women, having their words and thoughts taken seriously is, in and of itself, a major achievement: "Seeing my name, picture and words in the paper made me feel proud and pleased with my accomplishment. It renewed my faith in myself and my [writing] gift," wrote a woman in Pennsylvania's Muncy State Prison. "My family was so proud, as well as my partner."[504]

Furthermore, providing a regular forum for incarcerated women's writings undermined the alienation that prisons seek to foster. Prisons seek to efface all traces of a prisoner's individuality and self-determination. Thus, for women who are told when to get up, when to eat, what to eat, when to move and when to stay still, the act of expressing oneself—and the idea that their expression is heard by others—becomes not only a means of drawing attention to prison conditions but also an act of subversion against both their own lack of agency and the isolating effects of prison.

Inside/Outside provided an opportunity not only for women to express themselves but also to spotlight abuses in the prison system that remained unnoticed by both other media and many groups working around criminal justice issues. During its four years of existence, Inside/Outside covered working conditions in women's facilities, the dehumanizing treatment of children visiting their mothers, and prisoner suicides. Women used the column to alert outside feminists to the injustices they faced: Jamie Bowen wrote an article exposing the poorly trained staff, bad food, inadequate medical care and Kafka-esque bureaucracy for filing a grievance to complain at the privately run prison where she was held.[505] Sydney Heizer Villa, a woman incarcerated in Texas where any books referencing homosexuality are considered contraband, wrote an article about the rampant homophobia of both staff members and fellow prisoners.[506] Dawnya Ferdinandsen wrote about the suicide of her fellow prisoner Carol Bell at the Ohio Reformatory for Women, sparking an expose on the facility's poor mental health care.[507]

In addition, *Sojourner* offered free subscriptions to incarcerated women. Interest was startlingly high: within two years, the number of incarcerated female subscribers grew from twenty to over three hundred and, by the time *Sojourner* closed in late 2002, over 1,000 incarcerated women subscribed to the journal. Letters from prisoners revealed how much *Sojourner* had helped break through the isolation and alienation fostered by incarceration: "I wish to thank you for my subscription to *Sojourner*," wrote a woman at Kentucky Correctional Institution for Women. "It keeps me up to date on current issues that affect women daily."[508] Furthermore, the Inside/Outside section helped prisoners realize that the issues they faced were systemic rather than individual: "I thought no one else had the problems we face here with guards, medical, and basic human treat[ment]," stated "Elsie," a prisoner at Dwight Correctional Center in Illinois.[509]

Sojourner not only connected women in prison with each other, but also helped break the additional isolation that many lesbian and queer women feel in prison. In a system that fosters homophobia among both prisoners and staff, the recognition of lesbian, bisexual and transgender concerns is reassuring. "This prison is the only women's prison in Kentucky and the guards are very homophobic. If I sit too close to another woman it is a sexual write-up. The guards say that if they allow us to touch each other then they are promoting homosexuality," wrote another woman in the Kentucky Correctional Institute for Women. "You are my contact with reality and I thank you."[510]

Sojourner closed in 2002, leaving incarcerated women nationwide without a regular (and widely read) public forum for their voices.

Sojourner was not the only feminist magazine to attempt to break the silence around women in prison. In the 1970s, feminist journal *off our backs* regularly printed letters from Carol Crooks and other incarcerated women about their struggles. In February 2001, it published an issue specifically to women in prison. It solicited the stories of incarcerated women and devoted over three pages to their letters, some of which touched on prison overcrowding, the lack of counseling for abuse survivors, the lack of educational and vocational training and the isolation that prison imposes.

Although *off our backs* did not begin offering a regular column or even actively soliciting submissions from incarcerated women, it remained open to their voices.

In 2003, it published an article on the importance of vocational programs to women behind bars. Its author, Rhonda Leland, was a California prisoner who had graduated from one of these programs and who wanted to rally public opposition to the state's proposal to eliminate them.[511]

The next year, *off our backs* published a letter by Leland on behalf of her fellow prisoner Debra Holmes. After serving 20 years in prison, Holmes was scheduled to appear before the parole board. "The parole board will expect her to parole to the county of commitment, have a job offer ahead of time, and a place to reside. The board will expect Debra to walk out of prison after twenty years and have a pre-fabricated life fit to their design." Leland urged *off our backs* readers to write letters to the California Board of Prison Terms, halfway houses, social service agencies and prospective employers on Holmes' behalf. "She is a participant in women's support groups and long-term organizations. She is active in helping others and is a candidate for parole," Leland wrote. "I am requesting that each person who reads this article donate at least one hour and a few stamps to write letters of support. Let Debra know she is not alone or forgotten, please!"[512] By writing a letter to a nationally distributed journal, Leland not only raised awareness and garnered outside support for her friend but also broke through the sense of isolation shared by many behind bars.

Working with Prison Rights Groups

Women in prison have also reached out to prisoner rights groups to make their voices heard. Since 1996, women in California have regularly submitted short articles, art and poetry to *The Fire Inside*, the quarterly newsletter of advocacy group California Coalition for Women Prisoners. According to its mission statement, *The Fire Inside* defines itself as a space where both women and their supporters "communicate with each other and the broader public about the issues and experiences women prisoners face."[513]

Like the contributors of *Sojourner's* Inside/Outside column, the women writing for *The Fire Inside* often felt validated by seeing their words in print: until her death, prisoner organizer and domestic violence survivor Charisse Shumate was a regular contributor to the newsletter, often writing about her struggles to obtain adequate medical care not only for herself but for all of the women in the Central California Women's Facility. In addition to drawing public attention to the prison's negligent and sometimes life-threatening medical care, Shumate's writings "helped her alter her own perception of herself."[514] Whereas the act of being published and having their voices heard is important for all women in prison, it is particularly so for those whose self-esteem has been chipped away by years of domestic violence and other forms of regular abuse. The act of writing and being published becomes even more significant for women who have repeatedly been belittled, battered and silenced.

In 2002, the Northwest prisoner support group Break the Chains, which had concentrated on male political prisoners, began to recognize its inadvertent exclusion of incarcerated women. The group announced that each issue of its quarterly newsletter would devote four pages to writings from women at Coffee Creek Correctional Facility, Oregon's only women's prison. Until its demise in 2005, the group devoted a section of every newsletter to incarcerated women, raising their visibility among the Northwest prisoner support movement which, until that point, had primarily focused on men. "Response to the women's writings is really good from a distinct class of activists: Folks who were Black Bloc style anarchists at one point but are now more concerned with identity politics, race, gender and class," stated one Break the Chains organizer.[515] Including the voices and stories of incarcerated women raised awareness of these issues among readers who, in the past, had simply not considered them.

Like the women who had written for *Sojourner's* Inside/Outside column, Coffee Creek's prisoners wrote not only about their personal difficulties but also exposed invasive prison policies. Laura Maca, for instance, wrote a short article exposing the prison's new (yet unannounced) policy which allowed not only prison employees, but also state employees, law enforcement officials and other government agencies to track prisoners, family members and friends through photos taken during prison visits.

Creating their Own Media

Recognizing that forums for incarcerated women's voices are still too few, women have also sought to create their own media. At the Edna Mahan Correctional Facility for Women (EMCFW) in New Jersey, 24 prisoners put out *Perceptions*, a monthly newspaper for the women in that facility. The project began when Rebecca Sanford, a professor teaching weekly business-writing classes at the facility, learned that the prison's previous newspaper, *The Insider*, was defunct. She and another professor, Dr. Eleanor Novek, gained permission to start a newspaper from the facility's education department. However, at their first meeting, Charlotte Blackwell, the prison's warden, warned both women that *Perceptions* would not be allowed to become "a forum for a mass drawing together on issues." She cautioned that certain topics, such as prison medical care, were to be avoided.[516]

Although Sanford and Novek had initiated the project, the women at EMCFW took ownership of it. They met nearly every day to work on editing, typing, design and layout. The women also decided which subjects and stories were newsworthy. The paper's first issue was printed in February 2002.[517]

In the first issue, only one piece offered any criticism of any of the prison's conditions. One obvious drawback of running a newsletter within the facility and with the administration's approval was the need to censor any criticism of prison policy or conditions: the final decision on content was made by Charlotte Blackwell.[518] The women involved recognized this from the beginning: Dr. Novek recounted an early meeting with the journalism students. One student proposed a story about the warden's disrespect of the prisoner representatives assigned to bring her the other women's concerns. The other students immediately vetoed the idea, voicing concern that identifying critical issues would jeopardize the newspaper's existence.[519]

Despite these concerns, not all approved content painted the facility in a positive light. In an editorial, *Perceptions* writers broached the question of what they would and would not do if they (the prisoners themselves) were in charge of running a women's prison. Their fantasies revealed the absence of programming for older women and those in the maximum custody unit, emergency counseling and therapeutic interventions and opportunities for mother-child interactions. It also drew attention to the facility's overcrowding and increased potentials for violence and conflict among prisoners. In a subsequent issue, two prisoners interviewed the facility's education supervisor about the prison's age limit for college classes, both drawing attention to the exclusion of prisoners over the age of 24 from higher education programs and pressuring the supervisor to keep his promise to change this condition.[520]

As promised, writing directly critical of the prison has been censored: Marianne Brown submitted an essay criticizing the prison's waste of food. "The administration would not let me print it, but it's the truth."

According to Brown, Blackwell visited her personally and told her, "*Perceptions* is not the place to air out our dirty laundry. It is for the women to share positive things with one another."[521]

In addition, the "privilege" of having a forum for their voices is also tenuous. In 2006, the administration stopped both the journalism classes and *Perceptions*.[522]

However, having such an outlet for expression—even one with the possibility of administrative censorship—is still a rarity for most women in prison. When Yraida L. Guanipa attempted to establish a prisoner newsletter through the NAACP chapter at her federal prison, the administration refused to approve the project. "The camp administrator did not give us a reason," she wrote. "They do not need to. The answer was [simply that] the proposal was not approved and there are not [administrative] remedies available."[523]

Other women have sought to both circumvent administrative control and reach a wider audience. In 2002, women at Oregon's Coffee Creek Correctional Facility decided to create a zine written by and for women in prison. "My goal was to unite women prisoners and get their stories to people in the outside world," wrote Barrilee Bannister, whose earlier attempts to write for anarchist zines had resulted in disciplinary action and being labeled a gang member by prison authorities. "I wanted the voices of women in prison—who are also mothers, daughters, grandmothers, aunts and nieces—to be heard."[524]

Lacking access to equipment and supplies such as printers, copy machines and postage, Bannister asked women on the outside to publish and distribute *Tenacious: Art and Writings by Women in Prison*. Announcements of the zine's existence and its promise of free subscriptions to incarcerated women were sent to *Sojourner*'s prisoner subscription list and to those who requested books from the Women's Prison Book Project, an organization sending free reading material to incarcerated women nationwide. Both submissions and requests for subscriptions came from women across the country.

Free from the need to seek administrative approval, incarcerated women wrote about the difficulties of parenting from prison, dangerously inadequate health care, sexual assault by prison staff and the scarcity of educational and vocational opportunities, especially in comparison to their male counterparts. Although circulation remained small, the women's stories provoked public response. An account of harassment for reporting a prisoner-officer affair led to a letter-writing campaign spearheaded by Break the Chains members, who demanded an end to the harassment and that staff members be held accountable for their actions.

In another instance, the act of publishing also prompted a more personal response. Stephanie Walters Searight, a 27-year-old Michigan prisoner, wrote about discovering that she was HIV-positive when she entered prison. Her story had an unexpected result: "My last article has inspired my mom to travel the five states [from Georgia to Michigan] to visit. You'll never know what that means to me," she wrote in a note included with a subsequent submission. "It has been years since I have been able to see her."[525]

Tenacious also raised awareness about women in prison among individuals who had previously been uninvolved in prison activism. The women's social justice zine *Caryatid Rises* made women in prison its theme for one issue while the editor of the Midwestern mama-zine *Mad Lovin' Mama* decided to not only accept submissions from mothers in prison but also to look into doing support work for women imprisoned in her home state.

Not all prisoners are lucky enough to find sympathetic outsiders to help them get their words out. Hoping to persuade an outside church to support her endeavor, Yraida L. Guanipa designed a mock-up for a newsletter of articles written by women at Florida's federal prison in Coleman. However, despite the advocacy of at least one member, the church remained uninterested in the project.[526]

"This is not the first time that I have created a sample," Guanipa stated. In past years, she had submitted three other sample newsletters to both individuals and organizations that originally expressed interest in the idea. Despite their initial enthusiasm, all have ultimately turned down Guanipa's proposal.

However, Guanipa refused to give up: "I will keep trying until I find an organization or person to help me. I truly believe that we federal prisoners have better resources and we can help our sisters in state and county prisons."[527]

New Possibilities: Utilizing E-mail

In 2005, utilizing the Bureau of Prisons' new e-mail system for prisoners, Guanipa began sending out descriptions of life in FCC Coleman. "Prison Talk Online" (PTO) started with only five recipients and the idea that each would pass her e-mails to a wider audience who, in turn, could ask questions about her experiences or about the federal prison system in general.[517] One correspondent reposted Guanipa's words on a blog and, one year later, reported that the site—also named "Prison Talk Online"—received over 500 hits per week.[529] Like the women who write for *Tenacious*, Guanipa's mode of communication freed her from the confines of having to seek administrative approval, allowing her to write critically about her surroundings. Her first PTO detailed the preparations for a visit from prison officials from Iraq: "A week before their visit, the authorities ordered us to wax, paint and/or wash everything to make our prison look like a spotless heavenly prison (unrealistic)."[530] In a subsequent PTO, she detailed the dismal gynecological care: "They all wanted to perform a hysterectomy, I once questioned the authorities about that and they said that it was cheaper for the BOP [Bureau of Prisons] because the hysterectomy solves all female problems instead of providing gynecological services for 10-15-20-25 . . . years to a female prisoner (make your own conclusions)."[531]

Forbidden Words

Creating their own outlets of expression has not freed women entirely from the reality of prison censorship: less than two years after the inception of *Tenacious*, incarcerated women complained about not receiving their subscriptions. Despite rules requiring prison mailrooms to alert both the sender and the prisoner about rejected mail, several disposed of the publication without informing either. In addition, many mailrooms failed to return the zine to the sender. Thus, neither the outside editing collective nor the imprisoned subscribers were aware that *Tenacious* had been prohibited in certain facilities. "I thought you had gotten busy and forgot to send me a copy," wrote one contributor.[532]

In spring of 2004, Coffee Creek Correctional Facility banned the seventh issue. A piece that named and accused specific correctional officers of harassing a lesbian prisoner was deemed inflammatory, ("disrespects staff at Coffee Creek Correctional Facility") and was thus labeled "detrimental to the security, safety, health, good order or discipline of the facility."[533] The Pocatello Women's Correctional Center in Idaho rejected the zine specifically because it contained writings by other women in prison and thus could be considered inmate-to-inmate correspondence, which is banned in several states, including Idaho.

Other publications with articles criticizing, or even exposing, prison conditions have also been prohibited. Because of Dawnya Ferdinandsen's article about suicide, the Ohio Reformatory for Women (ORW) banned that particular issue of *Sojourner*. One prisoner at ORW complained, "I was called to the mailroom and told I could not have the paper as it was a risk to security, detrimental to inmates and a whole bunch of other negative b.s."[534] In addition, ORW officials confiscated another issue of *Sojourner* from Ferdinandsen stating that, although the journal had previously been allowed in, it now "had to go to the newspaper committee."[535]

Less than a year after she began PTO, Guanipa also encountered problems: "My PTO articles have been under heavy scrutiny by SOME correctional officers. Apparently some officers were offended with my writing and their decision was to hold off on some of my privileges."[536]

The privilege threatened was Guanipa's furlough, which would have allowed her to spend 36 hours outside the prison with her two sons. "My furlough was on hold because the unit manager (the highest authority in the camp) does not like my PTO articles," Guanipa wrote the following week.[537]

The threat of losing her furlough almost had the desired effect. "I can easily handle the rest of my sentence even if all of my privileges are taken away. But if any of the privileges taken away involves my family, I'd have to think twice."[538]

Guanipa ultimately did receive her 36-hour furlough. Perhaps because the threat never became a reality, she continued writing PTO, exposing the fraud, neglect and abuse perpetrated by prison staff and the official policies that allowed these behaviors to continue.[539]

Content, however, has not been the only reason prisons have prohibited prisoner-created media. In some instances, merely the fact that women are able to have their words printed is seen as threatening. In 1997, women participating in a writing workshop at the Northeast Prerelease Center, a medium/minimum security prison in Cleveland, Ohio, created *The Circle*, a chapbook of their finished works. However, when the writing instructors attempted to bring the chapbooks to the workshop, the guards refused to allow them to bring them in, stating that they needed permission from the warden first. "So we had to leave the books with the guards at the entryway that day and await word from the warden," recalled one instructor. One month later, the prison still had not granted permission and the women had still not seen the final product. The prison administration never gave a reason for denying the women access to their books.

Eventually, the instructors asked each participant for a family member's address and sent him or her the students' copies.[540]

Getting Their Words Out

The absence of other media indicates the continued lack of resources and support for incarcerated women's voices within both the radical feminist and prisoner rights movement.

In addition, prisoner-made media is not widely distributed, if it is distributed at all. *Perceptions* is not made available to people outside the Edna Mahan Correctional Facility. "Many have made their way outside the prison when writers send their articles home or to friends," said Rebecca Sanford.[541] Thus, while *Perceptions* provides an outlet for women to express their ideas and experiences, its lack of distribution to a wider audience prevents it from being a tool to raise awareness about—and possibly galvanize public response to—issues concerning women in prison.

The newsletter for Break the Chains was distributed by the group itself and not included on other literature lists of prisoner support groups or mail-order zine distributors. In addition, Break the Chains remained a regional group, focusing on those incarcerated in the Pacific Northwest. Thus, while providing women imprisoned in Oregon with a forum to share their concerns with each other and with their male counterparts, the newsletter's limited distribution prevented their stories from being widely read.

Despite its inclusion of women incarcerated across the country, the mailing list for *Tenacious* is similar in size. However, unlike the Break the Chains newsletter, copies of *Tenacious* are sold at several info-shops and small bookstores along the East Coast, such as Baltimore's Atomic Books, the DC-based Brian MacKenzie infoshop and Toronto's Uprising Bookstore. Several zine distributors—small, such as Dreamers' Distro, and large, such as Microcosm in the United States and Great Worm Express in Canada—also distribute *Tenacious*. Despite its slightly greater distribution and favorable reviews in widely read activist publications such as *Slug and Lettuce, HeartattaCk* and *Maximum Rocknroll*, requests for *Tenacious* from non-incarcerated individuals remain much fewer than those of women behind bars.

The Fire Inside, the newsletter of the California Coalition for Women Prisoners, is an exception to the limited distribution of prisoner-made media. It boasts a circulation of over 2,000 and has an online archive accessible to anyone with an Internet connection.[542] The newsletter's extensive circulation, as well as its connection to advocacy group California Coalition for Women Prisoners, is especially important given the California Department of Corrections' 1995 rule forbidding the media from arranging to speak with specific prisoners.[543] The ban left prisoner organizers unable to communicate with sympathetic journalists. Thus, *The Fire Inside*, launched the following year, became all the more crucial for women incarcerated in California to have their voices—and their complaints—heard.

Yraida Guanipa's "Prison Talk Online" is another exception. The blog dedicated to Guanipa's writings receives over 500 hits each week, indicating a consistent public interest in the experiences of women in prison. However, the online availability of *The Fire Inside* and "Prison Talk Online" are still rarities. The majority of incarcerated women lack access to the Internet. This lack of access often limits them to print media that they can (usually) receive but which has limited outside distribution.

The small-scale circulation of these media should not overshadow their importance. Both prison walls and society's assumptions about gender and incarceration often silence the voices of women. Media created by or willing to include the voices of these women are valuable tools in both raising public awareness and strengthening the women's own sense of self-worth and agency. Yraida Guanipa, who knows all too well the difficulties of having her voice heard by the mainstream media, agrees. "It's important for females to know that someone listens and that someone cares and that we are not rejected."[544]

"Prison officials do whatever they can to strip prisoners of their dignity and self-worth," stated Barrilee Bannister, one of the founders of *Tenacious*. "Writing is my way to escape the confines of prison and the debilitating ailments of prison life. It's me putting on boxing gloves and stepping into the rink of freedom of speech and opinion."[545]

RESISTANCE AMONG WOMEN IN IMMIGRANT DETENTION CENTERS

Although their immigration status and lack of outside visibility and support often render them more vulnerable to both abuse and retaliation than imprisoned female citizens, women in immigrant detention have also staged both individual and group acts of resistance to protest not only their conditions, but also the unjust policies causing their confinement.[546] Their actions remain largely invisible in discussions around prisoner rights and prisoner organizing.

Part of this neglect ties into the larger invisibility of immigrants. Like prisoners, immigrants are a largely unseen population of American society. When their existence is included in the public discourse, they are often demonized or blamed not only for their own difficulties but the ills of larger society as well. When they are depicted as individuals, the image is usually that of a Mexican or Central American male.[547] Immigrant women are often invisible.

"Before September 11, there were more pro-immigrant feelings, especially with the economic boom," Victor DuCouto of the MIRA (Massachusetts Immigrant and Refugee Advocacy) Coalition in Boston stated. "The Massachusetts Institute for a New Commonwealth (MassINC) and Citizens Bank published a report that explained that immigrants were a big part of the economic boom in Massachusetts. Ironically, on September 10, the presidents of Mexico and the United States were meeting to discuss amnesty . . . Legislation [was on the table] that would allow immigrants to pay $1,000 to INS to change their visa status instead of having to go back to their country of origin for three to ten years before reapplying."[548]

The newspaper of the Texas border town Laredo reflects the pre- and post-9/11 public sentiment. In May 2000, the *Laredo Morning Times* ran an article with the headline "Immigration Aids Strong Growth in Many U.S. Metropolitan Areas." The article cited data from the Census Bureau stating that the influx of immigrants helped the growth of urban economies.[549]

After September 11th, the sentiment shifted. By 2003, headline in the *Laredo Morning Times* showed an increase in public fears linking immigration with the threat of terrorism: "Poll Shows Security Important to U.S." blared a February 2003 headline.[550]

Families for a Secure America, a group against illegal immigration, has stated, "There is no way to differentiate an undocumented [immigrant] from a terrorist."[551] This organization is not alone in mixing issues of immigration and terrorism: politicians and government officials have used public fear of terrorism to push for harsher anti-immigrant measures. In October 2004, Homeland Security official Michael Garcia told the Associated Press that, despite having no supporting evidence, he feared that terrorists would try to used Mexican and Central American smuggling networks to slip people into the United States "I personally don't know . . . (of an) al-Qaida known terrorist trying to come through Mexico into the United States," Garcia told the Associated Press, which then ran the headline "Border Feared Vulnerable to Terrorists."[552] In March 2006, Tennessee senator Bill Frist introduced a bill to increase border guards and fencing and hasten deportation of undocumented immigrants. "Our country needs security at our borders in order to slow the flow of illegal immigration and make America safer from foreign criminals and terrorists," he stated.[553]

Such fear-mongering mirrors the hysteria around crime in the previous decades that has led to harsher prison sentences and public indifference over prison conditions. At the same time, by focusing the public's attention on the threat of terrorism, it renders immigrants and their issues invisible. In addition, fear of immigrant crimes and of terrorism have largely, if not almost exclusively, focused on male immigrants, leaving women out of the discourse altogether. Because the existence of female immigrants complicates a discussion that often links the issue of immigration to terrorism, they are often conveniently overlooked or omitted.

Detention

The sharp increase in immigrant detention did not begin with September 11. In 1996, the Anti-Terrorism and Effective Death Penalty Act (AEDPA) and the Illegal Immigration Reform and Immigrant Responsibility Act (IIRIRA) were passed. AEDPA required the mandatory detention of non-citizens convicted of a wide range of offenses, including minor drug charges. IIRIRA expanded the list of offenses that mandated detention. Judges were no longer able to consider an immigrant's circumstances, including family relationships and community ties, or the severity of the offense. In addition, these acts allowed the INS to indefinitely detain noncitizens who had been given a final order of deportation.[554]

In 1999, INS issued the Interior Enforcement Strategy. Ostensibly to prevent immigration-related crime and remove undocumented immigrants from the country, the strategy entailed actively searching for noncitizens in the prison system in order to expedite their deportations.[555] The statute of limitations was also abolished, meaning that those whose offenses had happened over a decade ago are now subject to deportation. Debi Sanders, the executive director of the Capital Area Immigrants Rights Coalition, recounted the case of "Hannah," a woman who has held a green card for 25 years and now, under the Interior Enforcement Strategy, was arrested, detained and placed in deportation hearings because 12 years earlier, she had stolen one shirt from a department store and been sentenced to community service.[556]

These acts dramatically increased the number of immigrants in detention even before 9/11: in 1994, the average daily population in INS detention was 5,532. By 2001, that number had more than tripled to an average daily of 13,210.[557] In 2006, the Department of Homeland Security's Office of the Inspector General estimated that 627,000 immigrants would enter state prisons and local jails and 25,000 more would enter the federal prison system in the following year.[558]

Between 1992 and 1995, women comprised 6% of immigrants with an order for formal removal (deportation). In 1996, that number doubled with women making up 12%. By 2000, this number had doubled again to 24%. According to the INS, most of this increase is "attributed to women from Mexico who attempted entry without proper documents or through fraud."[559] In May 2008, INS released a few basic statistics about detained immigrant women: "Women account for 10% of the FY08 ICE average daily population of 29,340 detainees," stated Kendra Wallace, the national Outreach Coordinator of the U.S. Immigrations and Customs Enforcement (ICE) agency. These numbers do not include women detained in the federal prison system or held by the Office of Refugee Resettlement.[560] The INS has not publicly released more detailed reports that classify detainees by both gender and country of origin. In 2005, a female detainee granted an interview with *The Fire Inside*, the newsletter of advocacy group California Coalition for Women Prisoners. She stated that there were 60 to 80 immigrant women facing deportation in the INS-contracted jail in California. She estimated that 65% of these women were of Asian descent, 30% were from Spanish-speaking countries and 5% were from other countries.[561]

All immigrant parents facing deportation face permanent separation from their U.S.-born children. However, much like citizen parents incarcerated in state and federal prisons, gender impacts the consequences of deportation.[562] When a father is detained and deported, the children often are left with the mother, who often struggles not only with the loss of the father's presence and income but sometimes must remit money to her deported spouse. While no statistics have been gathered (or released) about the issue, anecdotal evidence suggests that mothers facing deportation more often struggle with their American-born children's placement and future. Janet Sabel, the director of the immigration law unit of the Legal Aid Society, recalled that one mother, facing imminent deportation to Nicaragua, was told by immigration officials to leave her children with her husband, an abusive drug user. The mother managed to persuade the officer to grant her a few days to make other arrangements. During that time, a priest referred her to the Legal Aid Society, which reopened her case and stopped the deportation.[563]

This mother was lucky in persuading the immigration officer to delay her deportation, finding the Legal Aid Society and being able to remain with her children. Others have not been as fortunate.

Elvira Arellano was an undocumented immigrant working as a cleaning woman at O'Hare International Airport. She is also the single mother of a U.S.-born son. In 2002, after a post-9/11 security sweep at the airport, she was arrested and convicted of social security fraud. She was ordered to appear before immigration authorities on August 15, 2006. Instead, Arellano and her son took sanctuary in Chicago churches that provide refuge for undocumented immigrants.

In August 2007, Arellano began a speaking tour against her deportation, which would separate her from her son. She was arrested in Los Angeles after speaking at a rally and deported to Mexico. Her eight-year-old son remained in the United States.[564]

Just as women in U.S. prisons do not fit the stereotype of violent black male felons and are thus ignored by those who cannot reconcile the perception of women—as mothers, caretakers, etc.—as prisoners, women detained in INS facilities do not fit many of the preconceptions of detained immigrants and suspected terrorists. However, unlike many state departments of correctional services and the Bureau of Justice, the INS virtually never mentions gender in public reports about detainees. Thus, there is virtually no way to dispel or disprove public stereotypes of those held in INS detention facilities.

In the Name of Security . . .

Adding to the cloak of invisibility around female immigrant detainees, the goings-on in INS facilities are hidden from the outside world. For example, the administration at Florida's Krome Processing Center has continually denied access to the press whenever significant events, such as a hunger strike, occur. The agency has also continually refused to grant both journalists and human rights organizations access to Krome, thus preventing outside scrutiny. Furthermore, the INS has unofficially barred journalists from media that have previously covered the facility's inadequacies and abuses and who dare to challenge INS practices. In January 1996, then district director Walter D. Cadman turned down a request by 11 Miami journalists to tour Krome. Cadman's refusal was based on the fact that "nothing unusual had happened to warrant such coverage." The journalists appealed to INS Commissioner Doris Meissner. Three months later, on April 8, the INS granted five journalists a "sanitized tour of Krome." None of the original 11 petitioners were included.[565]

Similarly, human rights organizations and immigrant advocacy groups have also been denied access to detention centers and their immigrant inmates. The administration at the Avoyelles Parish Jail, a criminal correctional facility in rural Louisiana, denied Human Rights Watch both a tour of the jail and direct, private contact with its INS detainees in March 1997. York County Prison, a state prison in Pennsylvania which also serves as one of the nation's largest holding facilities for INS detainees, also denied requests from Human Rights Watch for access.[566]

Even when detainees' stories and complaints do reach the media and the outside world, they are often viewed with skepticism, especially given the hostile climate toward immigrants. After a 1995 riot at a privately run detention center in Elizabeth, New Jersey, drew media attention to the detainees' complaints about abusive conditions, the INS's contract compliance officer Norman Uzzle told the *New York Times*, "These people all attempted to enter the country illegally. You have to take what they say based on the fact that they have already lied to officers of the service."[567]

Conditions Within

Facilities that the INS uses to house its many female detainees mirror some of the worst aspects of state and federal prisons. Like many state and federal inmates, detainees are required to pay for all medical services, including visits to the doctor, Tylenol or any other medication. "You could not receive any medication unless you paid for it," stated "Sister," an immigrant who had finished her prison sentence only to be sent to an INS-contracted county jail while facing deportation hearings. "There were women who needed medication for chronic illnesses that could not afford it." In addition, she notes that detention centers often refuse to allow women to bring medication that had already been prescribed by the prison.[568]

Like prisons, the exorbitant phone rates at detention centers prevent many from keeping in touch with their children and loved ones on the outside. "Our families are charged anywhere between thirteen and fifteen dollars for a short local call," reported Sister.

In some instances, the dehumanizing conditions of state and federal prisons actually seem better than those in INS detention facilities. Sister recalled that, while she was incarcerated at a California state prison, she was able to have contact visits with her children. The jail that INS had contracted to house her only offered non-contact visits: "I chose not to have my children visit me at the [INS-contracted] jail because after 13 years of visiting me and touching me, I would have had to endure the pain of seeing them behind a glass partition and talking to them through the telephone line."[569]

Many detainees remain unaware of their rights; language barriers often prevent them from learning and asserting them. A Haitian woman at Turner Guilford Knight (TGK), a Florida jail that houses detainees, reported that she had no idea how to file a grievance because no one had explained the procedure to her in Creole.[570]

Detention officers have also used women's unfamiliarity with immigration and legal proceedings to sexually abuse them. The Krome Processing Center, one of the oldest and largest INS Service Processing Centers, has been the subject of federal investigations of alleged abuses since 1986.[571] Women reported that officers promised detainees that they would be released from detention if they engaged in sexual activities with them. Conversely, the officers told the detainees that they would be transferred to a county prison, deported or even killed if they failed to cooperate or dared to complain.[572] "Bernadette," a Haitian-born woman who spent seven months at Krome, reported that one officer regularly threatened women with deportation. He also warned that he would make them "disappear" into the Everglades.[573]

INS policy allows detainees to be transferred across the country, thus separating them from friends, family and immigration lawyers while they attempt to appeal their deportation sentences. This can have disastrous results: one asylum seeker, detained with her husband, was transferred from Florida to York County Prison in Pennsylvania. Her husband remained at Krome.

Upon his release, the husband traveled to Pennsylvania to bring her the documents that INS required for parole. His request to visit her was denied, but he was able to submit the required documentation. Although she was told that she would be released in two days, the INS instead transferred the woman back to Miami.

Lacking enough money to return to Miami, the husband was stranded in Pennsylvania. He missed his own immigration hearing as a result.[574]

INS officials transfer detainees to prevent organizing. Alex Sanchez, an immigrant from El Salvador who was detained in California for two years, reported, "If they [INS officials] thought that they [detainees] were up to something, or if they were trying to organize, they would send them places where their families will never be able to visit them."[575]

At the Turner Guilford Knight Correctional Center (TGK) in Florida, detainees reported that jail and INS officers had threatened them with transfer to prisons in other states, such as Louisiana, Pennsylvania, or California if they did not stop complaining about jail conditions.[576] One woman told the Women's Commission for Refugee Women and Children, an advocacy group for refugees and asylum seekers, that a TGK officer told her: "You keep complaining, so you're going to be transferred to a federal prison. Then you'll know what it's like to be with real criminals. You don't understand that you get the golden treatment here. Your next prison will be the worst place of all."[577]

These threats have often intimidated women into silence. Detainees at TGK told attorneys from the Women's Commission for Refugee Women and Children that other women had been transferred to Pennsylvania as retaliation for having participated in know-your-rights presentations with the Florida Immigrant Advocacy Center.[578]

In addition to having its own detention centers, the INS also contracts with local jails and state prisons to house some of its more than 20,000 detainees. More than 57% of immigrant detainees are held within over 312 local jails and state prisons that have contracts with the INS.[579] Women are more likely to be placed in local jails—and mixed with the general prison population—because the INS has less space reserved for women in its own service processing centers.[580]

The INS pays more per detainee than the state does for its prisoners. For example, the INS pays New Jersey's Passaic County Jail $77 dollars per day for each detainee. In contrast, the state pays $62 per day for its inmates.[581]

Despite the additional money that immigrant detainees bring, many of these facilities remain ill equipped to handle the special needs of immigrant populations. Many of these jails are located in rural areas where staff members may never have encountered non-English speaking people before the INS began paying them to hold detainees.[582] Detainees who do not speak English are often not provided with translation services. Those who speak more common languages, such as Spanish, may at least have access to fellow inmates or staff who can communicate with them. This was the case in the Clear Creek County Jail, a local Colorado jail that houses INS detainees: Sarah Daniel, a woman awaiting sentencing, remembered a woman from Peru who spoke no English. "Luckily there is another woman here who is bilingual or this little Peruvian lady would be screwed as most of the deputies here do not speak Spanish."[583]

However, many women do not speak languages commonly found in jails and prisons. The Women's Commission for Refugee Women and Children cites the case of a detainee from India who spoke only Gujarati. During her first week in detention, she had only spoken to someone in her native language twice. Furthermore, the woman "was completely unfamiliar with the concept of asylum . . . The INS had provided her with several immigration forms, including an explanation of the credible fear process, but they were all in English and she could not understand them. The INS had also provided her with a list of legal services, but again the list was in English and she did not understand it."[584] Chinese women held in the Kern County Jail in Lerdo, California, had never had the facility's rules explained to them in Chinese. The women were often placed in solitary confinement for minor rule infractions; one woman spent five days in solitary confinement for not using a pencil sharpener properly.[585]

Chinese women held at the Orleans Parish Prison in New Orleans also received little assistance. For the initial two months of a detention period of over two years, the INS provided some translation services. After those two months, however, the INS stated that language assistance was no longer necessary. The jail's medical forms had been translated into Chinese; the INS would provide translation only for medical emergencies. The primary language of the 10 to 13 detainees was Fujianese, not Mandarin. In addition, not all of the detainees were literate: their education levels ranged from no schooling to middle school.[586]

Even women who do speak English are treated harshly. RJ, who had been housed at the Clear Creek County Jail with INS detainees from

Mexico, Venezuela, Peru, Russia and South Korea, remembered that the guards' treatment varied, depending on the detainee's proficiency and accent. "People were treated as if they were of lower intelligence if they could not speak English fluently or 'correctly' all of the time," RJ recalled. "The guards would poke fun, dismiss, patronize, ignore inmates more often if this [lack of proficiency] was true of the inmate."[587]

Jail and prison administrators have resisted suggestions that services should be provided to accommodate the special needs of INS detainees. "We've bent over backwards," stated the warden of TGK. "We've cleaned and we've painted, but I can't treat the INS detainees any differently [than the jail inmates]."[588]

Detainees wear the same prison uniform and are subjected to handcuffing, shackling, insufficient food, 23-hour lockdown and strip searches. "It's a jail, so we have to strip search," stated the head of the Florida Department of Corrections. "Perhaps it's not appropriate for these women, but we have to follow the rules."[589]

Although in many respects immigrant detainees are treated the same as the prisoners around them, they often have less access to the facility's services and programs.[590] In addition, assistance provided to male detainees are often not extended to their female counterparts: in the York County Prison, two Mandarin interpreters were posted in the men's section to provide translation for the 118 men who had been detained after the *Golden Venture* ran aground.[591] The six Chinese women at York had to formally request an interpreter's assistance before one of the (male) interpreters was made available.[592]

Instances of Resistance

Women in INS facilities have also organized to protest their conditions of confinement. In August 2000, over 300 detainees at an INS center in Los Angeles organized a hunger strike to protest the outrageous conditions, including the mold covering the shower stalls, inadequate supplies of food and the lack of ventilation. Although the hunger strike lasted only one day, it garnered both media attention and some changes in the facility, such as the installation of industrial-strength fans.[593] Although the male detainees seemed to have been the key organizers of the strike, one later stated that the "women were the strongest group that participated."[594]

This is not the first—or only—time that male and female detainees have organized together to protest their conditions of confinement. Unlike state and federal prisons, an INS detention center can house both men and women in the same facility. Thus, unlike state and federal prisoners, male and female detainees have worked together to protest their conditions of confinement.

In August 1991, 150 men and 30 women detained at Krome protested not only the facility's conditions and abusive guards but also the lengths of their detention. The detainees sat in Krome's outside patio area all day, refusing not only to eat but also to enter the building for mandatory roll calls.[595]

On New Year's Eve, 1992, 119 men and 40 women detained at Krome began a hunger strike to protest the INS's policy of indefinitely detaining Haitian refugees while allowing Cuban asylum seekers to go free.[596] All but three of Krome's Haitian population participated, making up more than two-thirds of the facility's total population.

Although female detainees made up only one-third of the strike, they held fast to their protest. Eight days into the strike, 39 of the original 40 were still refusing to eat. According to the father of one woman, "She said she was very weak and couldn't talk long. I begged her to eat, but she said if she eats they will lose the struggle."[597] In response, Krome administrators shut off the water coolers in housing units and threatened to transfer the women to jails where they would be unable to receive family visits. INS officials also refused to allow news media into Krome during that time, stating that they feared media coverage would lengthen the strike.[598]

The strike had some effect: in the six months that followed, 88 of the 159 Haitian asylum seekers had been released from Krome.[599]

Resistance among Women in Immigrant Detention Centers

In 1993, the Chinese women detained at the Orleans Parish Prison in New Orleans staged a hunger strike against the lack of recreational activities available to them. The jail's outdoor exercise yard was paved, with no trees or grass, surrounded by a high fence. The women were often kept indoors for up to two weeks at a time. Inside, they had no access to craft supplies or reading materials. They often spent their entire day lying on their beds staring at the ceiling. Their hunger strike pressured the jail to provide Chinese-language videos.[600] While videos may seem like a trivial gain, access to recreation material in their language undercuts the bleakness of an indeterminate period of detention.

In 1995, 22 Chinese women at the Kern County Jail in California staged a hunger strike protesting the length of their detention. All had originally filed asylum claims, citing China's one-child policy. All had been held for over two years.

Nine of these 22 women refused to eat for 24 days. "I feel terrible now, but I won't stop because I want to be free of the jail," Tin Chan Wang told the *New York Times*. "There is no pain in dying, but it hurts when they keep you in jail."[601] The women broke their fast for one day, then resumed for another 26 days.[602]

Women have also acted individually to stop intolerable conditions. In 2000, Christina Madrazo, a transsexual from Mexico, filed an asylum claim based on persecution because of sexual orientation. Her asylum grant was initially granted, but after a fingerprint check revealed that she had been convicted of two misdemeanors it was rescinded. She was detained at Krome where she was raped by a guard.[603]

Madrazo filed a formal complaint—a rarity among women in state and federal prisons and even more so among immigrant detainees who do not know whether guards and staff truly have the power to transfer them to harsher facilities, release or deport them. She also filed a lawsuit against the U.S. government for subjecting her to the attack.

However, Madrazo's willingness to speak up did not come without a price. After reporting a second rape to INS officials, Madrazo was transferred to a psychiatric hospital where she was held for two months in a ward for severely psychotic people. For those two months, any time she wanted to go outside for air, she was placed in leg irons and handcuffs. Then, on July 24, 2000, she was abruptly released from detention with no explanation.[604]

Madrazo's outspokenness encouraged other women to voice their own tales of sexual abuse. A dozen women—including two who had been impregnated at Krome that year—came forward with stories of guards fondling them, propositioning them and threatening them with deportation if they refused or reported them. These complaints prompted an investigation by the FBI, the Office of Public Integrity, the Office of the Inspector General and the U.S. Attorney's office. Nine of the fifteen officers named were transferred to desk jobs. Two were convicted.[605]

In December 2000, the majority of Krome's female detainees were transferred to Turner Guilford Knight Correctional Center (TGK), a county jail for women awaiting trial on criminal charges. Some were placed in solitary confinement.[606] Citing a lack of beds at TGK, the INS transferred four groups of women to York County Prison in Pennsylvania. It also deported several women who had experienced or witnessed the staff's sexual abuse.[607]

Talking

Women have also challenged conditions within INS facilities simply by speaking out. Like women incarcerated in state and federal prisons, INS detainees are threatened with transfers and staff retaliation if they complain. Haitian women detained at TGK told the Women's Commission that an officer had threatened to place them in lockdown if they complained about their treatment.[608]

At Krome, a group of asylum seekers filed a written complaint against a guard who played her radio loudly and refused to turn the lights off at night while the women were trying to sleep. The next day, two male guards told the women that, because they had complained, they would not be released even if they passed their credible fear interviews.[609]

The threat worked: "The asylum seekers were petrified," another detainee later told the Women's Commission. "I told them to tell their lawyer, but they said they couldn't say anything or they would not pass their credible fear interviews and they would be sent home."[610] Some women would not speak with attorneys from the Women's Commission because they believed that the attorney-client room was bugged and that complaining about their treatment would result in being placed in solitary confinement.[611]

This fear is not unfounded: after a Mexican detainee filed a complaint about the denial of their rights, four officers physically grabbed her while she was watching television in the jail's common area and dragged her to a cell. She spent seven days in solitary confinement.[612]

Others have not allowed the threat of transfers or retaliations to keep them from speaking to immigrant advocacy groups, such as the Women's Commission for Refugee Women and Children and the Florida Immigrant Advocacy Center, or from filing complaints. In another instance, after reporting the abuses she had witnessed, "Ana" was transferred from Krome to Orleans Parish Prison in New Orleans. When she was returned to Krome two months later, a deportation officer told her, "You won't be released because I'll make sure that you stay here. I'll deport you and bar you from returning to the United States for ten years."[613]

Ana testified about the abuses at Krome before a grand jury. Despite the deportation officer's threats, she was subsequently released.[614]

Talking (or testifying)—especially despite threats and fears of retaliation and deportation (which often equals severe persecution or death in a woman's home country)—is a huge act of resistance. However, testimonies of immigrant detainees largely go unnoticed by the larger prison activist movement unless the detainee has garnered considerable publicity and attention. Compounding this invisibility is the fact that many of these reports are generated by advocacy groups supporting refugee and asylum seekers. These groups have no ties to the prison activist movement, making it less likely that their reports and work will be included in research and writing about incarcerated women. In addition, their reports often position detainees as less deserving of the inhuman conditions, mistreatment and abuse to which prisoners are routinely subjected. "Despite the fact that a significant percentage have committed no crime and are simply exercising their right to seek refugee protection in the United States, INS detainees are subject to harsh treatment and punitive conditions," wrote the Women's Commission for Refugee Women and Children in the Executive Summary of its 2000 report on sexual abuse at Krome.[615] Such a statement ignores the idea that, regardless of the reason she is being held, no person should be subjected to sexual harassment and assault, substandard health care and the other atrocities regularly found in prisons and detention centers.

SOME HISTORICAL BACKGROUND

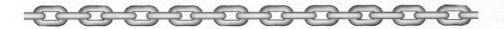

This is not a book about how individual women are singled out for unjust treatment and harsh punishments. Nor is it a book about how certain individuals respond to these injustices. These stories do not occur in a vacuum; they are symptomatic of a systemic problem called prison.

In the fall of 1965, in a special message to Congress, Lyndon B. Johnson declared a war on crime: "I hope that 1965 will be regarded as the year when this country began in earnest a thorough and effective war against crime."[616] In his 1973 State of the Union message, Richard Nixon vowed to continue and expand that war, linking the growing civil unrest to violent street crime.[617] Ronald Reagan further intensified the amount of policing and prisons with the "war on drugs." Both wars came at a time when economic conditions were deteriorating, particularly in communities of color; both served to lock poor people away before they could organize and challenge social conditions and the social order. Although mass incarceration is a relatively new phenomenon, the use of imprisonment as a means of social control, particularly of black and brown bodies, is not.

Changing the Color of Prison:
The Black Codes, Convict Lease System and Black Women

Following the abolition of slavery, former slave states passed new legislation regulating the behavior of newly freed blacks. These new

Black Codes criminalized a range of actions—such as vagrancy, being outside after a certain hour, absence from work and possessing a firearm—but only when the person charged was black. The codes also changed the gravity of an offense: following emancipation, when large numbers of newly freed black people stole to survive, petty thievery became a felony.

These codes changed the color and nature of imprisonment. Prior to the Civil War, between 1831 and 1859, when slavery was the primary (and most lucrative) method of controlling black people, only three of Tennessee's twenty-four women prisoners were black.[618] Of the white female prisoners, 45% had been convicted of larceny. After the war, however, white women were rarely imprisoned for larceny. This did not mean that larceny was no long an imprisonable offense: during that same time period, the most common offense among incarcerated black women, who had become the majority of women convicted, was larceny.[619] In 1868, 100% of the women in the Tennessee penitentiary were black.[620]

Similarly, historian Mary Ellen Curtin found that before the abolition of slavery, 99% of the prisoners in Alabama's state penitentiary were white. Within a short time period following the passing of the Black Codes, the overwhelming majority of state prisoners were black.[621] Between 1874 and 1877, the imprisonment rate for blacks in Mississippi and Georgia increased 300%. In other states, prisons whose previous populations had been all white were too small to house the number of emancipated blacks convicted of petty offenses.[622]

The Thirteenth Amendment to the Constitution, abolishing slavery and involuntary servitude, made an exception to those "duly convicted" of a crime. Thus, incarceration served a dual purpose: separating and warehousing "undesirables" and creating profits for people and companies seeking sources of cheap labor. In the South, a convict lease system developed in which crews of prisoners were leased from the state by a company to perform hard labor: in Mississippi, convicted blacks were returned to plantation work; in Alabama, many worked the coal mines.

The Codes also created a new class of prisoners in Alabama—the county convicts, men and women convicted of misdemeanors and sentenced to up to two years of hard labor.[623] Although only found guilty of misdemeanors, county convicts not only suffered similar conditions as their state counterparts, but also lacked outside supervision of their treatment. In addition, county convicts were held responsible for paying their own court costs as well as the fees incurred by the sheriff. The fees usually amounted to $50, a sum that most could not afford to pay. Instead, they worked off the fee by serving additional time at the rate of 30¢ per day.[624] Thus, even when the Codes did not change misdemeanor offenses into felonies, they still enabled the state to exploit black labor.

The convict lease system also enabled leasing corporations to influence the length of imprisonment. Good behavior was rewarded with "short time"—two months off every year of a prisoner's sentence. Contractors, however, had the power to issue reports of a prisoner's bad conduct and frequently did so to retain prisoners who had achieved some skill at mining. On one occasion, the number of reports aroused official suspicion: "I think that the problem of short time is trying to be solved by the contractors themselves," wrote J. D. Douglass, a secretary of Alabama's Department of Corrections, in 1888. "I wish you could see the report of Coalburg for June. The conduct of sixty-two is reported as Bad, in about half of which cases the offense is not given."[625]

Black women were not exempt from this new criminalization. Under the Black Codes, they too were sentenced to the convict lease system. Their gender, however, afforded them some respite from the labor meted out to men: the dozen or so women who had been leased to the Coalburg prison mine in Alabama, for example, were hired out as cooks and house servants rather than forced to work in the mines. Moreover, perhaps because they did not mine coal, contractors had less interest in retaining them; their sentences tended to be shorter than those of their male counterparts.[626]

Gender did not exclude them, however, from the brutal punishments of the prison camps: in 1888, several women prisoners testified before a state senate investigating committee about their treatment under the convict lease system. Every woman testified that she had been whipped during her sentence and had seen other women whipped frequently and repeatedly. Women were whipped for quarreling, fighting, talking back and being impertinent to officers. One woman, who had never picked cotton, was whipped because she could not pick 125 pounds in one day. Another was whipped for dancing on a Sunday.[627] In addition, a woman sentenced to a mining camp or prison farm often found herself the sole female among 50–100 male convicts. Adding to her vulnerability to rape and sexual abuse, she was often forced to live with the mining boss or prison manager.[628]

In non-slave states, incarceration remained the primary means of controlling and subordinating the black population: even before the Civil War, black women were arrested and convicted at higher rates than their white counterparts. Between 1797 and 1801, 44% of women imprisoned in New York State were black. In 1840, 49% of Ohio's female prisoners were black.[629] These numbers continued to increase, although not always proportionate to the changes in the general population: in Ohio, although the number of African Americans in the state rose from 2% to 5% between 1890 and 1930, the proportion of African-American women in prison increased from 26%–52%.[630]

Policing Gender Behavior

As seen above, women were not exempt from incarceration. In fact, imprisonment has often been used as a means of gender as well as social control. Just as the Black Codes criminalized actions only when enacted by black people, women were often arrested and imprisoned for defying societal expectations of feminine behavior: being drunk, engaging in pre- and extramarital sex, contracting a venereal disease, or keeping bad company.[631] Men, however, were neither arrested nor otherwise penalized for these same behaviors.

In addition, the idea of rehabilitating or reforming women who violated either the law or societal norms resulted in longer—often indeterminate—sentences than men convicted of the same offense. In 1869, Michigan enacted the country's first indeterminate sentencing law. The "three years law" empowered Zebulon R. Brockway, the superintendent of Detroit's House of Correction, to hold women convicted of prostitution for up to three years on the theory that these women would be reformed with extensive "retraining." However, the state legislature rejected Brockway's proposal for indeterminate sentencing for men.[632]

In 1913, Pennsylvania passed the Muncy Act, requiring that all women convicted of an offense punishable by more than one year be given an indeterminate sentence in the Muncy State Industrial Home for Women. Under this act, women were also not eligible for parole as early as men.[633] As late as 1966, the Superior Court of Pennsylvania ruled that the sentencing disparities under the Muncy Act did not constitute an infringement on women's constitutional rights, stating that men and women's "inherent physical and psychological differences justified differential treatment. Therefore it was deemed reasonable for women to receive longer sentences, especially because they supposedly received more effective rehabilitation while incarcerated."[634]

However, women have always constituted a relatively small percentage of those sentenced to prison. Until the late 19th century, these small numbers meant that women were sent to male prisons, to be housed sometimes in adjacent cells to men, more often in attics or cellars. They shared the same appalling conditions—overcrowding, poor food and harsh treatment. Unlike male prisoners, however, women had less access to the physician and chaplain and rarely, if ever, were permitted to go to workshops, mess halls or exercise yards. Women were blamed for any disruptions that their presence caused among the male prison population. Sexual abuse by both male prisoners and prison staff was not only common, but apparently acceptable: the Indiana state prison used female prisoners to run a prostitution service for male guards.[635]

The War on Drugs:
Targeting Small-Timers and Associates Means Targeting Women

In 1973, following Nixon's State of the Union message, New York State passed the country's first mandatory sentencing law: the Rockefeller Drug Laws required a sentence of 15 years to life for anyone convicted of selling two ounces or possessing four ounces of a narcotic regardless of circumstances or prior history. In 1973, 13,437 people were imprisoned in New York State; twenty years later, that number was 64,569.[636] The Rockefeller Drug Laws set a precedent for other states to follow. Today, all state and the federal governments have some form of mandatory sentencing in their books. Like the Black Codes, drug-related mandatory sentencing laws disproportion-ately affect poor people and people of color: although crack and powder cocaine have the same active ingredient, crack is marketed in less expensive quantities and in lower-income communities. Under the 1986 Anti-Drug Abuse Act, a five-gram sale of crack cocaine mandates a five-year federal sentence while a 500-gram sale of powder cocaine mandates the same sentence.[637] These disparities increased the proportion of people of color sent to prison: in 1980, African-Americans constituted 12% of the U.S. population but over 23% of all people arrested on drug charges. In 1990, four years after Congress had passed the Anti-Drug Abuse Act, African-Americans were still only 12% of the country's population but constituted more than 40% of those arrested for drugs *and* over 60% of those convicted.[638] The Act also enabled police and prosecutors to arrest and charge spouses and lovers with "conspiracy" for actions as simple as taking a phone message or signing for a package.[639]

Drug offenses are not the only offense carrying harsh penalties. In 1993, Washington State passed the nation's first Three Strikes law, mandating life imprisonment without parole for those convicted of a third felony. The next year, California followed suit. In 1995, Oregon passed Measure 11, sentencing anyone over the age of 15 convicted of a person-to-person crime to a mandatory sentence, regardless of prior history or degree of involvement.

Some Historical Background

Women, particularly poor women and women of color, have been hard-hit by these laws. In 1970, there were 5,600 women incarcerated nationwide.[640] By June 2001, that number had increased 2800% to 161,200.[641] In New York State, for instance, 400 women were imprisoned in 1973. As of January 1, 2008, 2,821 were behind bars, a 635% increase.[642]

Other social policies have worked to push poor women, particularly women of color, closer to prison. In 1996, President Bill Clinton signed the Personal Responsibility and Work Opportunity Reconciliation Act (PRWORA), drastically limiting welfare. Among its provisions, the PRWORA set a five-year lifetime limit on receiving welfare, excluded support for children born to mothers already on welfare, and required recipients to work after two years, regardless of other circumstances. In addition, it created a lifetime ban on welfare benefits for those convicted of drug felonies and those who had violated probation or parole, thus excluding over 100,000 women from welfare programs.[643] Several states also applied work requirements and time limits to those caring for the children of incarcerated women, approximately 60% of whom are female relatives. Thus, these women become ineligible for future benefits if they cannot afford to care for the children of their sisters, daughters, and other female relatives and must rely upon welfare assistance.[644]

By the end of the 1990s, the number of people receiving welfare (the majority of whom were women) had fallen 53%, or 6.5 million.[645] Approximately 40% of those who left or, more accurately, were pushed off welfare remained unemployed. Despite numerous evaluation studies, researchers of welfare "reform" policies remain uncertain about how those who have left currently make ends meet.[646] What is known is that in 1996, the number of women in prison rose by 9.1%, nearly double the increase in men sentenced to prison.[647] At the end of that year, 74,730 women were in state or federal prison. At the end of 2000, 91,612 women were incarcerated in state or federal prisons, a 108% increase since 1990.[648]

Resistance Behind Bars

Prisoners as Profit: Then and Now

Although gender did not allow a woman to escape imprisonment, harsh treatment or brutal punishments, under the convict lease system, it was a mitigating factor in the length of her imprisonment. In 1888, Alabama changed the way that its counties could lease its prisoners: instead of charging a flat rate for prisoners, regardless of gender, age, or ability, county governments had to classify prisoners according to their capacity for work. Counties began sending women prisoners to the state penitentiary at Wetumpka.[649] Because they earned less money for the leasing corporation, women escaped the additional time tacked onto the sentences of male prisoners. That same year, Alabama signed a 10-year contract with the Tennessee Coal and Iron Company (TCI), entitling the company to the labor of all male state prisoners and half of all (male) county prisoners. The company paid $18.50 per month per prisoner.[650]

With the advent of the private prison, however, gender has become irrelevant: corporations are paid a set daily fee for each prisoner regardless of gender, ability or any other factors. Between 1995 and 2004, the number of people in private prisons increased from 12,534 to 98,791.[651]

Reform and Its Limitations

The soaring increase in prisons, as well as the horrifying conditions within them, has prompted calls for reform. However, it is important to note the historical impact of reform: the prison itself was born from early reformers' calls to replace corporal and capital punishment with the extended loss of liberty. Imprisonment, reformers argued, would provide the opportunity for those convicted of crimes to reform themselves through hard work, silence and solitude. The Walnut Street Jail in Philadelphia opened in 1790 as a Quaker alternative to corporal punishment and execution and was emulated throughout the country.[652]

Separate prisons for women were also the result of well-intentioned calls for reform. In 1874, after Quaker reformers Sarah Smith and Rhoda Coffin led a campaign to end sexual abuse of women imprisoned at the (male) Indiana state prison, a separate women's prison was established. Other states followed suit and, by 1940, 23 states had established separate facilities to hold female prisoners.[653]

Although female prisons were seen as a much-needed reform over locking women in the cellars and attics of male penitentiaries, their existence led to an increase in the number of women sentenced to imprisonment. In Illinois, for example, the most dramatic increase occurred when the prison at Joliet opened a unit specifically for women. Despite the fact that no more than 10 women had ever been incarcerated at one time, the first female-only unit was a 100-cell building built in 1859. During the next decade, the total number of women sentenced to prison tripled.[654]

Similarly, in New York State, reformer (and commissioner of the New York State Board of Charities) Josephine Shaw Lowell's repeated calls for separate women's prisons resulted in the opening of the state's first reformatory in Hudson in 1887.[655] Within two years, Hudson had reached its capacity of 234; under Lowell's urging, the state legislature opened two other reformatories: Albion in 1893 and Bedford Hills in 1901.[656]

Even in these reformatories, women did not escape punishments that amounted to torture. Clifford Young, the chief inspector of the New York State Commission of Correction, recounted that in 1919 and 1920, women at Bedford Hills who were perceived as "refractory or hysterical . . . were handcuffed with arms behind the back, and with a second pair [of handcuffs] were fastened to the gratings so that their weight was on the toes or ball of the foot. While in this position their heads were forced down into a pail of water. The management contended that this was 'treatment,' not punishment."[657]

Both Albion and Bedford Hills continue to exist today: in January 2007, Albion held 1,106 women and Bedford Hills held 812.[658]

More recent calls for reforms have taken into account gender differences and issues particular to women. These, too, have strengthened an already-unjust system of incarceration. In 2006, California governor Arnold Schwarzenegger announced that the California Department of Corrections and Rehabilitation (CDCR) had identified 4,500 women who did not need to be imprisoned. Instead of releasing them, however, CDCR proposed building 4,500 new beds in what they called Female Rehabilitative Community Corrections Centers, essentially mini-prisons, in the urban areas where many of these women had lived before arrest.[659] The state legislature rejected the proposal, but in 2007 passed a modified version of the bill, AB76, which called for a "Female Offender Reform Master Plan" that would address the needs particular to its imprisoned female population rather than relying on the supposedly gender-neutral (but often designed for men) one-size-fits-all model. This "master plan" did not address the root causes of rising female incarceration: mandatory sentencing, racial profiling, poverty and the feminization of poverty, the lack of support systems for women leaving prison. Instead, the plan called for increased assessment and implementation of "gender specific rehabilitative programs" within existing prisons.

Calls for reform have failed to adequately address the factors leading to women's incarceration. Instead, they mask the inequities and injustices inherent in the prison system and have historically strengthened its capacity and ability to separate and punish those who transgress social mores, particularly the poor, people of color and other marginalized populations.

Even government entities have realized this: in 1973, the same year that Nixon began his efforts to intensify the War on Crime, the National Advisory Commission on Criminal Justice Standards and Goals stated that prisons fail to reduce or deter crime, provide only temporary protection to the community, and change the incarcerated person for the worse. It recommended that society use imprisonment only as a last resort.[660]

Some Historical Background

Just as some have recognized the injustices and brutality of prisons and called for widespread reforms, others have called for the abolition of the entire system. Prisons act not only as sites of social control but also, as demonstrated in the preceding chapters, as state-sanctioned sites of violence against women, particularly women of color, poor women and those who transgress social norms. Incarceration has not decreased crime; instead, "tough on crime" policies have led to the criminalization (or what Christian Parenti and others have referred to as "widening the net") of more activities, leading to higher rates of arrest, prosecution and incarceration while shifting money and resources away from other public entities, such as education, housing, health care, drug treatment, and other societal supports. The growing popularity of abolitionist thought can be seen in the expansion of organizations such as Critical Resistance, an organization fighting to end the need for a prison-industrial complex, and the formation of groups working to address issues of crime and victimization without relying on the police or prisons.[661]

While organizing and reenvisioning a world in which caging people is no longer necessary (or desirable), we cannot ignore the reality that over 100,000 women are currently locked within prisons. Numerous prison abolitionists have acknowledged this conundrum:

> A major challenge of this movement is to do the work that will create more humane, habitable environments for people in prison without bolstering the permanence of the prison system. How, then, do we accomplish this balancing act of passionately attending to the needs of prisoners—calling for less violent conditions, an end to sexual assault, improved physical and mental health care, greater access to drug programs, better educational work opportunities, unionization of prison labor, more connections with families and communities, shorter or alternative sentencing—and at the same time call for alternatives to sentencing altogether, no more prison construction, and abolitionist strategies that question the place of the prison in our future?

— Angela Davis, *Are Prisons Obsolete?*[662]

How do you balance responding to immediate need with a generational abolitionist approach?

— Alexander Lee, *TGI Justice Project*[663]

One way in which this can happen is by acknowledging, recognizing, publicizing and supporting the actions that incarcerated women themselves are taking to resist and change the conditions that they endure. While their actions may not challenge the presumed need for incarceration nor tear down the prison walls, they do disrupt the daily reality of incarceration and the continued invisibility of women held behind prison walls. These women speak and act at a price, making continued outside support essential to ensuring that their well-being is not further jeopardized. In addition, outside communication can encourage and inspire hope for those inside.

I was thinking about how we prisoners are very cut off from much of the rest of the world, including people who do not support the prison system or people who may be interested in our struggle. So I think that more communication via letters would help. I think that transaction would encourage resistance on both ends because it would strengthen information and knowledge both ways. I also think that hearing about efforts of resistance outside of prison would inspire and encourage us prisoners. Plus, through correspondence with inmates, people can see that many incidents that they read or hear about happen daily and it will really legitimize things. The communication between two humans concerning their hopes, ideas and their plights is what allows them to bond in resistance against a system that affects everyone in many different ways. As I mentioned, we inmates would be inspired to see another position of struggle and that, though they may differ, all struggles are shared. This would strengthen resistance both inside and outside of the prison gates.

— Rachel Galindo, letter from La Vista Correctional Facility in Colorado[664]

GLOSSARY

~~~~~~

Administrative Segregation: commonly known as Ad Seg. *See* Segregation.

Affidavit: formal sworn and signed statement of fact.

Anti-Terrorism and Effective Death Penalty Act (AEDPA): passed in 1996, AEDPA mandates detention of non-citizens convicted of a wide range of offenses, including minor drug charges. In addition, AEDPA (and IIRIRA) allowed the INS (now known as ICE) to indefinitely detain noncitizens who had been given a final order of deportation.

Bureau of Prisons (BOP): a subdivision of the U.S. Department of Justice responsible for the administration of the federal prison system.

CO: short for correctional officer. Euphemistic term for guard.

Cell extraction: procedure in which a number of guards, armed with chemical agents, riot gear, batons and/or stun guns, rush into a prisoner's cell to subdue and restrain her as quickly as possible. According to most jail and prison guidelines, cell extractions should be used only as a last resort and must be videotaped from start to finish.

Chain gang: group of prisoners chained together to perform menial or physically challenging labor, such as chipping stone, often along a highway or rail bed. It existed in the United States until the 1950s when it was phased out. In the 1990s, several states reintroduced the chain-gang system.

Class-action lawsuit: suit brought by one or more people on behalf of themselves and others who share the same issue(s).

Clemency: lessening of a penalty or prison sentence.

Cop-out: written complaint.

Department of Corrections (DOC): governmental agency that oversees the (state) prison system in a given state.

Good time: time off one's prison sentence for good behavior or working within the prison system.

Grievance: formal statement of complaint.

Illegal Immigration and Immigrant Responsibility Act (IIRIRA): Passed in 1996, IIRIRA expanded the list of offenses that mandated detention. Judges were no longer able to consider an immigrant's circumstances, including family relationships and community ties, or the severity of the offense. In addition, IIRIRA (and AEDPA) allowed the INS (now known as ICE) to indefinitely detain noncitizens who had been given a final order of deportation.

Inter-institutional visit: visit between two prisoners housed at different institutions.

Interior Enforcement Strategy: Ostensibly to prevent immigration-related crime and remove undocumented immigrants from the country, the strategy entailed actively searching for noncitizens in the prison system in order to expedite their deportations. The statute of limitations was also abolished, meaning that those whose offenses had happened over a decade ago are now subject to deportation.

Kite: written communication to prison staff.

Mandatory minimum laws: laws requiring mandatory prison sentences for certain offenses regardless of the person's previous criminal history (or lack thereof), the circumstances or any other factors.

Glossary

Measure 11: Oregon initiative passed in 1994 establishing mandatory minimum sentencing for offenses involving person-to-person violence, regardless of circumstances or the person's past criminal history (or lack thereof). Measure 11 applies to anyone over the age of 15, requiring juveniles over 15 charged with these crimes to be tried as adults.

Misconduct report: disciplinary measure taken when a prisoner violates a Posted Operational Rule (POR). PORs range from minor actions, such as putting feet on chairs, lying down in the yard, "slowpoking it" (walking too slowly) and not wearing a coat or robe over pajamas when going to and from the bathroom, to more serious infractions such as fighting and sexual activity (regardless of consent). Lending and bartering also incur write-ups. Receiving a write-up causes a prisoner to lose good time, keeping her in prison longer. Misconduct reports are also considered (negatively) by the parole board. Also known as write-ups.

Misdemeanor: less serious criminal action, usually one that warrants no more than a one-year prison sentence.

Preliminary injunction: court order restraining a party from going forward with a course of conduct. Preliminary injunctions are made in the early stages of a lawsuit before a determination has been made about the merits of a case. If the case is decided against the party that has been enjoined, then the injunction will usually be made permanent. If the case is decided in favor of the party that has been enjoined, the injunction will usually be dissolved or dismissed.

Prison family: type of prisoner social network in which prisoners adopt the roles of a hetero-patriarchal family (husband, wife, mother, father, sister, brother, etc). Prison families include heterosexual, bisexual and lesbian-identified prisoners.

Racial profiling: using a person's racial or ethnic background to determine whether she is more likely to commit a particular type of crime.

Segregation: punitive measure in which a prisoner is isolated in a cell for 23 to 23½ hours per day. Movement is extremely limited—a prisoner in segregation cannot take showers every day and is handcuffed each time she leaves the cell. She is allowed one hour of recreation each day in a yard that, according to one prisoner, is the size of a dog kennel. She is fed through a food slot in the door. The prisoner has no human contact except with prison staff. Hallucination, paranoia, aggression, self-mutilation and suicidal ideation are common results.

Settlement agreement: agreement reached by the parties to a dispute either before court actions have started or while litigation is before the court.

Shake-down: search in which a prisoner's cell is ripped apart, ostensibly in search of contraband.

Special Housing Unit (SHU): *See* Segregation.

Termination proceedings: proceedings taken by the state to end a parent's legal custody rights

Write-up: *See* Misconduct report.

RESOURCES

HEALTH

AIDS Educational Project – National Prison
Project of the ACLU
733 East 15th St. NW, Suite 620
Washington, DC 20005
202-393-4930
www.aclu.org/prison/index.html
Serves as a national resource center to provide educational materials, legal information and assistance to persons seeking information about AIDS in prison. Provides free packets of information to prisoners, including an educational pamphlet, *AIDS and Prisons: The Facts for Inmates and Officers* (in English, possibly available in Spanish, single copies free to prisoners) and a comprehensive *AIDS and Prison Bibliography* for $10.

For subscriptions, questions about HIV, and info about organizations near you that can help:
Prison Health News
c/o Philadelphia FIGHT
1233 Locust Street, 5th Floor
Philadelphia, PA 19107
All subscriptions are free.

Center for Health Justice
has a free national prisoner HIV prevention and treatment
hotline that accepts collect calls from inmates Mon.–Fri. 8 to
3 p.m. Provides HIV treatment and prevention info, support
for callers who are ill or newly diagnosed HIV+, and advocacy
support regarding medical care, medications, and other health
issues. In correctional facilities where we have programs,
prisoners can call the hotline to request a one-on-one counseling
session, get a referral for HIV testing, or to seek help with a prerelease health plan.
213-229-0979

Disability Rights Education and Defense Fund, Inc.
2212 6th St.
Berkeley, CA 94710
510-644-2555
www.dredf.org

Hepatitis C Awareness Project
PO Box 41803
Eugene, OR 97404
Newsletter, info packet. Offers seminars, workshops and support
groups both in and out of prison.

Hepatitis C Support Project
P.O. Box 427037
San Francisco, CA 94142-7037
Provides a free information booklet, as well as a free newsletter,
HCV Advocate.

HIV/Hepatitis C in Prison (HIP) Committee
California Prison Focus
2940 16th St. #307
San Francisco, CA 94103
Phone/fax: 510-665-1935

Jeff Dicks Medical Coalition
P.O. Box 343
Beechgrove, TN 37018
Advocacy for prisoners who need, and are not receiving, appropriate medical care.

National AIDS Treatment Advocacy Project (NATAP)
580 Broadway, #1010
New York, NY 10012
Will mail Hepatitis C and Hepatitis C Co-Infection Handbook.

National Black Women's Health Project
1237 Abernathy Blvd. SW
Atlanta, GA 30310
Health information (medical, social, political) available for African-American women. Write for newsletter.

POZ Magazine
PO Box 417
Mount Morris, IL 61054
Magazine about living with HIV. Free subscriptions for people with HIV who can't afford to pay for a subscription. All requests for free subscriptions must be signed and dated to meet postal regulations.

Prison Doula Project
c/o POWER
309 5th Ave SE
Olympia, WA 98501
birthattendants@gmail.com

Prisoners with AIDS Rights Advocacy Group
P.O. Box 2161
Jonesboro, GA 30237
Offers support, educational materials, referrals and political lobbying for prisoners with AIDS/HIV.

FOR INCARCERATED MOTHERS:

Aid to Children of Imprisoned Mothers
524 Larkin St. SW
Atlanta, GA 30313
Provides information to **all** incarcerated mothers. Direct social
services only to mothers in Atlanta area.

Center for Children with Incarcerated Parents
65 South Grand Ave.
Pasadena, CA 91105
Free educational materials for incarcerated parents and their children.

Children's Center
PO Box 803
Bedford Hills, NY 10507
Publishes *The Foster Care Handbook for Incarcerated Parents:
A Manual of Your Legal Rights and Responsibilities* and
Parenting from Inside/Out: The Voices of Mothers in Prison,
both written by women prisoners. Each costs $2.

Family and Corrections Network
32 Oak Grove
Palmyra, VA 22963
www.fcnetwork.org
Provides a resource list for incarcerated parents, their children and
their children's caregivers.

Mothers Reclaiming Our Children
4167 Normandies Ave.
Los Angeles, CA 90037
Working to create a nationwide program to provide support to
families, attend court hearings and trials, and work with attorneys.
Provides advocacy work for prisoners and their families.

National Indian Child Welfare Association
5100 SW Macadam Ave. #300, Portland, OR 97239
Can assist Native prisoners in navigating custody issues.

Resources

National Resource Center for Family Support Programs:
Family Resource Coalition
200 S. Michigan Ave., #1520
Chicago, IL 60604
Provides information about family programs.

Parent Resource Association
213 Fernbrook Ave.
Wyncotte, PA 19095
215-576-7961
Referrals and information to incarcerated parents. Family counseling to parolees.

Alabama only

Aid to Inmate Mothers, Inc.
PO Box 986
Montgomery, AL 36101
800-679-0246
www.inmatemoms.org
Monthly visitations of children at Julia Tutwiler Prison and Edwina Mitchell work release center in Wetumpka, AL. Also provides weekly support groups and services for domestic violence survivors at Tutwiler. Job readiness, literacy and transitional services.

California only

Legal Services for Prisoners with Children
1540 Market St., #490
San Francisco, CA 94102
415-255-7036
info@prisonerswithchildren.org
www.prisonerswithchildren.org
Referrals and resources for women.
Produces a custody manual for incarcerated parents.
No individual legal aid.

<u>Illinois only</u>

Chicago Legal Aid to Incarcerated Mothers
220 S. State St., Suite 830
Chicago, IL 60606
Support and assistance to women in prison. Legal assistance around parenting issues. Publishes *Handbook for Incarcerated Parents in Illinois.*

<u>Massachusetts only</u>

Aid to Incarcerated Mothers
32 Rutland St., 4th floor
Boston, MA 02118
607-536-0058
Pre- and post-release services for imprisoned mothers and their children, including case management, legal advocacy, support groups and referrals.

<u>New York only</u>

Hour Children, Inc.
36-11A 12th St.
Long Island City, NY 11106
718-433-4724
Provides foster care for children of incarcerated women. Works with incarcerated mothers and their children to strengthen family ties through parent education, enhanced visiting, transportation assistance, advocacy. Five community residential programs for women ex-prisoners and their children.

Incarcerated Mothers' Law Project
Women's Prison Association and Home
110 2nd Ave.
New York, NY 10003
Staff and volunteer attorneys teach women how to advocate for themselves and for their children in court and with foster care

agencies, in the community, and while incarcerated. Volunteer lawyers assist mothers in their efforts to maintain family ties and make good decisions about their children's care. Staff also work with clients in the community to assess the status of legal relationships with children, define goals, and prepare advocacy strategies.

Women's Prison Association and Home
110 2nd Ave.
New York, NY 10003
212-674-1163
www.wpaonline.org
Provides foster care prevention, counseling and housing placement assistance.

Washington State only

Incarcerated Mothers Advocacy Project (IMAP)
Seattle, Washington
360-480-4563
imap.legal@hotmail.com

Monthly presentations about family law at Washington Corrections Center for Women ("Purdy") and Mission Creek Corrections Center for Women. Law students present about general family law issues mothers face in prison, answer basic questions, and research questions from mothers in prison.

Biweekly Drop-In Legal Clinic, 2nd and 4th Monday of every month, 6:30–8:30 p.m., for formerly incarcerated mothers. Law students provide general legal info and, when possible, provide a facilitated referral to an attorney or social service provider who can provide more detailed assistance.

Location: JusticeWorks! Thrift & Gift
5101 Rainier Ave S #106, Seattle, WA 98118

<u>Washington, DC, only</u>

Our Place, DC
1236 Pennsylvania Ave. SE
Washington, DC 20003
202-548-2400
Provides transportation, overnight lodging, self-help support group, drop-in center, information, referrals, gifts for children, family reunification support, public education, advocacy, legal services for incarcerated and recently released women and their families.

FREE BOOKS & READING MATERIAL

Books Through Bars – NYC
c/o Bluestockings Bookstore
172 Allen St.
New York, NY 10002
Free, serving NY and other states as needed. Specializes in politics, history, literary fiction, and other educational books. No religious books.

Books Through Bars
4722 Baltimore Ave.
Philadelphia, PA 19143
Sends books to people imprisoned in all states except Oregon and Michigan. Request books by topic.

Chicago Books to Women in Prison
PO Box 14778
Chicago, IL 60614
http://chicagobwp.org
Sends books to women in prisons nationwide.

South Chicago ABC Zine Distro
2002 23rd Ave S
Minneapolis, MN 55404
womensprisonbookproject@gmail.com
Publishers and sends zines on a wide variety of subjects to people
in prison. Write for a catalog and sample zine.

Women's Prison Book Project
c/o Boneshaker Books
2441 Lyndale Ave. S.
Minneapolis, MN 55405
Ships to all states except OR, MI, CO, and WV. Free books to
women prisoners only. No county jail requests. Does not ship
hardback books. Free resource guide for women and transgender
prisoners. Encourages women and transgender prisoners to write
articles for their newsletter. Write for more details.

FOR LGBT PRISONERS

Black and Pink Project
Supports LGBTQ prisoners.
www.blackandpink.org

LockedOut
c/o Prison Book Project
P.O. Box 396
Amherst, MA 01004
Free resource guide for LGBTQ prisoners in the U.S.

Sinister Wisdom, Inc.
PO Box 3252
Berkeley, CA 94703
www.sinisterwisdom.org
Publishes work (prose, poetry, essays, graphics and book reviews)
by lesbians only. Free to women in prison.

Transgender, Gender Variant and Intersex (TGI)
Justice Project
1095 Market St., Suite 308
San Francisco, CA 94103
Works on alternative sentencing, advocacy for transgender prisoners
to access hormones, find attorneys and prepare cases for attorneys.
Prisoners can send confidential legal mail to the above address c/o
Alexander Lee, Attorney at Law.

New York only

Sylvia Rivera Law Project
322 8th Ave., 3rd floor
New York, NY 10001
212-337-8550
www.srlp.org
Free legal services to transgender and gender non-conforming
low-income people and people of color in New York City and
surrounding areas.

FOR SURVIVORS OF ABUSE

Free Battered Women/California Coalition for Women Prisoners
1540 Market St., Suite 490
San Francisco, California 94102 USA
415-255-7036 x320
fax: 415-552-3150
info@womenprisoners.org
www.womenprisoners.org
Advocates for the release of domestic violence survivors from state
prison. Only works with women incarcerated in California.

National Clearinghouse in Defense of Battered Women
125 South 9th St., Suite 302
Philadelphia, PA 19107
Information, referrals and legal assistance for battered women.
Works a lot with prisoners, free newsletter.

Resources

FOR IMMIGRANTS IN DETENTION OR PRISON

Immigrant Legal Resource Center
1663 Mission Street, Suite 602
San Francisco, CA 94103
www.ilrc.org
Legal help and advocacy for immigrants. Works with immigrant
detainees and prisoners.

California only
La Raza Centro Legal
474 Valencia St., Suite 295
San Francisco, CA 94103
ATTN: Detention Project
415-575-3500

PRISONER SUPPORT

ACLU National Prison Project
125 Broad St., 18th floor
New York, NY 10004
Handles major class-action lawsuits involving conditions in
federal or state prisons. Does not take on individual cases.

All of Us or None
C/o Legal Services for Prisoners with Children
1540 Market St., Suite 490
San Francisco, CA 94102
415-255-7036
www.allofusornone.org
A national organizing initiative of prisoners, former prisoners and
felons, to combat the many forms of discrimination they face as
the result of felony convictions. Has chapters in several California
cities as well as Oklahoma.

American Friends Service Committee Prison Watch Project
89 Market St., 6th floor
Newark, NJ 07102
973-643-3192
Fax: 973-643-8924
bkerness@afsc.org
Monitors human rights violations and abuse of prisoners in
U.S. federal and state prisons. Prisoners should send personal
testimony to Bonnie Kerness at the above address.

Critical Resistance
1904 Franklin St., Suite 504
Oakland, CA 94612
www.criticalresistance.org
Organization dedicated to fighting the expansion of the prison
system. Has chapters in Baltimore, Chicago, Gainesville, Los
Angeles, New Orleans, New York, Oakland, Tampa/St. Petersburg
and Washington, DC. Chapters work on diverse projects—such as
establishing "harm free zones" that don't rely on policing; prisoner
newspaper and radio projects; prisoner support; and local
organizing against prisons and policing and for true community
safety. Write for a complete list of programs and to get involved in
the movement.

D.R.I.V.E. Movement
drivemovement.org
Founded by death row prisoners, the DRIVE movement seeks
to unite the death row community to push forward and initiate a
change in conditions.

Innocence Project (National)
100 Fifth Ave., 3rd Floor
New York, NY 10011
Only handles cases where post-conviction DNA testing of
evidence can yield conclusive evidence of innocence.

Resources

Jericho Movement
PO Box 1272
New York, NY 10113
718-949-5153
Political prisoner support group working toward prison abolition.

National Network for Women in Prison
714 West California Blvd
Pasadena, CA 91105
Resources and advocacy work. Produces a free newsletter written
by former prisoners.

Prison Activist Resource Center
PO Box 339
Berkeley, CA 94701
www.prisonactivist.org
Does advocacy and prison support work. Free resources packet
for prisoners.

Project for Older Prisoners (POPS)
c/o Jonathan Turley
National Law Center
2000 H St. NW
Washington, DC 2002
Information for older prisoners.

Southern Center for Human Rights
83 Poplar St. N.W.
Atlanta, GA 30303-2122
www.schr.org
Represents prisoners and jail inmates in class action lawsuits
against conditions of confinement, degrading or discriminatory
treatment, denial of medical and mental health care, and other
constitutional violations.

Just Detention International
3325 Wilshire Blvd., Suite 340
Los Angeles, CA 90010
213-384-1400
www.justdetention.org

California only

California Coalition for Women Prisoners
1540 Market St. #490
San Francisco, CA 94102
415-255-7036 x314 • 415-552-3150
info@womenprisoners.org
www.womenprisoners.org
A grassroots racial-justice organization that challenges the institutional violence imposed on women and communities of color by prisons and the criminal justice system. Visits women in prison, publishes *The Fire Inside* newsletter, organizes annual protests, and does advocacy, education, outreach, and support for former prisoners.

Justice Now
1322 Webster St., Suite 210
Oakland, CA 94612
510-839-7654
Legal students assist California women prisoners with defense of parental rights, compassionate release, healthcare access, sentencing mitigation and placement in community programs.

This is not a comprehensive resource list. The following websites also maintain prisoner resource lists:

• **Prison Activist Resource Center:** www.prisonactivist.org

• **Critical Resistance:** www.criticalresistance.org

• **Prison Book Program's National Prisoner Resource List:**
  www.prisonbookprogram.org/nprl.php

• **Family and Corrections Network:** www.fcnetwork.org
  (for family resources only)

RECOMMENDED READING

~~~~~~

BOOKS

Atwood, Jane Evelyn
Too Much Time: Women in Prison
London: Phaidon, 2000.

For nine years, Atwood visited women's jails and prisons throughout the United States, Russia, France, Czechoslovakia, Switzerland, India, Spain and Israel, photographing their daily lives behind bars. In stark black-and-white, Atwood illustrates the horrors of prison life: the scars of self-mutilation, pregnant women giving birth while handcuffed and male guards forcibly stripping mentally ill women. Even her photos of the more prosaic routines—male guards frisking and strip-searching women, women dressing after a strip search or women tearfully watching their families leave the visiting room—reveal the regular humiliation and dehumanization that prisons, regardless of country, inflict upon those they hold within.

Cook, Sandy, and Susanne Davies, eds.
Harsh Punishment: International Experiences of
Women's Imprisonment
Boston: Northeastern University Press, 1999.

The editors, both lecturers at the School of Law and Legal Studies at Australia's LaTrobe University, chose to include the personal accounts of formerly and currently incarcerated women as well as the writings of scholars and prisoner rights activists. *Harsh Punishment* examines both the issues facing women imprisoned in the U.S., Canada, England, New Zealand, Poland and Thailand and the actions that they and their advocates are taking to address these issues.

Curtin, Mary Ellen
Black Prisoners and Their World, Alabama, 1865–1900
Carter G. Woodson Institute series in Black studies. Charlottesville: University Press of Virginia, 2000.

Curtin chronicles the rise of the Black Codes following the Civil War, the increasing incarceration of newly freed African Americans and the exploitation of their labor by prisons and private coal companies in nineteenth-century Alabama. Curtin devotes a chapter to African-American women, whose gender made their labor undesirable to coal companies and thus less profitable to the jails and prisons. She also describes and frames their refusal to obey prison rules as individual acts of resistance.

Davis, Angela
Are Prisons Obsolete?
New York: Seven Stories Press, 2003.

Davis, a renowned prison abolitionist and former prisoner, traces the history of the prison, its rise as a form of social control in the post–Civil War era, and argues for its eradication. For those who believe that prison abolition is an idealistic pipe dream, Davis draws parallels between today's movement to eliminate prisons with the movement to abolish slavery, pointing out that "the belief in the permanence of slavery was so widespread that even white abolitionists found it difficult to imagine black people as equals."

Diaz-Cotto, Juanita
Chicana Lives and Criminal Justice: Voices from El Barrio
Austin: University of Texas Press, 2006.

Chicana Lives is the first book to examine the issues confronting Chicanas in California's criminal justice system. Diaz quotes extensively from 29 women, thus allowing their stories to demonstrate how racism, abuse, violence and the war on drugs has devastated their lives and their communities. Diaz also explores lingual discrimination, a topic that has been largely absent from the current body of work on incarceration. She notes the increased incarceration of monolingual Spanish-speaking women as a result of the U.S. war on drugs. She also documents the women's efforts to challenge conditions at the Sybil Brand Institute, Los Angeles' women's jail and redefines individual actions—such as bilingual women translating for their monolingual peers—as resistance.

Diaz-Cotto, Juanita
Gender, Ethnicity and the State: Latina and Latino Prison Politics
Albany, NY: State University of New York Press, 1996.

In this groundbreaking work, Diaz-Cotto compares the post-Attica organizing strategies of Latinos and Latinas imprisoned in two maximum-security prisons in New York State. Despite its title, Diaz also chronicles the activism of non-Latina prisoners, such as African-American prisoner organizer Carol Crooks, whose beating sparked the 1974 August Rebellion.

Faith, Karlene
"The Santa Cruz Women's Prison Project, 1972–1976"
In *Schooling in a "Total Institution": Critical Perspectives on Prison Education*, edited by Howard S. Davidson, 173–192. Westport, CT: Bergin & Garvey, 1995.

Faith, a cofounder of the Santa Cruz Women's Prison Project, describes the four years of the project's existence. Faith details not only the program's courses, but also the difficulties of implementing a program, especially one that encouraged critical thinking, within a prison setting. She also recounts the program's impact on the women who participated and the women's protests during the times when the prison banned the program.

Faith, Karlene
Unruly Women: The Politics and Confinement of Resistance
Vancouver: Press Gang Publishers, 1993.

Faith traces the historical persecution of women who refuse to adhere to societal gender norms to the current criminalization of female "deviant behavior." She also examines the imprisonment of women in both the U.S. and Canada, including the notorious maximum-security P4W (Prison for Women). *Unruly Women* was published before the 1994 riot at P4W and the ensuing public outrage over prison brutality that led to the prison's close. Faith also devotes a section to both the Women's Prison Project and other acts of resistance among women imprisoned in California during the 1970s (including one instance in which she was taken as a "friendly hostage" while conducting interviews).

Gagne, Patricia
Battered Women's Justice: The Movement for Clemency and the Politics of Self-Defense
New York: Twayne Publishers, 1998.

Gagne examines the history and prevalence of domestic violence in the United States, the trials of battered women who defended themselves, the emergence of the shelter movement and, perhaps most interestingly for those seeking information about women's organizing behind bars, incarcerated women's efforts to gain clemency. Gagne places particular emphasis on the Celeste clemencies in Ohio, contrasting them with later, less successful, campaigns in other states.

Herivel, Tara, and Paul Wright
Prison Profiteers: Who Makes Money from Mass Incarceration
New York: New Press, 2007.

Prison Profiteers examines the private prison companies, investment banks, churches, guard unions, medical corporations, and other industries and individuals that benefit from mass imprisonment. While none of the articles are specifically tied to the impact on the rising number of incarcerated women, they each investigate little-known policies that affect everyone in U.S. prisons today and connect the dots between these practices and the entities that profit from them.

Recommended Reading

Kurshan, Nancy
"Women and Imprisonment in the U.S.: History and Current Reality"
Available online at: http://prisonactivist.org/women/women-and-imprisonment.html.

> Kurshan, a long-time prisoner rights activist, scholar and founder of the Committee to End the Marion Lockdown, provides a short history of female imprisonment in the U.S. She includes a one-page overview of women's resistance from the Civil War until the 1970s and calls upon other prisoner rights activists and researchers to continue researching and expanding this little-known history (or herstory).

Rafter, Nicole Hahn
Partial Justice: Women, Prisons, and Social Control
New Brunswick: Transaction Publishers, 1990.

> Rafter traces the history of the women's prison, from the early days of women's incarceration in the attics, cellars and corners of male penitentiaries to the establishment of separate facilities for women. She examines both the reformatory, which served as a mechanism to socially control the increasing number of white women living independently, and the women's penitentiary, which served to warehouse African Americans and other women seen as "irredeemable." Rafter gives historical examples illustrating how, even after the demise of the reformatory, the ideas of controlling and changing gender behavior continued to affect the sentencing structure for women.

Sudbury, Julia
Global Lockdown: Race, Gender, and the Prison-Industrial Complex
New York: Routledge, 2005.

> "Spiraling incarceration rates, rampant overcrowding, and systemic human rights violations are common features of women's prisons from Lagos to Los Angeles," writes Julia Sudbury, professor of ethnic studies at Mills College and editor of *Global Lockdown*. These 20 essays demonstrate how race, gender, colonization, globalization, neoliberalism and militarism have contributed to the dramatic increase

of women's incarceration worldwide. The tone of most of these essays, however, is fairly academic, potentially rendering the book inaccessible to readers unable or unwilling to read works full of academic language.

Talvi, Silja J. A.
Women Behind Bars: The Crisis of Women in the U.S. Prison System
Emeryville, CA: Seal Press, 2007.

Investigative journalist Silja Talvi visited women's prisons throughout the U.S. interviewing hundreds of women, as well as the prison officials who keep them. In extremely accessible language, Talvi reiterates the more commonly known conditions in women's prisons, such as overcrowding and abuse, but also exposes frightening new trends such as the growing implementation of privately run "God Pods" (units run by fundamentalist or evangelical Christian groups that push prisoners to convert) and the increasing use of interstate transfers to cope with the drastic numbers of women behind bars.

Women of the ACE Program at the Bedford Hills Correctional Facility
Breaking the Walls of Silence: AIDS and Women in a New York State Maximum Security Prison
Woodstock, NY: Overlook Press, 1998.

Collectively written by members of the AIDS Counseling and Education program at Bedford Hills, the book documents the organization's history, including the obstacles to organizing a peer education program within a prison, and shares its curriculum with those seeking to create similar programs in other prisons.

PERIODICALS

California Coalition for Women Prisoners
The Fire Inside: Newsletter of the California Coalition for Women Prisoners
San Francisco, CA: The Coalition, 1995 to present:
www.womenprisoners.org/fire

The quarterly publication of advocacy group California Coalition for Women Prisoners features the voices and daily experiences of women imprisoned throughout California as well as short articles by outside advocates. Although the articles are specifically about California women's prisons, many of the subjects and struggles can be applied to other states. Past issues have featured articles and editorials about the need for (and lack of) mental health care at Valley State Prison for Women, inadequate prison health care in general and the struggle against the state's plans to expand women's prisons.

"Inside/Outside"
Sojourner: The Women's Forum
Jamaica Plain, Mass. Sojourner, Inc., 1999–2002.

From July 1999 until its closing in late 2002, the feminist magazine *Sojourner: The Women's Forum* devoted a section to the issues faced by women imprisoned across the country. The section, entitled Inside/Outside, included investigative reporting of prison conditions as well as letters and articles by incarcerated women.

Prison Legal News
Seattle, WA: Prison Legal News, 1992 to present.

Founded in 1990 by two men incarcerated in Washington State, *Prison Legal News* is particularly useful for those seeking in-depth information on prisoners' litigation efforts. It also prints in-depth investigative articles about prison conditions, such as excessive force, mail censorship, visiting, telephones, religious freedom, free speech, prison rape, abuse of women prisoners, retaliation, the Prison Legal Reform Act (PLRA), medical treatment, AIDS, the death penalty, control units, use of prison labor, etc.

Prison News Service
Toronto: PSC Publishers, 1987–1996.

The Canadian-based *Prison News Service* offered news, analysis and commentary from prisoners in both the United States and Canada. The archives of the tabloid-sized quarterly is a wealth of information about prisoner organizing, such as Linda Evans's work around AIDS at the Federal Correctional Institution in Pleasanton, California and Marcia Bunney's continued activities as a jailhouse lawyer. The 1995 issue includes coverage of the inquiry into conditions at Canada's P4W and correspondence from women held inside.

Tenacious: Writings from Women in Prison
Brooklyn, NY: Black Star Publishing, 2002 to present.

Feeling that their voices and experiences were not being heard by both their male counterparts and the larger outside world, women imprisoned in Oregon's Coffee Creek Correctional Facility started the zine *Tenacious: Art and Writings by Women in Prison*. The zine is not limited to women incarcerated in Oregon; since its inception, it has included the writings and art of women imprisoned throughout the country. Early issues describe sexual harassment and abuse, the lack of vocational programming, and living with HIV. Later issues include mothers' reflections on lengthy separations from their children, Colorado's new prison farm worker program and descriptions of living in segregation. (Full disclosure: I am the outside person the women approached to compile, copy and distribute this zine.)

REPORTS

Fine, Michelle, Kathy Boudin, Iris Bowen, Judith Clark, Donna Hylton, Migdalia Martinez, "Missy," Rosemarie Roberts, Pamela Smart, Maria Torre and Debora Upegui
Changing Minds: The Impact of College in a Maximum Security Prison
New York: Ronald Ridgeway, 2001.
web.gc.cuny.edu/che/changingminds.html.

From 1997 to 2000, CUNY professor Michelle Fine and eight women incarcerated in New York's Bedford Hills Correctional Facility conducted interviews with prisoners participating in the prison's College Bound program, the students' children and prison staff about the effects of having a higher education program in a women's prison. Although the report focuses mainly on the effect of education on recidivism, interviewees also talk about how education has affected other issues such as anger management, substance abuse, HIV/AIDS, domestic violence, sexual abuse, parenting support and prenatal care.

Recommended Reading

Human Rights Watch Women's Project
All Too Familiar: Sexual Abuse of Women in U.S. State Prisons
Washington, DC: Human Rights Watch, 1996.
www.aclu.org/hrc/PrisonsStates.pdf.

Title VII of the Civil Rights Act of 1964 guaranteed equal employment regardless of gender, allowing women to work at male prisons and men to work at female prisons. Thirty-two years later, in 1996, Human Rights Watch released a 510-page report detailing the prevalence of staff sexual abuse in eleven women's state prisons. The report also describes each prison system's response (or lack thereof) to staff sexual abuse and issues policy recommendations to both the federal government and each specific state department of corrections.

Human Rights Watch
Locked Away: Immigration Detainees in Jail in the United States
September 1998. www.hrw.org/reports98/us-immig/Ins989-05.htm.

In 1998, the U.S. Immigration and Naturalization Service (INS) housed more than 60% of its 15,000 detainees in local jails throughout the country. Based on interviews with more than two hundred detainees held in seven different states, hundreds of letters and telephone calls from other detainees jailed around the country, INS officials, jail officials, immigration judges, immigrant rights advocates, and attorneys, the report lists the numerous injustices and hardships that immigrant detainees, including refugees and asylum seekers, face when held in local jails.

Little, Cheryl, and Joan Friedland
Krome's Invisible Prisoners: Cycles of Abuse and Neglect
Miami, FL: Florida Immigrant Advocacy Center, Inc., 1996.

Prepared by attorneys from the Florida Immigrant Advocacy Center, *Krome's Invisible Prisoners* details the horrific conditions facing immigrants detained at Florida's Krome Service Processing Center, including overcrowding, lack of access to legal counsel, unsanitary living conditions, inadequate medical care and lack of access to basic necessities.

Women's Commission for Refugee Women and Children
*Behind Locked Doors: Abuse of Refugee Women at the Krome
Detention Center*
New York: Women's Commission for Refugee Women and Children, 2000
www.womensrefugeecommission.org/reports/doc_download/272-
behind-locked-doorsabuse-of-refugee-women-at-the-krome-
detention-center.

In 2000, the Women's Commission for Refugee Women and Children
assessed conditions at the Krome Service Processing Center. The
report reiterated many of the complaints about conditions that FIAC
found four years earlier; in addition, it described the widespread sexual
abuse of female detainees by Krome staff members and the atmosphere
of fear and intimidation engendered by those abuses and staff threats of
deportation, transfers to county jails and prisons, and even death.

Women's Commission for Refugee Women and Children
A Cry for Help: Chinese Women in INS Detention
New York: 1995.

In 1993, the *Golden Venture*, a ship smuggling over 300 Chinese
from China's Fujian Province, ran aground off Rockaway Beach,
New York. The media ran stories about the smuggling of people
from mainland China to the U.S. and their exploitation by "snake-
heads" (smugglers with ties to Chinese gangs), but soon forgot about
the actual people involved. Two years later, the Women's Commission
released a report documenting the conditions of the 10 to 13 women
aboard the *Golden Venture* who were subsequently sent to the
Orleans Parish Prison in Louisiana.

Women's Commission for Refugee Women and Children
*Innocents in Jail: INS Moves Refugee Women from Krome to Turner
Guilford Knight Correctional Center Miami*
New York: 2001.
www.womenscommission.org/pdf/us_tgk.pdf.

In December 2000, following complaints of sexual abuse of female
detainees at Krome Service Processing Center, the INS relocated

female detainees to the Turner Guilford Knight (TGK) Correctional Center, a Miami-Dade County jail. Although the transfer would, according to the INS, "ensure those detainees the most safe, secure, and humane detention conditions possible," interviews with detainees revealed that TGK was also unable to accommodate their legal, health, linguistic, and cultural needs and, aside from segregating immigrant detainees in two cell pods, subjected them to the same demeaning treatment as the jail's prisoners.

Women's Commission for Refugee Women and Children
Liberty Denied: Women Seeking Asylum Imprisoned in the United States.
New York: 1997.
http://womensrefugeecommission.org/docs/liberty.pdf.

Liberty Denied reflects a two-year investigation of the treatment of women seeking asylum in the United States. Many of these women have fled gender-based persecution, including gang rape by military forces, forced marriage, or female genital mutilation. Asylum seekers are frequently jailed for months, and even years, with little contact with the outside world. Like its previous reports about Krome and TGK, the Women's Commission found that women asylum seekers frequently endure prolonged detention and face physical and verbal abuse by both INS officials and prison staff.

A NOTE ABOUT TRANSGENDER, TRANSSEXUAL, INTERSEX AND GENDER-VARIANT PEOPLE IN PRISON

There are no official records on the number of transgender, intersex or gender-variant people behind bars. In 2000, based on the fact that 70 prisoners were on hormone treatment in New York State prisons and 17 in New York City jails, researcher Darren Rosenblum gave a "vague estimate" that the number of imprisoned transgendered people was in the low thousands.[1] In 1997, San Francisco's Department of Health found that over 30% of transgender women of color in the city had been incarcerated within the past year."[2] From April to June 2008, researchers conducting a demographic assessment of transgender prisoners for the CDCR interviewed over 300 transgender people in California's male prisons alone.[3]

The reasons behind these numbers are not simply that a greater number of transgender, transsexual and gender non-conforming people engage in actions that are illegal. As Alexander Lee of the Transgender, Gender Variant and Intersex Project points out, "The reasons why TGI people become prisoners in California are the same reasons why people of color, low-income people, homeless people, sex workers and immigrants become prisoners."[4] Widespread social stigma against transsexual, intersex and other gender non-conforming people leads to pervasive discrimination in housing, employment, health care, education, public benefits and social services. Discrimination and violence also prevent transgender people from accessing the social safety nets—such as shelters, foster care, Medicaid and public entitlements—that would enable them to survive without turning to illegal activities. This lack of access pushes a disproportionate number of transgender youth and adults into criminalized means of survival, such as sex work, drug sales or theft. Trans and gender non-conforming people are also more likely to be arrested for poverty-related offenses such as loitering, turnstile-jumping and sleeping outside. Entrenched social stigma and transphobia also lead to pervasive violence and physical brutality from family members, community members and police.[5] Transgender women are particularly at risk for police entrapment and violence because of the widely held stereotype of transgender women as sex workers.[6] As a result, transgender people are disproportionately poor, homeless, criminalized and imprisoned.

Once arrested and convicted, many transgender people are sentenced to prison based on their birth-assigned gender or genitalia. Transgender women who live and identify as women, but who were labeled male at birth, are generally placed in male prisons. Transgender men are generally placed in female prisons.[7] While transgender people face the same negligent, sometimes life-threatening health care system as other prisoners, their health needs are often exacerbated by the prison's refusal to continue hormone therapy. Because gender-related hormone prescriptions are not covered by Medicaid or by many private health insurance companies, many transgender and gender-variant people rely on less formal channels. However, prisons often deny hormone access to those without a formal prescription. In some states, such as Pennsylvania and, until 2011, Wisconsin, even having a prescription does not guarantee being allowed to continue hormone therapy.[8] The denial or irregular delivery of hormones can cause a range of physical, emotional or psychological harm. For transgender women, whose bodies are accustomed to regular estrogen intake, withdrawal can cause heart problems, irregular blood pressure, hot flashes, anxiety, panic attacks, hair loss and difficulty with short-term memory and concentration. For transgender men, interrupted hormone access can cause depression, lethargy, mood swings, sleep disturbance and anemia.[9]

Authorities in both men's and women's prisons target transgender, gender non-conforming and intersex people, subjecting them to verbal harassment, humiliation, excessive strip searches and isolation as well as refusing to recognize their gender identities.[10] Transgender women placed in male prisons are at great risk of sexual assault: one study found that 59% of transgender women in California's male prisons had been sexually assaulted while incarcerated compared to 4% of the male-identified population.[11] Transgender women in male prisons also face the threat of forced prostitution by both prison staff and other prisoners. Gabriel Arkles, the staff attorney at the Sylvia Rivera Law Project, testified during a U.S. Department of Justice hearing about rape in prison:

> A common form of sexual abuse of transgender, intersex, and gender non-conforming people in prison is forced prostitution. In these systems, correction officers bring transgender women to the cell of male inmates and lock them in for the male inmate to have sex with. The male inmate will then pay the correction officer in some way, for example with cigarettes or money. The correction officer sometimes gives a small cut to the woman and brings her back to her cell.

> The rape and sexual exploitation of transgender, intersex, and gender non-conforming people in some facilities is very open. Sometimes all or almost all the staff and officials in a particular facility know about the abuse, but even those who do not participate in it maintain a rigid conspiracy of silence.[12]

In other male prisons, officers practice "V-coding"—placing transgender and transsexual women in cells with sexually aggressive men. Kim Love who experienced this first-hand during her three years in California's male prison system, observed that "without the sexual tension being brought down, the prisoners would probably overturn that place. Because there's more prisoners than there is COs. They use us [to keep the peace]."[13]

As a seeming "solution" about the placement of transgender and gender-variant people, other prisons regularly place them in solitary confinement, ostensibly for safety purposes. However, being in solitary confinement (often labeled "protective custody") reduces access to recreational and educational programming and increases psychological stress as a result of the extreme isolation, and makes people more vulnerable to staff sexual abuse and other misconduct.[14]

Inside women's prisons, transgender men do not face the same threat of sexual or physical assault from other prisoners. However, staff members in women's prisons target transgender, gender non-conforming, and intersex people with verbal harassment, humiliation, excessive strip searches, isolation and a refusal to recognize their gender identities.[15] "Sally," a woman incarcerated in Indiana recalled the experience of her friend C, who was in the process of transition, including breast removal and hormone therapy. "The prison refused to prescribe continued hormones," C's friend recalled. "Conservative officers were more harsh with C. Female guards treated her as a sexual predator and male guards treated her as a weak/gay man, a threat to their own sexuality."[16]

Transgender men and those who are perceived to have traditional masculine qualities are disproportionately blamed and punished as the aggressor in any violent conflict, regardless of circumstance.[17] At La Vista Correctional Facility in Colorado, those who present as gender-variant or masculine are called "boy-girls." "Officers watch them more closely," noted RJ. "Boy-girls and gender-variant individuals tend to be viewed as trouble."[18] Closer scrutiny of gender non-conforming women is not limited to La Vista. "Sally" notes that the guards pay close attention to romantic and sexual relationships involving masculine-appearing prisoners. "These are the couples more likely to get caught having sexual contact and therefore punished, which further solidifies the prison officials' views of the 'studs' as sexual predators. This gives them an easy excuse to single them out by moving the trans/masculine partner around more frequently if they see a relationship forming or keep them in seg longer for discipline resulting from a sexual contact or battery charge when caught with their girlfriends. These relationships form probably a quarter of the women put in segregation." Sally noted that, in addition, staff and administrators question masculine-appearing women about their sexuality. One administrators asks them if they were molested as children and then tells them that they are simply "sexually confused."[19]

Prisons have always been used as a means of controlling women's gender behavior.[20] As late as the twentieth century, women could be incarcerated for defying gender norms. Women's prisons continue to reinforce gender roles and behaviors in both their rules and, in some cases, by institutionalizing separate, often more punitive, units for gender non-conforming prisoners.

During the 1970s, staff at the Sybil Brand Institute for Women, the county jail in Los Angeles, separated butch and masculine-appearing women into Cell Block 4200 or "the Daddy Tank." Prison staff sent women to this unit who had "short haircuts or no make-up, those wearing trousers with flies, jockey shorts, T-shirts or turned-up socks, those who spread their legs when they sit, and those who hold a cigarette between thumb and forefingers."[21] Women reported that conditions in the Daddy Tank were "three or four times worse than in other sections of the jail—women there had the least privileges, were assigned the dirtiest jobs and placed in segregation without warning.[22] Staff members would often greet women from the Daddy Tank by saying, "Here come the boys" and "I see we have the men with us today."[23]

In June 1972, non-incarcerated lesbian activists picketed outside the jail to protest the Daddy Tank, demanding its closure.[24] SBI officials refused to close the Daddy Tank altogether. Instead, they moved the women into Cell Block 3000 or "the Daddy Dorm." Women were housed in a dormitory-style setting instead of individual cells, permitted access to an open dayroom, and became newly eligible for classes and programs. However, one woman reported, "They just pulled a few femmes out of the general population" to make the punishment of gender non-conforming people less visible.[25]

Segregating lesbians, particularly the masculine-appearing and gender non-conforming ones, continued at SBI until the 1980s.[26]

This procedure was not limited to Sybil Brand. The county jail in neighboring San Bernardino County also isolated masculine-appearing people during the 1980s. "Charlie Morningstar," a man who had been female-assigned at birth, recounted spending eighteen months in various isolation cells at opposite ends of the jail. "The guards would move me all the time between all of those isolation cells. Sometimes in the middle of the night they would come and move me to another isolation cell."[27]

Such discriminatory practices continue today. In 2009, the Fluvanna Correctional Center for Women in Virginia began separating prisoners who wore "loose-fitting clothes, short hair or [had] otherwise masculine looks." The women were sent to the "butch wing," also known as the "little boys' wing," "locker room wing" or "studs' wing." Prisoners stated that they were verbally harassed by staff who would make remarks such as, "Here come the little boys," when they were escorted to eat.[28]

In 2011, the Colorado Department of Corrections closed Fort Lyons, a men's prison that housed men confined to wheelchairs and the transgender women assigned to push their wheelchairs. Both groups were transferred to La Vista, where a unit was converted into "a prison within a prison" especially for them. The transgender women were housed with the men. "They will not house them with us because, although some have breasts and live as women, they have not had full surgical change of genitals. Because of this, they are considered as men and housed as such by DOC," reported RJ. "They have spraypainted the windows to prevent us from seeing in or them from looking out. There is a fence with its own razor wire and a locked gate around their living unit. They have separate times for recreation, library, eating and visits. If any of the men or trans women have to travel from one part of the facility to another, our movement will be ceased."[29]

In the first edition of *Resistance Behind Bars*, there was a conspicuous absence of stories from transgender, transsexual, intersex and Two-Spirit people in prison. The first (and only) story occurs on page 155 in the chapter "Resistance in Immigrant Detention." From 2001 to 2008,

I found nothing about incarcerated transgender women's organizing or about cisgender women's organizing in solidarity with their transgender peers. The closest I found was the May 2007 story of Victoria Arellano, a 23-year-old transgender immigrant from Mexico. Arellano was sent to the San Pedro Processing Center in California after being arrested on a traffic charge. ICE officials classified Arellano as a man and sent her to the men's dormitory.

Arellano had AIDS. Before her arrest and detention, she was in good health and had been taking antibiotics to prevent pulmonary infections from developing into treatment-resistant pneumonia. At San Pedro, officials denied Arellano her medications. They also repeatedly ignored her requests to see a doctor. As Arellano's health deteriorated, the men in her dormitory took care of her. They used their own towels to cool her fevers, used cardboard boxes to collect her vomit and, as her condition worsened, eighty of the men staged a strike. They refused to get in line for the nightly head count, chanting "Hospital," until the prison nurse agreed to take her to the infirmary.[30] While I found Arellano's experience compelling, it was a story of male prisoners organizing on behalf of the transgender woman in their dormitory.[31] Thus, I did not include it in my book.

Several months after I sent my manuscript to PM Press, I came across the story of Nikki Lee Diamond, a transgender woman. When sentencing her to prison, the judge ruled that she was to be sent to the California Institution for Women (CIW). Upon Diamond's arrival at CIW, she should have undergone the routine physical examination and pap smear given to all new women. Instead, the nurse refused to examine her, leaving the room instead. A guard then escorted Diamond to the prison's hospital unit and placed her in a cage-like cell. The prison's chief medical officer and psychiatrist approached Diamond and stated, "I am here to tell you that this is a prison for women, not for those who just think they are women."

Refusing to allow the doctor to intimidate her, Diamond retorted, "And psychiatry is a profession for qualified doctors, not just those who get their licenses out of a Cracker Jack box."[32] When the prison's chief deputy warden told her that he was sending her to the men's medical prison at Vacaville, Diamond again refused to be intimidated:

> I stood and faced my adversary. "You may be the chief deputy warden, but I am the great-great-great-great-great-great-great granddaughter of the chief medicine woman of the Huron tribe of the Iroquois nation, and I am certain that the superior court judge who sentenced me to this seven-to-life sentence at the California Institution for Women would not take too kindly to your snubbing his decision and sending me elsewhere. He ordered me to be examined by a doctor and a nurse, who deemed me female, and I was housed with the other females in that county jail for my nine-month stay. If you insist on negating his decision, I will advise my attorney to inform the judge." I turned my back and sat down on the bed.[33]

Diamond was ultimately able to serve her sentence in a women's prison. While some of the women verbally harassed her, Diamond found support from other women. They showed her where things were located in the prison and taught her how the system worked.

Diamond's experience has not paved the way for other transgender, intersex or gender-variant people to claim the same right. Transgender women are, more often than not, placed in male prisons and have had to fight for even the most basic rights and protections.

In 1989, Dee Farmer, a transgender woman, was transferred to the federal maximum-security prison for men in Terre Haute, Indiana. Despite Farmer's feminine appearance, which included surgically enhanced breasts, prison officials placed her in general population where she was repeatedly beaten and raped and, as a result, infected with HIV. Farmer sued the prison, charging that prison officials' "deliberate indifference" to the substantial risk of harm violated her Eighth Amendment right against cruel and unusual punishment. The Supreme Court agreed, ruling that prison officials who are "deliberately indifferent" to substantial risks of serious harm are liable under the Eighth Amendment. However, prison officials were not liable unless they had *actual subjective* knowledge that the transgender person was at risk and then failed to act on that knowledge: "[A] prison official cannot be found liable under the Eighth Amendment for denying an inmate humane conditions of confinement unless the official knows of and disregards an excessive risk to inmate health on safety; the official must both be aware of facts from which the inference could be drawn that a substantial risk of harm exists, and he must also draw the inference."[34] The ruling, thus worded, did not push other jail and prison officials to more carefully consider the safety of transgender, transsexual and gender-variant prisoners under their custody.

Following her arrest on December 17, 2002, Kelly McAllister, a pre-operative transsexual, was placed in a cell with a larger male inmate who brutally raped her. McAllister did not allow jail officials to escape responsibility. She filed a claim against Sacramento County, its district attorney and the sheriff's department for jeopardizing her safety by ignoring her transgender status and placing her in a cell with a man.[35]

In 2003, Donna Dawn Konitzer, a transgender woman incarcerated in Wisconsin, filed suit in federal court charging the Wisconsin Department of Corrections (WDOC) with subjecting her to cruel and unusual punishment by not allowing her to have surgery that would complete her transition to a woman. Although they provided her with hormone therapy, prison officials refused Konitzer's requests to wear female undergarments, to refer to her as a woman, and to use make-up, body hair removal products and an anti-baldness treatment. In May 2010, a district court ruled that a jury could find that prison officials "were deliberately indifferent to Konitzer's serious medical needs" by refusing her the real-life experience as a woman as part of treating her gender identity disorder because Konowitz's gender identity disorder was a formal medical diagnosis. On September 1, 2010, WDOC agreed to settle the case. In the settlement, WDOC agreed:

▷ to contract "with an outside medical specialist with expertise in endocrinology or gender identity disorder to independently evaluate" Konitzer

▷ to provide, on a one-time basis, state-issued bras and underwear consistent with those provided to female prisoners and to allow Konitzer to buy bras and female underwear at the prison's canteen

▷ to continue providing hormone therapy as well as medical and mental health care

▷ to ensure Konitzer's privacy when using the shower and toilet

▷ to pay $5,000 to cover Konitzer's legal fees and restitution

▷ to provide her with a six-month treatment of Propecia to fight baldness and to allow her to buy subsequent treatments in the prison canteen[36]

In other states, though, transgender women continue to fight to even receive hormone treatment. Since 2006, Anastasia Seger, a male-to-female pre-operative transsexual incarcerated in Arkansas, has been struggling to receive hormone therapy treatment. Because Seger had relied on less formal channels and had no legal prescription before her arrest and incarceration, the prison refused to allow her to continue.

Seger did not allow prison policy to discourage her. She wrote numerous letters to staff, such as the mental health counselor and prison psychiatrist, and to administrators, such as the head of mental health and the DOC director. She also filed numerous grievances and a civil suit. When her civil suit was dismissed as frivolous, she appealed. When her appeal was dismissed, she began a campaign to change the prison's policy.[37] In addition, she wrote about her struggles for the Black and Pink newsletter both to inform the general public and to let other transsexual prisoners that they were not alone.

Transgender, transsexual and gender non-conforming people have also challenged prison policies and practices in other ways. Prisoners at California's Valley State Prison for Women started a support group for transgender men and masculine women who are harassed because of their appearance. The group not only offers support, but shares information and resources with each other.[38] After noting the absence of discussion and advocacy around gender identity issues in the prison where he is housed, "Charlie Morningstar" started the Two Spirits Wellness Group. The group grew from six to fifteen people in less than two years. "We talk about first recognizing," Morningstar describes. "We do that to reaffirm identity to everyone else, and to encourage other people within our group to say who they are."[39] Morningstar also talks about his own experiences with others in the group, as a man who was assigned female at birth. "There are some people who did not really know who they were, they hadn't explored that they were transgender males. They had just considered themselves gay, or masculine lesbians, and because of the stigma they couldn't admit it to themselves that they really were males." In addition to simply breaking the silence around gender identity issues, the group also talks about sex, the risks of having sex while in prison and the right to receive hormone treatment while incarcerated in California.[40] People incarcerated in other prisons may also have similar support groups which have not received outside attention.[41]

Narratives of transgender, gender variant and intersex people's resistance in prisons are rare. This should not be interpreted to mean that they do not resist prison abuses. Instead, researchers, activists and abolitionists should see the conspicuous absence of transgender, gender variant and intersex stories of resistance behind bars as a challenge to dig further, figure out why such tales are absent and do what is needed to both end the silence and support their struggles.[42]

---

1 Darren Rosenblum, "'Trapped' in Sing Sing: Transgendered Prisoners Caught in the Gender Binarism." *Michigan Journal of Gender & Law* 6 (2000): 517.

2 Tali Woodward, "Life in Hell: In California Prisons, an Unconventional Gender Identity Can Be Like an Added Sentence," *San Francisco Bay Guardian*, March 21, 2006, http://www.sfbg.com/40/24/cover_life.html.

3 Lori Sexton, Valerie Jenness, Jennifer Sumner, *Where the Margins Meet: A Demographic Assessment of Transgender Inmates*, http://ucicorrections.seweb.uci.edu/sites/ucicorrections.seweb.uci.edu/files/A%20Demographic%20Assessment%20of%20Transgender%20Inmates%20in%20Men%27s%20Prisons.pdf.

4 Alexander Lee, "Gendered Crime and Punishment: Strategies to Protect Transgender, Gender Variant and Intersex People in America's Prisons," *GIC Tip Journal* IV 3 no. 4 (2004): 4. http://www.gicofcolo.org/Upload/TIP/ PDF/2004/tip_2004_summer.pdf.

5 Sylvia Rivera Law Project, *"It's War in Here": A Report on the Treatment of Transgender and Intersex People in New York State Men's Prisons* (2007): 11–12, 15. http://srlp.org/resources/pubs/warinhere.

6 Lee, "Gendered Crime and Punishment," 4.

7 Ibid.

8 In 2005, Wisconsin passed a law barring prison doctors from providing transgender prisoners with medically necessary hormone therapy or sex reassignment surgery. The ACLU and Lambda Legal sued on behalf of Kari Sundstrom and Andrea Fields, both of whom sought to continue hormone therapy while incarcerated. On August 5, 2011, the U.S. Court of Appeals for the Seventh Circuit upheld the right of transgender people to receive medical care while incarcerated. See ACLU Press Release, "ACLU and Lambda Legal Sued to Allow Transgender Inmates to Receive Hormone Treatments," August 5, 2011. http://www.aclu.org/lgbt-rights/federal-court-upholds-transgender-peoples-right-access-medical-treatment-prison.

9 Pascal Emmer, Adrian Lowe, and R. Barrett Marshall, *This Is a Prison, Glitter Is Not Allowed: Experiences of Trans and Gender Variant People in Pennsylvania's Prison Systems*, Philadelphia: Hearts on a Wire Collective (2011): 18. http:// www.scribd.com/doc/56677078/This-is-a-Prison-Glitter-is-Not-Allowed

10 Ibid., 32.

11 Gabriel Arkles, "Intersections of Transgender Lives and the Law: Safety and Solidarity Across Gender Lines: Rethinking Segregation of Transgender People in Detention," *Temple Political and Civil Rights Law Review* 18 (2009): 517.

12 Sylvia Rivera Law Project, 25–26. Cites Gabriel Arkles, Prison Rape Elimination Act testimony, August 15, 2005. The Sylvia Rivera Law Project is a program providing free legal help to trans, intersex and gender non-conforming people in New York City.

13 blake nemec, "No One Enters Like Them: Health, Gender Variance, and the PIC," in *Captive Genders: Trans Embodiment and the Prison Industrial Complex*, ed., E. Stanley and N. Smith (Oakland, CA: AK Press, 2011): 229, 222.

14 See Arkles. Arkles notes that, had ICE officials segregated Victoria Arellano from the men with whom she was confined, she would have had no one to advocate for her at all.

15 Pascal et al., *This Is a Prison, Glitter Is Not Allowed*, 32.

16 "Sally," letter to the author, May 30, 2011.

17 Pascal et al., *This Is a Prison, Glitter Is Not Allowed*.

18 RJ, letter to the author, July 10, 2011. Fearing lawsuits, CDOC requires all staff who may work with transgender, transsexual and gender-variant people to undergo sensitivity trainings. RJ, who asked guards at La Vista about these trainings, reports, "He [the first officer] mentioned that they have to pat down the trans women who have breasts with their thumbs so there can be no mistake

about boob-grabbing . . . The second officer said they learn about 'gender identity disorder,' which trans people are presumed to have. He also told me that they cannot refer to them with gender-loaded titles like sir or maam. They have to use neutral words like 'Inmate Such and Such' or DOC numbers. To me, the training seemed less of considering the needs of DOC populations and more of, 'Okay, these are our game moves to avoid lawsuits.'" (RJ, letter to the author, August 6, 2011)

19 "Sally," letter to the author, May 30, 2011. As of her letter, two women filed grievances about the administrator's behavior. Others, she noted, have not for fear of longer time in segregation.

20 Juvenile courts and juvenile detention centers today continue to regulate gender behavior and punish deviations from gender norms. Often, release dates from youth prisons are determined by successful completion of the prison's rehabilitative programming, which often attempts to force queer and trans youth to comply with heteronormative and gender norms. This means longer prison terms for queer and trans youth. Fore more, see Wesley Ware's "Rounding Up the Homosexuals" in *Captive Genders: Trans Embodiment and the Prison Industrial Complex*, ed., E. Stanley and N. Smith (Oakland, CA: AK Press, 2011).

21 Jeanne Cordova, "Prison Reform—New Freedoms for Daddy-Tanked Lesbians," *Lesbian Tide* 7 (1977): 6.

22 Regina Kunzel, "Lessons in Being Gay: Queer Encounters in Gay and Lesbian Prison Activism," *Radical History Review* 100 (2008): 5.

23 Cordova, 7.

24 "We Mean Business: Predicting the End of a So-Called Model Prison," *Lesbian Tide* 1 (1972): 1.

25 Kunzel, 16.

26 Juanita Díaz-Cotto, *Chicana Lives and Criminal Justice: Voices From El Barrio* (Austin: University of Texas Press, 2006), 251–52.

27 "Charlie Morningstar," in *Inside This Place, Not Of It: Narratives from Women's Prisons*, ed. Robin Levi and Ayelet Waldman (San Francisco: Voice of Witness/McSweeney's Books, 2011), 194.

28 Dena Potter, "Virginia Women's Prison Segregated Lesbians, Others," *Huffington Post*, June 10, 2009, http://www.huffingtonpost.com/2009/06/10/virginia-womens-prison-se_n_213967.html. The prison's warden, Barbara Wheeler, retired soon after news about the butch wing and other discriminatory practices became public. The Associated Press reported that the practice was also stopped following inquiries from the press and Republican Senator Ruff. See "Virginia Prison May Have Segregated Women for Appearances," WHSV, June 20, 2009, http://www.whsv.com/virginiaap/headlines/47604932.html.

29 RJ, letter to the author, July 25, 2011.

30 Arellano died of pneumonia and meningitis on July 20, 2007. Both could have been prevented had prison authorities not denied Arellano her medications. Sandra Hernandez. "A Lethal Limbo." *Los Angeles Times*, June 1, 2008, http://articles.latimes.com/2008/jun/01/opinion/op-hernandez1. See also Sandra Hernandez, "Denied Medication, AIDS Patient Dies in Custody." *Daily Journal,*

August 9, 2007, http://www.culturekitchen.com/shreya_mandal/forum/denied_medication_aids_patient_dies_in_0.

31 Gabriel Arkles described another instance in which men rallied to support the transgender woman on their unit: "One trans woman client of mine filed a grievance against a guard who verbally abused her, calling her a faggot, making degrading sexual remarks about her body parts, and threatening to kill her. The men incarcerated in the cells to either side of her chose to testify against the guard, exposing themselves to the risk of retaliation. In fact, that guard and a friend of his beat one of these men severely a few days later shouting that this was what he got for being a witness against him." See Arkles, "Safety and Solidarity," 530.

32 Nikki Lee Diamond, "Behind These Mascaraed Eyes: Passing Life in Prison," in *Nobody Passes: Rejecting the Rules of Gender and Conformity*, ed. Mattilda Bernstein Sycamore (Emeryville, CA: Seal Press, 2006), 197–99.

33 Ibid, 199.

34 *Farmer v Brennan*, 511 U.S. 837 (US Sup Ct, 1994).

35 National Transgender Advocacy Coalition, "Transgendered Woman Raped in Sacramento Jail Files Claim," December 18, 2002, http://www.ntac.org/pr/release.asp?did=59.

36 "Wisconsin DOC Settles Transgender Prisoner's Lawsuit," *Prison Legal News* 22, no.5 (2011): 31. The article notes that "In November 2010, Konitzer moved to void the settlement on the basis that it had been coerced. Konitzer said the withdrawal of her legal team in June 2010, with a trial date set for only two weeks later, caused the coercion. WDOC spokesman Tim LeMonds said the agency considered the settlement to be a 'binding contract.' The district court denied Konitzer's motion to void the settlement, and she filed an appeal with the Seventh Circuit, which remains pending." See: *Konitzer v. Bartow*, 2:03-cv- 00717-CNC (2003), http://dockets.justia.com/docket/wisconsin/wiedce/2:2003cv00717/31608/.

37 Anastasia L. Seger, "The Struggle for Trans Healthcare in Prison," *Black and Pink* (2011): 4.

38 Lori Girshick, "Out of Compliance: Masculine-identified People in Women's Prisons," in *Captive Genders*, ed., Stanley and Smith, 204.

39 Morningstar, 201.

40 Morningstar, 202.

41 Black and Pink, an "open family of LGBTQ prisoners and "free world" allies who support each other," offers print-outs for LGBTQ people trying to start a support group in prison. See http://www.blackandpink.org/ for more information.

42 Another report that includes the voices and experiences of gay, lesbian, transgender and intersex people in (male) prisons include the Montreal Prisoner Correspondence Project's 2008 *Imprisoned Pride: How Queer and Trans Prisoners Get Written Out of Mainstream Pride Movements*: http://prisonercorrespondenceproject.files.wordpress.com/2009/01/imprisonedpride.pdf. See also *Captive Genders*, ed., Stanley and Smith, and Joey L. Mogul, Andrea J. Ritchie, and Kay Whitlock. *Queer (in)justice: The Criminalization of LGBT People in the United States* (Boston: Beacon Press, 2011).

EPILOGUE

These stories are only the tip of the iceberg. After *Resistance Behind Bars* was published, I traveled around the country to present and facilitate discussions about resistance and organizing in women's prisons. Sharing these stories opened the door to many more. Some had been well documented but ultimately forgotten; others existed only in the memories of their participants.

When I visited the University of North Carolina in Chapel Hill, I found an amazing, yet long-forgotten, rebellion in the library archives. In 1954, an 18-year-old Black woman named Eleanor Rush was incarcerated at the North Carolina Women's Prison in Raleigh. She was placed in solitary confinement for six days. On the seventh day, Eleanor Rush was not fed for over sixteen hours. After 16 hours, she began yelling that she was hungry and wanted food. In response, the guards bound and gagged her, dislocating her neck in the process. Half an hour later, Eleanor Rush was dead.

The next morning, when the other women in the prison gathered in the yard, another woman in the solitary confinement unit yelled the news about Rush's death from her window. The women in the yard surrounded the staff members supervising their activities and demanded answers about Rush's death. When they didn't get them, the women—both the black and the white women—rioted.

The riot lasted three and a half hours. When Raleigh police and guards from the men's Central Prison arrived to quell the riot and herd the 350 women into their cells, the women continued to protest, throwing objects against the walls and making noise.[1]

The women's riot brought outside attention to Rush's death and, as a result of their actions:

▷ The State Bureau of Investigation ordered a probe into Rush's death rather than accept the prison's explanation that Rush, while bound and gagged, had dislocated her own neck and committed suicide.

▷ Nothing in the prison rules explicitly prohibited the use of improvised gags. After the riot and probe, the State Prisons Director explicitly banned the use of gags and iron claws (metal handcuffs that can squeeze tightly).

▷ The prison administration was required to pay $3,000 to Rush's mother. At that time, $3,000 was more than half the yearly salary of the prison warden.

▷ Prison superintendent Ivan D. Hinton, who, along with three other prison staff members, had bound and gagged Eleanor Rush, was replaced by Elizabeth McCubbin, the Executive Director of the Family and Children's Service Agency. Her hiring indicated a shift from a punitive model to a more social work–oriented approach.

At the probe, the women themselves testified that they had realized that the prison would attempt to sweep Rush's death under the rug. They had rioted to ensure that Rush's death was not dismissed and that the circumstances would not be repeated.

Despite these gains and despite the fact that the riot, the investigation, and its results made headlines for weeks, if not months, both Eleanor Rush and the rebellion have been forgotten by prison justice and prisoner rights advocates today.

Epilogue

The 1954 riot was not the only riot in a women's prison that, at the time, caught outside attention but has since been forgotten by history. In the first edition of *Resistance Behind Bars*, I briefly described a 1975 riot at the California Institute for Women (CIW). At a bookstore event in San Francisco, I met a woman named Sin Soracco, whose first words to me were: "You wrote about the riot I was in!" She then went on to describe the aftermath of the riot: Although the prison was placed on lockdown, the women managed to circulate a document on which everyone wrote their suggestions for important changes in how the prison operated. "One point that everyone agreed on was that no one should do longer than five years [in prison] because, after five years, it's very difficult to acclimate to being back outside," she recalled. The document became the women's own Ten Points. In addition to advocating a five-year limit on all prison sentences, they demanded improved health care, food, education, maternity care and family visits as well as an end to the arbitrary methods of penalizing women for infractions, the use of solitary confinement, brutal sentencing, overcrowding and staff sadism.

The riot also caught the attention of the California legislature. Two legislators visited the prison where the women presented their demands. The legislators asked that two women speak to the entire assembly about SB42, an upcoming determinate sentencing law. The women at CIW chose Sin, who described herself as a "completely ordinary, smart-assed convict" who was also politically conscious. The warden chose the woman who worked as her secretary. "She was a lovely Afro-Hawaiian lady who was professional, dainty, well-spoken," Sin remembered, "but what they didn't realize was that she was friends with *me*." Both women spoke to the concerns that the women at CIW had about sentencing and prison conditions.

More than thirty years later, Sin still feels that the riot—and the women's subsequent efforts—were significant. "It was a small step in ordinary criminals who had never felt a sense of power being able to do something. It was dramatic, it was a lot of fun and it was, in some cases, slightly effective." Their actions also showed the prison administration, the legislature and even the prisoners themselves that the women would not be dismissed.[2]

Many stories of resistance never leave the prison walls. In an informal conversation, former political prisoner Rita "Bo" Brown recounted that, in the early 1980s, women imprisoned in Nevada took action against the prison's psychiatrist who had been prescribing psychotropic medication to women who did not need it. As a result, one woman died. When the psychiatrist next visited the prison, the women threw chairs, tables, and anything they could lift, driving him not only off-premises but also off the job. Not only was the psychiatrist replaced (by the prison's first woman psychiatrist who did not share her predecessor's enthusiasm for drugging patients), but so were the prison's doctor, warden, assistant warden, and other higher-ups in the prison administration.

Unlike the 1954 riot in North Carolina or the 1975 Christmas riot, this action did not make the news. Brown learned of it only after arriving at the prison itself two months later.

Women have also resisted unfair and capricious prison rules in other, less visible ways. Christina Voight, incarcerated at Bedford Hills during the late 1990s, recounted two such rebellions. "Usually, virtually no one eats at the dining hall," Voight recalled. "The women cook their own food." Women used this reality to their advantage to protest the prison's new policy of denying them access to ice. A call went out for every woman to go to the dining hall for their meals. Although legally required to do so, the prison was unaccustomed and unprepared to feed the entire population. After two days, the prison administration capitulated, reinstating the women's ability to have ice.

Another time, the prison instituted a rule mandating that every woman wear the prison-issued sneakers rather than be able to choose her own footwear. The women once again found a creative way to protest: Every woman filed a request for a medical visit, asking to see the doctor about their feet. Once again, the administration backed down.

Epilogue

While ice and footwear may seem like trivial concerns to outside eyes, it is important to recognize that such issues become much more important in the context of an environment in which virtually every aspect of a woman's life—when to wake, when to shower, when to eat, and even when to move—is so strictly controlled. That women fight for these seemingly small rights—especially at great risk to themselves and the few privileges that they have—is testament to their individual and collective strength and resilience. Voight also noted that, during her incarceration at Bedford Hills, the prison administration punished individual organizing by taking away the woman's right to receive visits. Given that the majority of the women were mothers, few wanted to risk losing their ability to see their children. "However," she added, "when all the women organize, the prison can't put everyone in lockdown and take away everyone's visits."[3]

Since the publication of *Resistance Behind Bars*, women's resistance and organizing have continued. In 2010, women incarcerated in Colorado protested against the "labia lift" policy at the Denver Women's Correctional Facility (DWCF). In addition to being strip-searched after leaving their prison jobs or visits, women were forced to spread their labia. Women wrote letters and told family members in efforts to draw public attention to this new policy:

> This letter is to bring attention to the strip search procedure and the areas that are currently in question . . . I don't really know how to politely say what needs to be said, so please excuse the harsh bluntness in the rest of this letter.

> To strip naked, show the inside of your mouth, shake out your hair, lift your breasts, feet and fat rolls, turn away from the officer, grab and spread your butt cheeks, bend over and cough hard enough to flex, then relax the muscles inside your vagina has been the "norm" and expected strip search. That process alone is already quite humiliating. Now, without any notice or warning of any kind, DWCF has implemented a new step to this search. Depending on which officer is conducting the search, the new step varies. Female inmates are now to spread the labia, lift the

hood and expose the clitoris. This step has been titled the "labia lift." The inmate may be asked to do this while bending over after she has coughed, or to turn around and lift one leg onto a chair to be able to "widen" herself more, or to sit (on a toilet or a chair naked) and spread herself or to stand up and move her feet apart, leaning her shoulders back and then spread her labia.[4]

The search was particularly traumatizing for women who had survived past sexual assault and abuse. "How can I be a rape 'survivor' if I have to continue to go through the motions over and over?" asked one woman. Although even recounting the details of the search was harrowing, Terrina Flora-Alexander was determined to alert people on the outside about this new procedure, writing her story over the course of a week ("I had to have someone else type this because I couldn't do it," she noted).[5]

In addition to telling family members and outside supporters, women also directly challenged this new procedure. "Many of us have exhausted our Administrative remedies in [trying to challenge] the 'Labia lift' strip search procedure," wrote Krystal Voss, incarcerated at DWCF.[6] When the women's grievances were denied, one woman collected letters from the other women to send to a journalist friend. In July 2010, media coverage roused the attention of the ACLU. Women at DWCF wrote to the ACLU, each telling her story of humiliation when forced to spread her labia for the guard. The ACLU sent a letter to Ari Zavaras, head of the CDOC, charging that these searches raised serious concerns under the Fourth and Eighth Amendments. That letter prompted DWCF officials to revise their search policy to eliminate the labia lift (and the threat of a lawsuit and court injunction).[7]

Women in other states also continue to speak out and expose abusive and often exploitative practices, again at great risk to themselves. In Arizona, the Department of Corrections has contracted its prisoners to work for private agricultural businesses for almost twenty years.[8] In 2011, women on the Perryville Unit were assigned to Martori Farms, an Arizona farm corporation that supplies fresh fruits and vegetables to vendors across the United States (Martori is the exclusive supplier to Walmart's 2,470 Supercenter and Neighborhood Market stores).[9] According to one worker, the farm paid its imprisoned laborers $7.35 per hour, of which Arizona Correctional Industries took 30% for "rent," another 30% for a woman's retention fund for her release, and 6% for other deductions. These deductions left the woman with three dollars per hour. In contrast, the cleaning jobs available inside the prison pay 40 cents per hour with 6% deducted for the woman's expenses and no money set aside in a retention fund for her release.[10] For women with little to no outside support or future prospects, the Martori jobs offer the most desirable pay. They have, however, not been without problems. According to another woman who worked on the farm crews:

> They wake us up between 2:30 and 3 am and *kick us out* of our housing unit by 3:30 am. We get fed at four am. Our work supervisors show up between five am and eight am. Then it's an hour to a one-and-a-half hour drive to the job site. Then we work eight hours regardless of conditions . . . We work in the fields hoeing weeds and thinning plants . . . Currently we are forced to work in the blazing sun for eight hours. We run out of water several times a day. We ran out of sunscreen several times a week. They don't check medical backgrounds or ages before they pull women for these jobs. Many of us cannot do it! If we stop working and sit on the bus or even just take an unauthorized break we get a *major* ticket which takes away our 'good time'!!!
>
> We are told we get two fifteen-minute breaks and a half-hour lunch like a normal job, but it's more like ten minutes and twenty minutes. They constantly yell at us we are too slow and to speed up because we are costing $150 an acre in labor and that's not acceptable.[11]

Although Martori Farms contracts with the local fire departments to provide medical attention for injuries on the farm, farm supervisors have not always allowed women to stop work when they need medical care. When "N" complained of chest pains, the farm representative refused to allow her to stop working. The next day, an hour after returning to work, she began experiencing chest pains. The farm representative told her, "Come on, the big bosses are here. You'll be in trouble if you stop. It's not break time. Work, work, work." "N" complied, working while in pain until the break. She resumed working for another half hour before she experienced even more severe pains: "I have a steady deep dull pain with sharp stabbing pains periodically . . . Then all of a sudden I can't even lift the hoe in the air. My arms are no longer strong enough. By now the chest pains are so bad it's knocking the wind out of me. I'm straight seeing stars. I tell our substitute boss officer I can't do it no more. I'm having really bad chest pains. I can't even lift the hoe anymore." The man accused her of faking these pains, but allowed her to stop working. While the woman was receiving medical attention, another farm representative stated, "Oh, so now they're gonna start faking f***ing heart attacks to not work. Great."[12]

In addition, the prison has ignored women's medical conditions when assigning them to the farm crews. "N" was sent to West Valley Hospital where an emergency room doctor ordered that she be exempt from the farm work crew and any other physical exertion for three to four days. However, when "N" was returned to the prison that day, the nurse told her that they could not honor the doctor's order and ordered her back to work.

Although Martori Farms' relatively high pay is attractive to prisoners at Perryville, many women have not accepted the accompanying abuses as part of the job description. They have lodged complaints to prison administrators:

> Women have made their complaints on inmate letters and verbally to the lieutenant, sergeant, captains, deputy warden, counselors, supervisors, and the major. Their solution was to give us an extra sack lunch and agree to feed us breakfast Saturday mornings . . . Food is not what we were asking for. Though   being fed on Saturdays is nice. Yah! They were not feeding us Saturdays because that's a day Kitchen opens late because they give brunch on weekends. No lunch so we were

getting screwed! But as of this past Saturday they said they would feed us before work! Let's see how long it lasts.

Women have also stood up to unfair demands from the bosses at the farm. "N" recounted:

> On Wednesday I go to work . . . it's the second day in a row we are doing weeds. [I'm] up to my chest trying to weed to save a minimal amount of watermelon plants. Needless to say the work was excessively hard to put it mildly. So I must confess the day before I was "on one" so to speak. My haunted mind was lost in the past and so I was just trucking through the weeds, plowing them down not even connecting with my physical exertion and pain. The next day I was completely exhausted and physically broke down!! I was in so much pain because the day before I did like double the work everyone else did. So anyways, the Martori Farm representative was pushing me so hard trying to get me to produce the same results as the day before . . . [He] has everyone at minimum teamed up helping each other plow through these weeds. Well everyone but me that is. I repeatedly asked him to give me a partner. I kept telling him that I was in pain. I also went as far as to tell him that I don't think I can do this anymore, to *please* give me a partner also. His response was "No. You're strong. You can do it by yourself." I told him [this was] not true. I overexerted myself yesterday because I was going through some things. Now I'm hurt and need help . . . He thought my pleas were funny. I hated to degrade myself and plea so I stopped and continued.

After "N" had finished her assigned row, the farm representative demanded that she finish weeding two other rows. When she again requested a weeding partner, stating that she was in pain, the representative replied, "When you get to the end, I'll think about it."

> By this time, all the girls are finishing their rows because they're all teamed up with two or three girls per row. Except me. So there are only two whole rows left on the field by now and he already placed six girls per row. That's twelve women on two

rows. And I can't even get one helper. That's *ridiculous* . . . I tell him "All joking aside, all the others are finishing. Can I please get a helper?" He tells me "Seriously no joking. When you get to the end, I'll think about it." At that point I'm pretty upset and broke down. I looked at him and said "Is that right?" I paused staring at him waiting for him to stop his male chauvinist domination games or whatever he's playing. When he didn't say anything but just stared, I told him, "Fine. I'm done. I can't do this anymore. I'm hurt and struggling through this. After what happened to me before I would think you would provide me help when I need it. Since you won't look out for my health and well-being, I will. Someone has to. I'm done for today. I'm going to sit on the bus."

The supervisor demanded that she return to work, threatening to have the prison issue her disciplinary tickets which would result in a loss of good time and other privileges. She refused.

At this point I'm so angry that this jerk would make me lose everything because I'm not submissive and I don't obey him like the women back in Mexico do that I admit I blew up and acted unprofessional. I told him "F*** you and your tickets. Go write them if you want. In fact I'll write them for you to make sure you get the facts straight." . . .

At this point the two women who were on the bus got all riled up and were yelling, "That's not fair. She's your best worker and you're going to punish her with tickets!!!" "She's hurt. I heard her asking for help all day!" "We've been sitting on the bus for over an hour and we're not getting tickets, why is she the only one getting a ticket?"[13]

Not only did "N" stand up for herself, but the other women defended her actions at the risk of being ticketed as well. Their combined efforts ensured that "N" was not issued a ticket in retaliation for standing up for herself.[14]

Women have also alerted outside advocates and activists about these inhumane conditions, again at great risk to themselves. If not for their courage in speaking out, the outside world would remain unaware of the exploitation on the farm and the women's actions to challenge and change this reality.

A Quiet Kind of Resistance

As always, women continue to organize in less visible ways. At a 2010 film screening and discussion about women in prison, I met Tina Reynolds, a formerly incarcerated woman, mother, and the cofounder of Women on the Rise Telling HerStory.

Reynolds had entered the New York State prison system while seven months pregnant for a parole violation. Determined not to lose her baby to the foster care system, she asked the women around her how she could keep custody of her child. "I began using the lines of communication among women in prison to find out who I could speak to, what applications I had to fill out, who I should get the counselor to call if I wanted to get into an alternatives-to-incarceration program, when I should apply to the nursery program, what were the stipulations and criteria. I began to find a quiet kind of resistance that was very much real in the jail and in the prison."

That quiet kind of resistance was, in fact, the women's organizing against policies and practices that deemed them unfit to be mothers. When Reynolds was transferred to Bedford Hills, she visited the prison's women's center to consult Sister Elaine and apply for the prison's nursery program. Sister Elaine was not at the center that day, so Reynolds told her story to the women who were there.

> The women didn't make any judgment about me. I told them my story. I told them that I had been arrested sixty times, that I had seven children, that I'd been in and out of prison . . . Talking to women who maybe had committed one crime and were there for years, there was no judgment. There was no "Didn't you get it right the first time?" There wasn't any of that. It was their intent to get everything down about me so that they could make a case for me to Sister Elaine because they had her ear. To advocate on

my behalf and on behalf of me having that opportunity even if they didn't get a chance to keep their children or if they didn't get a chance to see their children ...

They saw me as a woman having a baby who deserved that right. I was in awe of that. They believed in me and my potential long before I believed in me and my potential. I was in awe of that as well.

Reynolds' parole violation left her ineligible for Bedford's nursery program. Sister Elaine arranged for her to interview for the nursery program at Taconic Correctional Facility, the medium-security prison across the street. Soon after her interview, Reynolds gave birth to her son. The women at Bedford cleaned out a closet, furnishing it with a crib and a cot, thus allowing Reynolds to keep her newborn son with her rather than having him placed in foster care while awaiting a response from Taconic.

Reynolds was accepted and transferred into Taconic's nursery program two weeks later.

We all got along and we built a family there in Taconic. While I was in programming, I had to send my son to the Children's Center and sisters that were doing time took care of my son. I thought that was such an interchange that was needed because here were women who didn't have their children and they could give their love to mine and to other women's babies who were there.

Kai received so much love and so much support. He was nine months when we left and he was already walking. He and I walked out of the prison together. At that moment, I knew that, because I was leaving women behind that have not had that experience, that I had that I had to do something.[15]

Not Stopping at the Prison Gate

Women's efforts to challenge and change conditions have not ended with their release. In January 2007, Yraida Guanipa was released after over a decade in the federal prison system. She continued to speak out against the deplorable conditions inside as well as the policies that continue to funnel so many people into the system. In 2008, Guanipa traveled to New York City where she and I both spoke on a panel about gender, prison and resistance. Later that year, she attended Critical Resistance's tenth anniversary conference where she shared her experiences with dance as a prison survival strategy, showing attendees the dance techniques that enabled her to endure over a decade behind bars. After twelve years at the Central California Women's Facility, Beverly Henry was released in 2009. She too continues to publicly speak out against prison atrocities. I had the honor of being a guest on Rose Aguilar's radio show with Beverly only a few months after her release from prison.

Formerly incarcerated women have also worked collectively, forming groups to support the women still inside. In 1987, after being released from prison, Bo Brown founded the Out of Control Lesbian Committee to Support Women Political Prisoners, a group of Bay Area queer women who organized outside resistance to the Lexington Control Unit for Women. After the control unit was closed, the committee continued to raise and send funds to enable women political prisoners to meet their basic needs while in prison. They also continued educating the larger public about political prisoners in the United States.[16] "In all my years inside, there was never a period of more than several weeks when I didn't at least have people sending me stamps and letters," Bo said in 1997. "I know that people don't have to be left alone and isolated. People don't have to be forgotten in those pits. We know how to do it— because it was done for me and I owe my community much for that."[17]

After her release, Tina Reynolds worked with several New York City organizations that advocate on behalf of incarcerated women. In 2003, while traveling with a friend, whose children's father had been incarcerated for years, Reynolds and her friend realized that women— and their experiences—were absent from many of the discussions and meetings around prison policy and prisoner justice. "We [realized that we] not only have to become present in these meetings and conversations, but we have to change the perspective of women and how they've been impacted. We have to offer solutions to these systems that are intertwined in regards to the criminal justice system."

That year, Reynolds and her friend invited fifteen formerly incarcerated women to a weekend-long retreat. "They all came with their own experiences. Some had spent twenty-seven years in prison, like Susan Hallett.[18] Some had spent less time than that. Some had just come home within six months. Some had been working in the criminal justice and human services fields for ten years. Some had just gotten a job. Some of them didn't have a job." At the retreat, the women came up with the idea of an organization led and run by formerly incarcerated women. At first, the women met on a monthly basis and offered each other mutual support and resources. They also began speaking about their experiences at different events, bringing incarcerated women's voices into discussions about prisoner justice.[19] In 2004, the women formed WORTH (Women on the Rise Telling HerStory), an organization of formerly and currently incarcerated women in New York City.[20]

From its inception, WORTH members worked on a variety of issues, all of which were informed by their own experiences of incarceration. It developed its Sister Inside program to reach women in New York State prisons. "We identify leaders in the prison or they self-identify through our communications with them," Reynolds explained. "They report on conditions of confinement and policies and practices not being upheld in prison. We [WORTH members outside of prison] send surveys in that will help us with the policy initiative that we're developing . . . These are ways in which we connect with our Sister Inside members to build leadership, to actively have them involved in the work that we're doing in the community, to include their voices and their thoughts and their concerns in the work that we do. Sometimes the information that they give us actually pushes us to develop an initiative."

Having experienced incarceration themselves, WORTH members understand the challenges that women face upon their release from prison. To help women prepare to meet these challenges, WORTH members developed RiseUp!, a reentry program for women with less than six months before their release from New York's Bayview Correctional Facility. "We feel like that is the way in which women should be supported," stated Tina. "Peer-led groups work better. We know what we need to offer each other so that we're successful and we felt, from the onset, that if we were successful, we could certainly offer support to women so that they could be successful. It's the power of example and us [formerly incarcerated women] as role models." The program—which addresses issues women face, such as education, mental and emotional health and family relationships as well as more typical reentry issues—is the first in New York State's prison system to be developed and led by formerly incarcerated women.

Reynolds recognizes that, to the outside eye, WORTH's everyday work with women behind bars "may seem soft. We impact women in a way that's feasible within the system we're working in. It [our work] doesn't usurp them in a way where we're saying, 'Okay, hold a rally' or 'Stop eating food.' [Instead] we're saying, 'Become leaders. This is how you do this. Support your sisters and let them know that we're here. Reach out to your families. Become involved. Answer these surveys; your answers inform us on how to do the work and so *you* are an integral part of this. So our approach is not soft."[21]

This seemingly "soft" approach has led to concrete changes for women in the New York State prison system. In 2008, after the Bureau of Prisons changed its policy to prohibit shackling pregnant prisoners while in labor, WORTH members took action to change New York State policy. They allied with legislators, attorneys and advocates who had not experienced incarceration to pass a bill prohibiting shackling incarcerated women during labor.[22] "We did a lot of organizing, we did a lot of collecting stories, we did a lot of speaking to the media," Reynolds recalled.[23]

On July 9, 2009, after the state legislature had approved the bill, WORTH members organized a rally of over a hundred people outside the governor's office to pressure him to sign the bill. Formerly incarcerated women who had been shackled while in labor spoke about their experiences. The women and their supporters wore purple ribbons around their wrists to symbolize shackles.[24] However, the response of passersby was disappointing. "We didn't realize that people didn't know what shackling was or anything about the handcuffing of pregnant women," Reynolds remembered. Armed with this realization, women wore simulated pregnant bellies and shackles at the following rally on August 18, 2009. "That [image] alone started getting responses of the people walking by. They were like, 'Are you kidding me? Are you for real? This really happens?'" Before the end of the rally, Paterson appeared and promised to sign the anti-shackling bill into law.[25]

WORTH's work had an impact beyond the New York State prison system. In 2011, two years after New York State had passed its anti-shackling legislation, the Massachusetts legislature held hearings on "An Act Relative to Safe Pregnancies and Related Health Care for Female Inmates," a bill banning any type of restraints for women in labor. The bill would also improve prenatal care and allow pregnant women to draw up custody plans for their children. A coalition, including NARAL, Planned Parenthood and the ACLU, formed to advocate for the bill. "In part, it is thanks to Tina and other women in New York that created momentum for bills like this, that the coalition was prompted to get behind this bill," stated Lois Ahrens, a Massachusetts-based organizer and the founder and director of the Real Cost of Prisons Project.[26]

Formerly Incarcerated and Convicted People Build a Movement

On February 28, 2011, more than fifty formerly incarcerated people from around the country convened in Alabama for a weekend of discussion and strategizing. All had worked on issues affecting incarcerated and formerly incarcerated people in their respective states. Reynolds was one of the original twenty people who began the discussion leading to the convening. She pointed out that, at that time, fourteen states had anti-shackling legislation, that several states have passed Ban the Box legislation, and that some states have lifted their prohibitions against people in prison and on parole being able to vote. These gains were a direct result of the organizing and advocacy by people who had been in prison and their allies. At the convening, attendees asked themselves and each other, "How do we bring people together and align people with the work that they're doing individually from a collective perspective?"[27]

The Formerly Incarcerated and Convicted People's Movement emerged from the inaugural meeting. Its goal is to organize a national movement to restore formerly incarcerated people's civil rights, halt prison expansion, demand an end to mass incarceration, eliminate prison abuses and protect the dignity of family members and their communities. The organizers drew connections between the Civil Rights movement of the 1960s and their own movement for civil and human rights, illustrating the connection by walking across the Edmund Pettus Bridge in Selma, Alabama, the site of the 1964 Bloody Sunday March.[28]

Returning to their respective home states, members of the Formerly Incarcerated and Convicted People's Movement continued to build together. "We've held rallies and acknowledged prison actions. We've collectively held events on historic days. For instance, the War on Drugs was enacted on June 17, 1971. All of us held an event within our respective states around the War on Drugs. When the prisons in Georgia had their strike, we recognized that. We just recognized the fortieth anniversary of the Attica uprising. We've recognized the Pelican Bay hunger strike. We've recognized the common issues that people who have been incarcerated have stood up and fought against in building this movement. The commonalities in our collective actions have brought us together to end mass incarceration," stated Reynolds.[29]

On November 2, 2011, the Formerly Incarcerated and Convicted People's Movement convened again in Los Angeles for a second national gathering. Over 270 people from twenty states converged for a one-day conference to share their experiences and vision and to strategize fighting against policies leading to racial profiling, gang labeling, inhumane sentencing, voter disenfranchisement and hiring discrimination. The conference included not only seasoned organizers like Tina Reynolds, but also women who were new to prison justice organizing like "Pilar" who had never before been in a public space with hundreds of people who shared her experience. Even women who had organized in their home states like Mercedes Smith, a formerly incarcerated woman and currently the outreach coordinator for WORTH, were impressed. "I thought it was the greatest thing I had ever heard—a *movement* that was made up of nothing but formerly incarcerated people. It had to be a powerful movement and I wanted to be a part of it," she recalled. "Once I got there, it showed me how important the work is that I do and it made me eager to come home and jump back into it."[30]

The one-day convening was packed with trainings on juvenile justice and youth organizing, Ban the Box, voter disenfranchisement, gender issues and other issues. Attendees learned about the issues, organizing and, in some cases, successes in other states.

"I knew they existed, but I didn't know there were that many [formerly incarcerated people fighting for change]," reflected Smith. "I met a lot of people. I know that in numbers come strength and there were so many of us. I left L.A. feeling totally amazed at everything, even though I do this work here in New York. I came home ready to take on bigger things."[31]

At the convening, attendees also adopted a national platform for the Movement. The platform addresses fourteen points related to incarceration:

I. We Demand an End to Mass Incarceration;
II. We Demand Equality and Opportunity for All People;
III. We Demand the Right to Vote;
IV. We Demand Respect and Dignity for Our Children;
V. We Demand Community Development, Not Prison Profit;
VI. End Immigration Detention and Deportation;
VII. End Racial Profiling Inside Prison and in Our Communities;
VIII. End Extortion and Slavery in Prisons;
IX. End Sexual Harassment of People in Prisons;

X. Human Contact Is a Human Right;
XI. End Cruel and Unusual Punishment;
XII. We Demand Proper Medical Treatment;
XIII. End the Incarceration of Children;
XIV. Free Our Political Prisoners.[32]

"While the platform points are broad, we believe we've at least touched on all of the aspects that people have experienced while doing time in prison and beyond," Reynolds noted, adding that the platform, although ratified by the conference attendees, is still a work-in-progress. "The issues addressed in the platform are the basic foundational issues involving the inhumane and oppressive treatment within the criminal justice system. We are taking a stand and saying that we're going to stop it, that things need to change."[33]

By the end of the conference, attendees set a goal of registering one million voters in 2012. However, one should not mistake restoring voting rights as the end goal. Through these gatherings and this movement, formerly incarcerated people are making connections, building relationships and organizing not only across state lines, but also across divides of race, gender, gender identity, sexuality and age. Smith remembered, with excitement, "I met so many good people there. I can't wait to have the opportunity to see them again, to see where they're at now and what they're doing."[34] These relationships have the potential for organizing on a mass scale to not just chip away, but effectively abolish large portions of the prison-industrial complex.

"It's not [just] about us having the right to vote," explained Reynolds. "It's having an opportunity to be part of this movement, to talk about a political analysis [of incarceration], to talk about education, to talk about the history of incarceration and how it's impacted us during the last forty years with the War on Drugs."[35]

"Pilar" agrees, pointing out, "The end point is not simply inclusion in the polity or recognition of citizenship. That is simply not enough because life has taught us that citizenship is not a guarantee of rights."

She notes, "Part of the movement seeks to restore political and civil rights, such as voting, but the larger goal is abolition."[36]

"The movement has to be built by the people who have been directly impacted," stated Reynolds. "It has to be a commitment to knowing that our criminal justice system denies people their human rights and that it is the closest thing to slavery that still exists in our country. It has to be a movement that doesn't stop."[37]

1 Lin Holloway, "Bare Prison Torture," *New Journal and Guide*, September 4, 1954.

2 Sin Soracco, "Resistance, Solidarity and Women's Prisons" (Reading, Green Arcade, San Francisco, CA, May 5, 2011).

3 Christina Voight. "The Real Cost of Prisons Project" (Museum of Comic and Cartoon Art, NYC, September 19, 2005).

4 Terrina Flora-Alexander, letter to the author, January 17, 2010, to January 25, 2010.

5 Ibid.

6 Alan Prendergast, "'Labia Lift' and Other Humiliations Described in Letter from Prison," *Denver Westword* Blogs, May 24, 2010, http://blogs.westword.com/latestword/2010/05/labia_lift_and_other_humiliations_described_in_letter_from_prison.php.

7 Krystal Voss, "Fighting the 'Labia Lift,'" *Women and Prison: A Site for Resistance*, http://womenandprison.org/sexuality/view/fighting_the_labia_lift/. American Civil Liberties Union, "Denver Women's Correctional Facility Ends Degrading Body Cavity Searches After ACLU Letter," September 24, 2010 (press release), http://www.aclu.org/prisoners-rights/denver-womens-correctional-facility-ends-degrading-body-cavity-searches-after-aclu-.

8 Nicole Hill, "With Fewer Migrant Workers, Farmers Turn to Prison Labor," *Alternet*, August 22, 2007, http://www.alternet.org/story/60497/with_fewer_migrant_workers%2C_farmers_turn_to_prison_labor

9 Walmart, "16-Year Relationship Between Wal-Mart and Arizona Business Grows, Thrives," September 7, 2007 (press release), http://walmartstores.com/pressroom/news/6702.aspx. The 2,470 figure is as of August 1, 2007.

10 "Q," letter to the author, September 6, 2011.

11 "N," letter to the author, April 24, 2011.

12 Ibid.

13 "N," letter to the author, May 7, 2011.

14 A woman who had also worked on the farm crew reported that in July 2011, several weeks after news stories about Martori Farms' use of prison labor circulated on the Internet, ADOC had temporarily stopped the farm crews until October.

15 Tina Reynolds, interview with the author, September 15, 2011.

Epilogue

16 *Out of Control Lesbian Committee to Support Women Political Prisoners,*
http://home.mindspring.com/~outoftime/.

17 Daniel Burton Rose, "Guerrillas in Our Midst," *George Jackson Brigade Information Project,* http://www.gjbip.org/GIOM.htm.

18 Susan Hallett was one of the founding members of WORTH and secured WORTH's initial funding from the Long Termers' Committee at Bedford Hills. Upon her release, Susan worked as a fierce legal advocate at the Legal Action Center for ten years. During that time, she helped thousands of formerly incarcerated people overcome hurdles to reentry. Susan also served as the program analyst for Legal Action Center's national project, National Helping Individuals with criminal records Reenter through Employment (H.I.R.E.) Network, which aims to increase employment opportunities for people with criminal records. She helped create a comprehensive Resource and Assistance web page that has been visited by millions of individuals who seek resources and help in their state.

19 Tina Reynolds, interview with the author, September 15, 2011.

20 Carole Eady (co-chair of WORTH), "History of Women on the Rise Telling HerStory (WORTH)." Unpublished document sent to author.

21 Reynolds interview, September 15, 2011.

22 Tina Reynolds, "Women's Voices." The New York Department of Correctional Services (DOCS) opposed the bill, first contending that it did not shackle women in labor and that, if it did, the department was capable of addressing the problem independently. Anna Clark, "Giving Birth in Chains: The Shackling of Incarcerated Women During Labor and Delivery," *Women and Prison: A Site for Resistance,* http://womenandprison.org/motherhood/view/giving_birth_in_chains_the_shackling_of_incarcerated_women_during_labor_and/.

23 Reynolds interview, September 15, 2011.

24 Tina Reynolds, "WORTH Pushes to Stop the Shackling of New Mothers," *North Star Fund Community Blog,* July 14, 2009. http://northstarfund.org/blog/2009/07/worth-rally.php. Jacquie Simone, "Unbinding Pregnant Inmates: Activists Call for Paterson to Sign Anti-Shackling Bill," *New York IndyMedia Center,* July 13, 2009. http://nyc.indymedia.org/es/2009/07/106424.html.

25 "Anti-Shackling Advocacy a Success," Correctional Association of New York," August 26, 2009, http://www.correctionalassociation.org/news/Anti-Shackling_Advocacy_Success_Aug09.htm. "New Law Bans Shackling of Incarcerated Women in Labor," *Correctional Association Bulletin,* Fall 2009, 1–2. Helena Zhu, "Governor to Save Jailed Mothers from Shackling During Labor," The Epoch Times, August 18, 2009, http://www.theepochtimes.com/n2/content/view/21196/.

26 Lois Ahrens, e-mail to the author, October 2, 2011.

27 Tina Reynolds, interview with the author, September 15, 2011.

28 On Sunday, March 7, 1964, six hundred Civil Rights activists attempted to march from Selma to Montgomery to protest the police murder of fellow demonstrator Jimmie Lee Jackson and to demand their rights. As the marchers crossed the Edmund Pettus Bridge, they were brutally attacked by white state

troopers, many of whom had been deputized that very morning. Seventeen marchers were hospitalized, leading to the naming of the day "Bloody Sunday." After a federal district court issued a restraining order preventing a second march across the bridge, a third march was successfully organized and carried out. These events made the bridge a symbol of the Civil Rights struggle.

29 In December 2010, thousands of people in Georgia state prisons held a six-day strike, refusing to leave their cells to report to work or other activities. Their demands included decent wages (Georgia does not pay its imprisoned laborers at all), educational opportunities, improved medical care, an end to cruel and unusual punishment, access to families and just parole decisions. It was the largest prison protest in the United States until the Pelican Bay prisoner hunger strikes in 2011. On July 1, 2011, prisoners at the maximum-security Pelican Bay State Prison's Security Housing Unit (SHU) launched a hunger strike. The strike lasted three weeks and involved approximately six thousand people in thirteen California state prisons. Their demands included an end to group punishments and a drastic overhaul to the criteria used for indefinite SHU placement. The strike was stopped on July 20 after the CDCR promised to review its SHU criteria. On September 26, 2011, prisoners resumed their hunger strike, stating that the CDCR had not acted in good faith. The strike lasted three weeks and spread to over twelve thousand people incarcerated in California and out-of-state. It was stopped when the CDCR again promised to change its criteria for SHU placement and to review the placement of every person currently in the SHU.

30 Tina Reynolds, Mercedes Smith, Doris (members of WORTH), interview with the author, November 18, 2011.

31 Smith, interview.

32 For the full platform of the Formerly Incarcerated and Convicted People's Movement, see their website: http://ficpmovement.wordpress.com/about/ficpm-national-platform/

33 Reynolds, interview, November 18, 2011.

34 Smith, interview.

35 Reynolds, interview, November 18, 2011.

36 Pilar, "Reflections of the Formerly Incarcerated and Convicted People's Movement," *Tenacious* 24 (Fall–Winter 2011): 34.

37 Tina, interview, September 15, 2011.

NOTES

1 Two of the girls were black lesbian lovers. In a scenario that would be repeated 13 years later in the case of the New Jersey Four, they had been out with friends when they encountered a cab driver who had tried to grab one of them. Her friends intervened, the cab driver called the police and the girls were arrested for assault. I don't remember if the judge refused to set bail or if he set it too high for their families to pay, but both of my cellmates were subsequently sent to Rikers Island.

2 Angela Davis, *Are Prisons Obsolete?* (New York: Seven Stories Press, 2003), 20.

3 I kid you not. The Oregon Department of Corrections rejects anything that has been drawn or written with crayon.

4 Allen J. Beck and Paige M. Harrison, *Prisoners in 2000,* special report for the Department of Justice, August 2001, 1, http://bjs.ojp.usdoj.gov/content/pub/pdf/p00.pdf.

5 Heather C. West, *Prison Inmates at Midyear 2009—Statistical Tables,* Bureau of Justice, June 2010, 4, http://bjs.ojp.usdoj.gov/content/pub/pdf/pim09st.pdf.

6 Ibid., 2.

7 American Civil Liberties Union (ACLU), "ACLU Applauds Senate Reintroduction of Racial Profiling Bill, Urges Congress to Finally Pass Comprehensive Legislation Next Year," December 19, 2005, http://www.aclu.org/racialjustice/racialprofiling/23090prs20051219.html.

8 Barbara Bloom, Barbara Owen, and Stephanie Covington, *Gender-Responsive Strategies: Research, Practice, and Guiding Principles for Women Offenders* (National Institute of Corrections, 2003) 8, http://www.nicic.org/pubs/2003/018017.pdf.

9 Tracy Snell and Lawrence Greenfeld, *Women Offenders,* special report for the Department of Justice, December 1999, 5, http://ojp.usdoj.gov/bjs/pub/pdf/wo.pdf.

10 Ibid.

11 C. W. Harlow, *Education and Correctional Populations,* special report for the Department of Justice, 2003.

12 Christopher J. Mumola, *Incarcerated Parents and Their Children*, special report for the Department of Justice, August 2000, 6.

13 Tracy Snell and Lawrence Greenfeld, *Women Offenders*, special report for the Department of Justice, December 1999, 5, http://ojp.usdoj.gov/bjs/pub/pdf/wo.pdf.

14 Heather C. West and William J. Sabol, *Prisoners in 2007*, Bureau of Justice Statistics, U.S. Department of Justice, December 2008, revised February 12, 2009, 21.

15 U.S. Department of Justice, *Prior Abuse Reported by Inmates and Probationers*, April 1999, 2. See also Doris J. James' *Profile of Jail Inmates*, 2002, special report for the Department of Justice, July 2004, 10.

16 U.S. Department of Justice, *Survey of State Inmates*, 1991, May 1993, 6.

17 In 2004, the Rockefeller Drug Laws were amended. Under the Drug Law Reform Act (DLRA), prisoners with the most severe sentences could apply to be re-sentenced to a term allowed by the new law. The DLRA also increased good-time allowances for everyone else already serving drug sentences. The DLRA did not increase the power of judges to place addicts into treatment programs or provide money to increase the availability of community-based drug treatment. Instead, it expanded eligibility for prison-based drug treatment. One year later, the Legal Aid Society found that not only was the re-sentencing process much slower than expected, but that District Attorneys were often fighting re-sentencing and asking for higher sentences. Furthermore, the New York State Department of Correctional Services had not expanded its drug treatment program as required. (See Legal Aid Society, "One Year Later: New York's Experience with Drug Law Reform," http://www.drugpolicy.org/docUploads/DLRA_FactSheet_1.pdf.)

18 Women in Prison Project of the Correctional Association of New York, *Imprisonment and Families Fact Sheet* (New York: March 2007), http://www.correctionalassociation.org/WIPP/publications/families%20Fact%20Sheet%202007.pdf.

19 Marc Mauer, Cathy Potler, and Richard Wolf, *Gender and Justice: Women, Drugs and Sentencing Policy* (Washington, DC: The Sentencing Project 1999), http://www.sentencingproject.org/doc/File/Drug%20Policy/dp_genderandjustice.pdf.

20 Drug Policy Alliance, "Race and the Drug War," http://www.drugpolicy.org/communities/race.

21 Renowned prison abolitionist Angela Davis was an associate professor at UCLA when she first became involved with prisoner support. Her participation in the Black Panther Party and Black Liberation movement led her to the struggle to free the Soledad Brothers and to her correspondence with George Jackson. The United Prisoners' Union in California was formed in 1970 by attorneys and (male) ex-prisoners. By 1973, it had split into two groups: the Prisoners' Union, which confined itself to prison issues, and the United Prisoners' Union, which allied itself with the more radical Bay Area groups. See Eric Cummins, *The Rise and Fall of California's Radical Prison Movement*, (Stanford, CA: Stanford University Press, 1994). In 1972, the American Civil Liberties Union formed the National Prison Project, which used class-action litigation

and public education to defend prisoners' rights. In 1971, prisoners at the maximum-security Green Haven Correctional Facility formed the Green Haven Prisoners Labor Union. Members petitioned the Public Employees Relation Board (PERB) of New York for recognition. PERB denied the petition, ruling that prisoners were not public employees and thus had no right to organize or collectively bargain under the Public Employees' Fair Employment Act. [see Mark Dowie, "Unionizing Prison Labor," *Social Policy*, 4 no.1 (July/August 1973): 56-60].

22 In 1969, Boston university professor Elizabeth Barker brought her university debating team to Norfolk Prison for a practice debate. "Beyond her expectations, the prisoner team bested the university team and, learning that she was an English professor, proceeded to deluge her with their poetry." The experience influenced her to coordinate a series of college courses at the prison during the 1970s. (Dante Germanotta, "Prison Education: A Contextual Analysis," in *Schooling in a "Total Institution": Critical Perspectives on Prison Education*, ed. Howard S. Davidson (Westport, CN: Bergin & Garvey, 1995), 117. Throughout the 1970s, Peter Linebaugh taught Marxism in men's prisons in New Hampshire, Massachusetts, Illinois and New York. (See Peter Linebaugh, "Freeing the Birds, Erasing Images, Burning Lamps: How I Learned to Teach in Prison," in *Schooling in a "Total Institution,"* 65-89.) Karlene Faith taught a political science course to the men in California's Soledad Prison in 1970. Upon learning that her students knew nothing about their female counterparts, Faith focused her attention on incarcerated women, organizing the Santa Cruz Women's Prison Project to bring university classes to women at the California Institution for Women from 1972 to 1976. (See Karlene Faith, "The Santa Cruz Women's Prison Project, 1972–1976," in *Schooling in a "Total Institution,"* 173–192.).

23 Both Barrilee Bannister and Dawn Amos, white women, were sentenced under their respective states' mandatory minimum laws for violent crimes, and are only two of many women who contradict the stereotype of the young, black, male predator. In California, 54% of the women in prison were sentenced for drug offenses in comparison to 38% of the state's total population. In Minnesota, 27% of women in prison were sentenced for drug offenses in comparison to 5% of the state's total population. (The Sentencing Project, *Gender and Justice: Women, Drugs and Sentencing Policy.* http://www.sentencingproject.org/ Admin/Documents/publications/dp_genderandjustice.pdf.

24 Diaz-Cotto details the seeming paradox of women prisoners and the Department of Corrections' reaction to their transgression of societal expectations in her section on Bedford Hills Correctional Facility in Juanita Diaz-Cotto, *Gender, Ethnicity and the State* (Albany, NY: State University of New York Press, 1996).

25 Owen admits that she developed a visible rapport with prison staff to facilitate her interviews with the prisoners. This obvious rapport may have led to distrust by prisoners engaged in organizing and other acts of resistance, resulting in either silence about their actions or a total decline to be interviewed. Similarly,

prison staff may have steered her away from "problem" women so as not to expose any gross violations or abuse occurring within the institution.

26 One issue particular to female prisoners is the distribution of sanitary napkins. For instance, in New York State prisons, each woman is allocated a set number of napkins per year. Because of the scarce supply, many women are forced to reuse and share them. [Human Rights Watch Women's Project, *All Too Familiar: Sexual Abuse of Women in U.S. State Prisons* (Washington, DC: Human Rights Watch, 1996). Cites interview with Rhea S. Mallet, The Correctional Association of New York, January 30, 1996.].

27 Beth E. Richie and Kay Tsenin, *Female Offenders, Pornography and Prostitution, Child Abuse and Neglect,* research forum on women and girls in the justice system for the Department of Justice, 1999.

28 Caroline Wolf Harlow, *Prior Abuse Reported by Inmates and Probationers,* special report for the U.S. Department of Justice, April 1999, 1.

29 Barbara Owen, *"In the Mix": Struggle and Survival in a Women's Prison* (Albany, NY: State University of New York Press, 1998), 164.

30 Letter to the author from Dwight Correctional Center, Illinois, March 20, 2002.

31 Tricia's sister, e-mail to the author, March 28, 2008.

32 Cassandra Shaylor, "'It's Like Living in a Black Hole': Women of Color and Solitary Confinement in the Prison-Industrial Complex" in *Feminist Legal Theory: An Anti-Essentialist Reader,* ed. Nancy E. Dowd and Michelle S. Jacobs (New York: NYU Press, 2003), 317–18.

33 Ibid., 320. The court determined the women's placement unconstitutional since they were housed in the control unit because of their political beliefs. It did NOT rule that control units constituted cruel and unusual punishment. The U.S. Court of Appeals then ruled that prisons are free to use political associations and beliefs to justify different and harsher treatment.

34 Victoria Lynn Simms, *Behind These Walls: A Woman's Perspective* (Unpublished work, 2001).

35 Bannister Barrilee, "Censorship Leads to Harassment at Coffee Creek Correctional Facility," *Tenacious: Art and Writings from Women in Prison* 11 (Spring 2007): 7–10. Construction on Coffee Creek Correctional Facility did not begin until 2000. The minimum-custody facility was not opened until October 2001 and the medium-custody facility, where Bannister was originally transferred from Eastern Oregon Correctional Institution, was not open until April 2002. See http://www.oregon.gov/DOC/OPS/PRISON/docs/pdf/cccf_fact_sheet.pdf.

36 Tricia's sister, e-mail to the author, March 27, 2008.

37 Melvin Claxton, Ronald J. Hansen and Norman Sinclair, "Guards Assault Female Inmates," *The Detroit News* (May 22, 2005), http://detnews.com/2005/specialreport/0505/24/A01-189215.htm.

38 Ibid.

39 Marcia Bunney, "One Life in Prison: Perception, Reflection and Empowerment," in *Harsh Punishment: International Experiences of Women's Imprisonment,* ed. Sandy Cook and Susanne Davies (Boston: Northeastern

Notes

University Press, 1999), 29–30. A jailhouse lawyer is a prisoner who uses his or her knowledge of the law to assist other prisoners with their grievances and cases.

40 lois landis, "Letter," *off our backs* xxxi:2 (February 2001): 11.

41 Nancy Kurshan, "Women and Imprisonment in the U.S.: History and Current Reality," http://prisonactivist.org/women/women-and-imprisonment.html.

42 Reformatories existed primarily for white working-class women. Black women continued to be seen as immoral or amoral and thus unredeemable and were sentenced to custodial prisons.

43 Jill McCorkel, "Criminally Dependent? Gender, Punishment and Welfare Reform," *Social Politics* 11, no.3 (Fall 2004): 402.

44 lois landis, "Letter," *off our backs* xxxi:2 (February 2001): 11.

45 Virginia High Brislin, *The Effect of Immediate Versus Delayed Separation from Infants on Several Dimensions of Inmate-Mothers' Perception and Enactment of the Maternal Role* (Lexington, KY: 1984), 3.

46 "Repression at Bedford Hills Prison," *off our backs* 4, no.12 (December 31, 1974): 4.

47 Juanita Diaz-Cotto, Gender, *Ethnicity and the State: Latina and Latino Prison Politics* (Albany, NY: State University of New York Press, 1996), 324–5.

48 Karlene Faith, *Unruly Women: The Politics and Confinement of Resistance* (Vancouver: Press Gang Publishers, 1993), 235.

49 Laura Whitehorn, "Resistance at Lexington," in *Criminal Injustice: Confronting the Prison Crisis*, ed. Elihu Rosenblatt (Boston, MA: South End Press, 1996), 109.

50 National Lawyers Guild Prison Law Project, "re: Alert: Intervention and Aid for Women at FCI Dublin in California," e-mail to the Prison Activist Resource Center, November 1, 1995. According to Paul Laird, the executive assistant to the Warden, the women were charged with a number of different incidents, including refusal to leave areas, refusal to go to their rooms, "insolence" and arson. He did not state how many had been found guilty of these charges, only that those who had, were subjected to disciplinary transfers, forfeit of good time, or disciplinary segregation of up to 60 days.

51 Karlene Faith, "The Santa Cruz Women's Prison Project, 1972–1976," in *Schooling in a Total Institution*, ed. Howard S. Davidson (Westport, CT: Bergin & Garvey, 1995), 174.

52 Juanita Diaz-Cotto, *Gender, Ethnicity and the State: Latina and Latino Prison Politics* (Albany, NY: State University of New York Press, 1996), 318.

53 *New York Times*, "Women Inmates Battle Guards in North Carolina," June 17, 1975.

54 *New York Times*, "Officers Charge Women Inmates Staging North Carolina Protest," June 20, 1975.

55 Juanita Diaz-Cotto, *Gender, Ethnicity and the State: Latina and Latino Prison Politics* (Albany, NY: State University of New York Press, 1996), 5.

56 For more information on prison family groups among women, see Angela Davis's autobiography, Jocelyn Pollock-Byrne's *Women, Prison and Crime*, and Diaz-Cotto, *Gender, Ethnicity and the State*. However, according to

Diaz-Cotto, the existence of such prison family groups did, in some instances, facilitate inmate organizing: "While individual prisoners might not care much about organizing to reform prison conditions, when requested to do so by other family members, they typed petitions, translated grievances, collected evidence of guard abuses, and passed messages to prisoners in other housing areas." (Diaz-Cotto, 302).

57 lois landis, "Letter," *off our backs* xxxi:2 (February 2001): 11.

58 Kathy Boudin, "Participatory Literacy Education Behind Bars: AIDS Opens the Door," *Harvard Educational Review* 63, no. 2 (Summer 1993): 209.

59 Dawn Amos, letter to the author, March 15, 2002.

60 "Elsie," letter to the author, January 2, 2002.

61 Christopher J. Mumola, *Incarcerated Parents and Their Children*, special report for the Department of Justice, August 2000, 4.

62 Nancy Kurshan, "Women and Imprisonment in the U.S.: History and Current Reality," http://prisonactivist.org/women/women-and-imprisonment.html.

63 Kebby Warner, letter to the author, August 9, 2002.

64 "Roberta," letter to the author, August 26, 2002.

65 Kebby Warner, letter to the author, June 28, 2006.

66 Barrilee Bannister, letter to the author, postmarked June 2002.

67 Barrilee Bannister, letter to the author, October 22, 2002.

68 RJ, letter to the author, January 29, 2008.

69 Marcia Bunney, "One Life in Prison: Perception, Reflection and Empowerment," in *Harsh Punishment: International Experiences of Women's Imprisonment*, ed. Sandy Cook and Susanne Davies (Boston: Northeastern University Press, 1999), 19–20.

70 Kathy Boudin, "Participatory Literacy Education Behind Bars: AIDS Opens the Door," *Harvard Educational Review* 63. no. 2 (Summer 1993): 207–232.

71 Ibid., 221.

72 Kebby Warner, letter to the author, March 20, 2002.

73 Tom Lowenstein, "Collateral Damage," *The American Prospect Online*, January 1, 2001, http://www.prospect.org/cs/articles?article=collateral_damage_010101.

74 Dawn Amos, letter to the author, July 15, 2001.

75 "Elsie," letter to the author, July 2002. Margaret, letter to the author, May 21, 2002.

76 "Elsie," letter to the author, July 2002.

77 Kebby Warner, letter to the author, July 14, 2002.

78 John E. Dannenberg, "Prison Drinking Water and Wastewater Pollution Threaten Environmental Safety Nationwide," *Prison Legal News*, http://www.prisonlegalnews.org/(S(w1xtk455tcloxv550me3xxmu))/displayArticle.aspx?articleid=19162&AspxAutoDetectCookieSupport=1. Helen Caples, letter to the author, March 16, 2008.

Notes

79 Women of the ACE Program at the Bedford Hills Correctional Facility, *Breaking the Walls of Silence: AIDS and Women in a New York State Maximum Security Prison* (Woodstock, NY: Overlook Press, 1998), 35.

80 Kathy Boudin and Judith Clark, "A Community Of Women Organize Themselves To Cope With The AIDS Crisis: A Case Study From Bedford Hill Correctional Facility," *Columbia Journal of Gender and the Law* 1, no.1 (January 31, 1991).

81 Ibid., 51.

82 Ibid., 100–101.

83 Susie Day, "Fighting AIDS, Refusing Powerlessness in Prison (an interview/ collaborative book review with AIDS peer counsellor and political prisoner Laura Whitehorn)," *Sojourner: The Women's Forum* 24, no 9: 17. Linda Evans and Laura Whitehorn, along with Marilyn Buck, Susan Rosenberg and others, were convicted in the Resistance Conspiracy to attack the U.S. Capitol, the Navy War College, and other government and corporate targets. Whitehorn was released in August 1999 and continues to work around the issues of AIDS in prison and the release of all political prisoners.

84 Marcia Bunney, "Finding Self-Respect for Battered Women," *Frontiers of Justice: Coddling or Common Sense?* Vol. II (Brunswick, ME: Biddle Publishing, 1998). Available Online at: http://www.lairdcarlson.com/celldoor/00102/Bun00102BatteredWomen.htm.

85 Elizabeth Lund, "Putting Drama into Prison's Stark Life," *Christian Science Monitor*, July 5, 2001.

86 Patricia Gagne, *Battered Women's Justice: The Movement for Clemency and the Politics of Self-Defense* (New York: Twayne Publishers, 1998), 93.

87 Ibid., 92.

88 Ibid., 93.

89 Ibid., 92.

90 Ibid.

91 Ibid., 95.

92 Jane Gross, "Abused Women Who Kill Now Seek Way Out of Cells," *New York Times*, September 15, 1992.

93 Jill E. Adams, "Unlocking Liberty: Is California's Habeas Law the Key to Freeing Unjustly Imprisoned Battered Women?" *Berkeley Women's Law Journal* 19, no.1 (2004): 238. Of the three women granted clemency, Wilson released only one. He reduced the sentences of the other two women.

94 Elizabeth Ann Dermody Leonard, "Convicted Survivors: The Imprisonment of Battered Women Who Kill" (PhD diss., University of California, Riverside, 1997). Available Online at: http://www.freebatteredwomen.org/pdfs/convsurv.pdf.

95 For more about the group, see http://www.freebatteredwomen.org.

96 Letter to author from Pocatello Women's Correctional Center, April 15, 2005.

97 Kathy Boudin, "Participatory Literacy Education Behind Bars: AIDS Opens the Door," *Harvard Educational Review* 63. no. 2 (Summer 1993): 228.

98 Women of the ACE Program at the Bedford Hills Correctional Facility, *Breaking the Walls of Silence: AIDS and Women in a New York State Maximum Security Prison* (Woodstock, NY: Overlook Press, 1998), 71.

99 "Chowchilla Retaliates Against NLG Jailhouse Lawyer Marcia Bunney," *Prison News Service* 51 (May/June 1995): 2.

100 Donna Willmott, "'Am I Gonna Die in Here?' Medical Neglect in California Women's Prisons," *Sojourner: The Women's Forum* 26, no. 7 (March 2001): 23.

101 Willmott, 23. Judy Ricci died on November 30, 2004. She had been released from CCWF in June 2004. For more information, see Judy Greenspan's memorial in "Judy Ricci Presente! 1960–2004," *Out of Time* 75 (February 2005): 4.

102 Barrilee Bannister, letter to the author, May 15, 2005.

103 Anonymous, letter to the author, October 20, 2007.

104 Women of the ACE Program at the Bedford Hills Correctional Facility, *Breaking the Walls of Silence: AIDS and Women in a New York State Maximum Security Prison* (Woodstock, NY: Overlook Press, 1998), 131.

105 Laura M. Maruschak, *Medical Problems of Prisoners*; and Maruschak, *Medical Problems of Jail Inmates*, Bureau of Justice Statistics, U.S. Department of Justice, November 2006, 1.

106 James Boudouris, *Parents in Prison: Addressing the Needs of Families* (Lanham, MD: American Correctional Association, 1996), 11.

107 Rebecca Project for Human Rights, and National Women's Law Center. 2010. *Mothers Behind Bars: A State-by-State Report Card and Analysis of Federal Policies on Conditions of Confinement for Pregnant and Parenting Women and the Effect on Their Children*. Washington, DC: Rebecca Project for Human Rights.

108 Rita Hammer, Barbara Moynihan and Elaine Pagliaros, *Forensic Nursing: A Handbook for Practice* (Sudbury, MA: Jones and Bartlett Publishers, 2006), 646.

109 "Inside the Women's Prisons of California," *Revolutionary Worker* 911, 1997.

110 Amnesty International, *"Not Part of My Sentence": Violations of the Human Rights of Women in Custody* (New York: Amnesty International, 1999), 10. http://www.amnestyusa.org/node/57783.

111 Ibid., 11.

112 SPARK Reproductive Justice NOW, *Giving Birth Behind Bars: A Guide to Achieving Reproductive Justice for Incarcerated Women*. Atlanta: SPARK Reproductive Justice Now, 2011.

113 Jocelyn Pollock-Byrne, *Women, Prison and Crime* (Pacific Grove, CA: Brooks/Cole Publishing Co., 1990), 147–52.

114 Ayelet Waldman, "Mothers in Chains," *Salon*, May 23, 2005, http://dir.salon.com/story/mwt/col/waldman/2005/05/23/prison/index.html.

115 "Statement by Dr. William F. Schulz, Executive Director of Amnesty International USA," *National Jeff Dicks Medical Coalition Newsletter* (October 2002): 8.

116 Cassie Pierson, "$350,000 Award to Sherrie Chapman." *The Fire Inside* 16 (December 2000), http://www.womenprisoners.org/fire/000228.html.

Notes

Cynthia Cooper, "A Cancer Grows." *The Nation,* May 2002, 6, http://www.thenation.com/article/cancer-grows.

117 "Deficient Diagnosis," *Tenacious: Writings from Women in Prison* 2 (Fall 2002): 13.

118 Bloom, Owen and Covington cite L. Acoca, "Defusing the Time Bomb: Understanding and Meeting the Growing Health Care Needs of Incarcerated Women in America," *Crime and Delinquency* 44, no.1: 49–70 and D. S. Young, "Contributing Factors to Poor Health Among Incarcerated Women: A Conceptual Model," *Affilia* 11, no. 4: 440–461.

119 "Deficient Diagnosis," *Tenacious: Writings from Women in Prison* 2 (Fall 2002): 13.

120 Ellen Richardson, "Medical Conditions at Valley State Prison for Women," *The Fire Inside* 17 (March 2001): 5, http://www.womenprisoners.org/fire/000209.html.

121 Jerrye Broomhall, letter to the author, June 13, 2008.

122 Kirsten, e-mail to the author, March 16, 2008.

123 Dan Pens, "Bag'm, Tag'm and Bury'm: Wisconsin Prisoners Dying for Health Care," *Prison Legal News* 12, no. 2 (2001): 1–2.

124 Donna Willmott, "'Am I Gonna Die in Here?' Medical Neglect in California Women's Prisons," *Sojourner: The Women's Forum* 26, no. 7 (March 2001): 22.

125 Darlene Dixon, "Private Health Care in Prisons: Take it or Leave It," *Sojourner: The Women's Forum* 27, no. 7 (2002): 15.

126 Paul von Zielbauer, "As Health Care in Jails Goes Private, Ten Days Can Be a Death Sentence," *New York Times,* February 27, 2005.

127 Correctional Medical Services, Locations, http://www.cmsstl.com/About-Corizon/Locations/

128 Correctional Medical Services, History, www.cmsstl.com/about-us/history.asp.

129 Correctional Medical Services, Locations: http://www.cmsstl.com/About-Corizon/Locations/.

130 Wyl S. Hilton, "Sick on the Inside: Correctional HMOs and the Coming Prison Plague," *Prison Profiteers: Who Makes Money from Mass Incarceration,* ed. Tara Herivel and Paul Wright (New York: New Press, 2007), 186.

131 Hilton, "Sick on the Inside," 187.

132 Stephanie Walters, "Let My Voice Be Heard," *Tenacious: Art and Writings from Women in Prison* 11 (Spring 2007).

133 Stephanie Walters Searight, letter to the author, August 30, 2007.

134 Women of the ACE Program at the Bedford Hills Correctional Facility, *Breaking the Walls of Silence: AIDS and Women in a New York State Maximum Security Prison* (Woodstock, NY: Overlook Press, 1998), 23.

135 Bloom, Owen and Covington cite Acoca, "Defusing the Time Bomb."

136 AIDS Action, "Incarcerated Populations and HIV/AIDS," Policy Facts, July 2001, http://img.thebody.com/legacyAssets/37/72/incarcerated.pdf.

137 Women in Prison Project, *Incarcerated Women and HIV/Hepatitis C Fact Sheet.*

138 Kathy Boudin and Judith Clark, "A Community Of Women Organize Themselves To Cope With The AIDS Crisis: A Case Study From Bedford Hill Correctional Facility," *Columbia Journal of Gender and the Law* 1, no.1, Jan 31, 1991. Cites New York State Department of Health, AIDS in New York State, 1989.

139 Ibid.

140 Women of the ACE Program at the Bedford Hills Correctional Facility, *Breaking the Walls of Silence: AIDS and Women in a New York State Maximum Security Prison* (Woodstock, NY: Overlook Press, 1998), 17.

141 Kathy Boudin and Judith Clark, "A Community Of Women Organize Themselves To Cope With The AIDS Crisis: A Case Study From Bedford Hill Correctional Facility," *Columbia Journal of Gender and the Law* 1, no.1, Jan 31, 1991.

142 When ACE received a grant from $250,000 from the New York AIDS Institute, both Boudin and Clark were hired as ACE's team of 12 prisoner staff members. Eight months later, both were removed by the Bedford Hills administration, who felt that the two had "undue influence." Both continued to be active as (unpaid) ACE members. In September 1991, one was reinstated on staff and the other removed from the program. The article does not specify what happened to whom.

143 Women of the ACE Program at the Bedford Hills Correctional Facility, *Breaking the Walls of Silence: AIDS and Women in a New York State Maximum Security Prison* (Woodstock, NY: Overlook Press, 1998), 54.

144 ACE, 66–7.

145 Kathy Boudin and Judith Clark, "A Community Of Women Organize Themselves To Cope With The AIDS Crisis: A Case Study From Bedford Hill Correctional Facility," *Columbia Journal of Gender and the Law* 1, no.1, Jan 31, 1991.

146 Michael Gruzuk, "Breaking the Walls of Silence," WNYC Arts and Community radio program, July 30, 1999. The stigma of HIV/AIDS is still prevalent in most prisons, sometimes even in those facilities with peer education programs. At Oklahoma's Mabel Bassett Correctional Center, the HIV peer education program is often disrupted for months by staff turnover, construction and other outside factors. Jerrye Broomhall, who acts as a peer educator when the program is functioning, reports, "the level of ignorance is shocking. Stuff like, 'I don't want to wash my clothes after her, what if her panties were bloody.' People don't want to share cells, meals, so most women just keep their status a secret." (Jerrye Broomhall, letter to the author, October 2, 2007.)

147 Resistance in Brooklyn, *Enemies of the State: A frank discussion of past political movements, victories and errors, and the current political climate for revolutionary struggle within the U.S.A. with European-American political prisoners Marilyn Buck, David Gilbert and Laura Whitehorn* (Brooklyn, NY: 1998).

148 Laura Whitehorn was charged and convicted of "conspiracy to oppose, protest and change the policies and practices of the United States government in

domestic and international matters by violence and illegal means." She spent 14 years in prison and was released on parole on August 6, 1999.

149 Beverly Henry, letter to the author, May 27, 2002.

150 Joann Walker, "Medical Treatment at Chowchilla," *Criminal Injustice: Confronting the Prison Crisis*, ed. Elihu Rosenblatt (Boston, MA: South End Press, 1996), 124. Walker died on July 13, 1994, two months after winning compassionate release from CCWF.

151 Tim Murphy, "Getting Out Alive," *POZ*, April 2004, http://www.poz.com/articles/153_238.shtml.

152 Kathy Boudin and Judith Clark, "A Community Of Women Organize Themselves To Cope With The AIDS Crisis: A Case Study From Bedford Hill Correctional Facility," *Columbia Journal of Gender and the Law* 1, no.1, Jan 31, 1991.

153 Cynthia Chandler, "Death and Dying in America: The Prison Industrial Complex's Impact on Women's Health," *Berkeley Women's Law Journal* 18 (January 31, 2003). See California Department of Corrections, Department Operations Manual, page 753. http://www.cdcr.ca.gov/Regulations/Adult_Operations/docs/DOM/Ch_10_Final_DOM-rev.pdf.

154 "Dedication," *The Fire Inside* 4 (1997), http://www.womenprisoners.org/fire/000482.html.

155 "California Agrees to Settle Inmates' HIV Privacy Claims," *AIDS Policy and Law 12*, no.17 (1997). On July 31, 2000, in light of evidence of tampering with medical files to prepare for the assessors' visits, the Department of Health Services' reports citing CCWF's failure to comply with regulations, and the CDC's failure to retest prisoners who had received fraudulent lab results, the plaintiffs' attorney submitted a motion to reopen discovery in the case. The motion was denied by Judge Shubb and the case was dismissed in August 2000. (See "Strategies for Change: Litigation," http://www.prisonerswithchildren.org/litigation.htm.)

156 Cassie M. Pierson, *Memorial for Charisse Shumate*, spoken at the First Unitarian Church, San Francisco, CA, September 23, 2001.

157 Charisse Shumate, "The Pros and Cons of Being a Lead Plaintiff," *The Fire Inside* 6 (December 1997), http://www.womenprisoners.org/fire/000464.html.

158 Prisoner from Central Correctional Women's Facility, letter to the author, March 3, 2002.

159 A. Clay Thompson, "Cancer in the Cells," *San Francisco Bay Guardian*, February 24, 1999. Sherrie Chapman died on December 12, 2002.

160 Lauren E. Glaze and Laura M. Maruschak, *Parents in Prison and Their Minor Children*, Bureau of Justice Statistics, U.S. Department of Justice, August 2008, 5.

161 Judy Greenspan, Beverly Henry, Theresa Martinez, Judy Ricci, Charisse Shumate, and Jess West, "The State of Prison Healthcare Activism: Fighting the HIV and Hepatitis C Epidemics," in *States of Confinement: Policing, Detention and Prisons*, ed. Joy James (New York: Palgrave, 2002).

162 Tim Murphy, "Getting Out Alive," POZ, April 2004, http://www.poz.com/articles/153_238.shtml.

163 Donna Willmott, "'Am I Gonna Die in Here?' Medical Neglect in California Women's Prisons," *Sojourner: The Women's Forum* 26, no. 7 (March 2001): 23.

164 Delores Garcia, "The Out of Sight Out of Mind Skilled Nursing Facility." Article circulated by Judy Greenspan in an e-mail to the Prison Activist Resource Center listserv, July 18, 2002. Garcia has since been released from prison. She continues to speak out about conditions inside.

165 *National Jeff Dicks Medical Coalition newsletter*, "Women Prisoners Have the Right to Fight Medical Neglect: Stop the Retaliation Against Dee Garcia, Prisoner Organizer, " October 2002, 8-9.

166 Glaze and Maruschak, *Parents in Prison and Their Minor Children*, 2. At the end of 1999, an estimated 126,100 children had a mother in state or federal prison. Advocates for both children and prisoners believe that the actual number is much higher. No agency is required to gather specific data on children of prisoners. In addition, the threat of losing their children prompts many mothers to keep silent about those left in the care of relatives or friends. "There is such a lack of data that we don't know how many incarcerated women have children, how many of these children are in foster care, how many inmates have a family court matter," stated Tamar Kraft-Stolar, the director of the Women in Prison Project of the Correctional Association of New York. "The [New York] State Department of Correctional Services doesn't track this information." (Sasha Nyary, "Foster Children with Mothers in Jail," *Gotham Gazette*, March 2004, http:// www.gothamgazette.com/article/children/20040303/2/901.

167 Glaze and Maruschak, *Parents in Prison and Their Minor Children*, 2.

168 Ibid., 5.

169 Ibid., 5.

170 Jeremy Travis, Elizabeth Cincotta McBride and Amy L. Solomon, *Families Left Behind: The Hidden Costs of Incarceration and Reentry*, Urban Institute, Justice Policy Center, October 2003. Revised June 2005, 4.

171 Karlene Faith, *Unruly Women: The Politics and Confinement of Resistance* (Vancouver: Press Gang Publishers, 1993), 204. Cites Serapio R. Zalba, *Women Prisoners and their Families* (Sacramento, CA: Department of Social Welfare and Corrections, 1964).

172 Zelma Weston Henriques, *Imprisoned Mothers and their Children: A Descriptive and Analytical Study* (Lanham, MD: University Press of America, 1982), 132.

173 The Women in Prison Project of the Correctional Association observed: "Notably, the ASFA time frame results neither from research on child development nor on the effects of long-term foster care on children, but solely from congressional compromise." The original bill proposed 18 months. An amendment to the bill proposed 12 months. The compromise reached was 15 months. See Julie Kowitz-Margolies and Tamar Kraft-Stolar, "When 'Free' Means Losing Your Mother: The Collision of Child Welfare and the Incarceration of Women in New York State," 54, footnote 95, http://www.correctionalassociation.org/publications/download/wipp/reports/When_Free_Rpt_Feb_2006.pdf

Notes

174 The Women in Prison Project of the Correctional Association of New York, *Imprisonment and Families Fact Sheet*, 1. In New York State, for instance, the median minimum sentence for women is 36 months, thus making ASFA's impact profound. (State of New York Department of Correctional Services, *Descriptive Statistics of Women Under DOCS' Custody on 10-29-05*.) See also Julie Kowitz, "Prison Moms Have a Hard Time Seeing their Kids," *Newsday*, May 21, 2002.

175 Two states, Nebraska and New Mexico, exclude incarcerated parents from ASFA's time frame if the only reason to file for termination is because the parent is in prison. See Neb. Rev. Stat. 43-292.02(2)(b) and N.M. Stat. Ann. 1978, 32A-4-28(d).

176 Kebby Warner, letter to the author, April 29, 2001.

177 Philip M. Genty, "Damage to Family Relationships as a Collateral Consequence of Parental Incarceration," *Fordham Law Journal* 30, no. 5 (July 2003): 1671. Arlene F. Lee, Philip M. Genty and Mimi Laver, *The Impact of the Adoption and Safe Families Act on Children of Incarcerated Parents* (Washington, DC: Child Welfare League of America Press, 2005), 20, http://www.fcnetwork.org/Resource%20Center/cop_pubimpact.pdf.

178 Christopher J. Mumola, *Incarcerated Parents and Their Children*, special report for the Department of Justice, August 2000, 5.

179 Mumola, 6. Cites Bloom and Steinhart, Table 2-10.

180 Barrilee Bannister, letter to the author, postmarked January 26, 2001.

181 Barrilee Bannister, letter to the author, March 8, 2002.

182 Barrilee Bannister, letter to the author, March 2, 2001.

183 Jocelyn Pollock-Byrne, *Women, Prison and Crime* (Pacific Grove, CA: Brooks/Cole Publishing Co., 1990), 173. Cites *Pitts v. Meese*, 684 F. Supp. 303 (1987).

184 Kimberly Burke, "Do I Have to Stand For This?" *Sojourner: The Women's Forum* 28, no. 2 (Fall 2002): 15.

185 Silja J.A. Talvi, "What We Do to Women in Prison: An Interview with Ellen Barry," *Sojourner: The Women's Forum* 24, no. 9 (May 1999). Reprinted in *Z Magazine*, http://zena.secureforum.com/Znet/zmag/july00talvi.htm.

186 Yraida L. Guanipa, e-mail to the author, September 17, 2005.

187 Yraida L. Guanipa, e-mail to the author, October 6, 2005.

188 Julie Kowitz, "Prison Moms Have Hard Time Seeing their Kids," *Newsday*, May 21, 2002.

189 The policy change was a response to a 1994 incident at the (male) Muskegon Correctional Facility. A three-year-old girl had been brought for a visit by her mother, a friend of a man incarcerated there. She had wandered away from their table and had been assaulted by another prisoner. Although this had occurred in a male facility, MDOC's Director's Office Memorandum 1995–58 applied to both male and female prisons.

190 *Overton v Bazzetta*, 539 U.S. (2003), http://supct.law.cornell.edu/supct/html/02-94.ZS.html.

191 In Texas, state prisoners can call home once every 90 days for 5 minutes only if they have remained (disciplinary) case free for the prior 90 days. The call

is collect and an officer listens in on an extension. At the Federal Medical Center facility in Carswell, Texas, a 15-minute call costs $3.45. Again, a prison employee monitors the phone conversation.

192 Yraida L. Guanipa, e-mail to the author, September 17, 2005.

193 Yraida L. Guanipa, e-mail to the author, October 25, 2005.

194 Mother at Colorado Women's Correctional Facility, letter to the author, October 29, 2002.

195 Mother at Colorado Women's Correctional Facility, letter to the author, October 19, 2004.

196 Mother at Colorado Women's Correctional Facility, letters to the author, April 25, 2003 and October 14, 2003.

197 Mother at Colorado Women's Correctional Facility, letter to the author, October 14, 2003.

198 Ibid.

199 Mother at Colorado Women's Correctional Facility, letter to the author, May 4, 2006.

200 Mother at Colorado Women's Correctional Facility, letter to the author, June 22, 2008.

201 "Roberta," letter to the author, postmarked July 7, 2004.

202 "Roberta," letter to the author, postmarked December 31, 2004.

203 Mother at Colorado Women's Correctional Facility, letter to the author, September 28, 2001.

204 Chuck Armsbury, "Supreme Court to Rule on Mother/Child Love," www.november.org/razorwire/rzold/20/20028.html.
Yraida L. Guanipa, letter to the author, May 8, 2005 and June 11, 2005.

205 Armsbury, "Supreme Court to Rule on Mother/Child Love."

206 Tom Lowenstein, "Collateral Damage," *The American Prospect Online*, January 1, 2001, http://www.prospect.org/cs/articles?article=collateral_damage_010101.

207 Barbara Bloom, Barbara Owen, and Stephanie Covington, *Gender-Responsive Strategies: Research, Practice, and Guiding Principles for Women Offenders* (National Institute of Corrections, 2003) 6, http://www.nicic.org/pubs/2003/018017.pdf.

208 Kebby Warner, letter to the author, April 29, 2001.

209 Marianne Brown, *Woman is the Word* (prison writing class project), 39.

210 Marianne Brown, letter to Devon Brown, commissioner of New Jersey State Prison, June 18, 2003. *Woman is the Word*, 47.

211 Ibid.

212 Brown, 50. Brown and her son were able to have a one-hour, fifteen-minute video conference on July 25, 2003. They were granted a second visit in September 2003.

213 Ibid.

214 RJ, letter to the author, April 24, 2006.

215 This is not to say that women prisoners have not disrupted daily operations to protest changes in prison policy that adversely affect communication and contact with their families. As mentioned in the Overview, in 1975, women at

a California prison protested the cancellation of family visits by gathering in the yard, breaking windows, making a ruckus and burning Christmas trees in a "solidarity" bonfire.

216 Merry Morash, Timothy S. Bynum and Barbara A. Koons, *Women Offenders: Programming Needs and Promising Approaches*, report to the U.S. Department of Justice, August 1998, 8.

217 Jean Harris, *Stranger in Two Worlds* (New York: MacMillan Publishing Company, 1986), 286.

218 Kathy Boudin and Roslyn Smith, "Alive Behind the Labels: Women in Prison," *Sisterhood Is Forever: The Women's Anthology for the New Millennium* ed. Robin Morgan (New York: Washington Square Press, 2003), 257.

219 Kathy Boudin, "The Children's Center Programs of Bedford Hills Correctional Facility," *Maternal Ties: A Selection of Programs for Female Offenders*, ed. Cynthia Blinn (Lanham, MD: American Correctional Association, 1997), 68.

220 The success of the programs at Bedford Hills is documented by books, articles and manuals written by prisoner participants. Unlike the writings and publications of most prisoner activists, these documents are more widely accepted and acknowledged by general society.

221 For more information about the Incarcerated Mothers' Law Project, go to: http://www.wpaonline.org/about/history.htm. The Women's Prison Association is a non-profit organization, providing services to women returning from prison to the New York City area. It also administers the AIDS peer education programs at both Bedford Hills and Taconic Correctional Facilities and discharge planning services to women leaving Rikers Island: http://www.wpaonline.org. Volunteers of Legal Services (VOLS) recruits volunteer lawyers and law firms to provide legal services needed by children, the elderly poor, incarcerated mothers and people with AIDS: http://www.volsprobono.org

222 Yraida L. Guanipa, e-mail to the author, December 15, 2005.

223 Ibid.

224 Yraida L. Guanipa, e-mail to the author, February 11, 2006.

225 Yraida L. Guanipa, e-mail to the author, December 15, 2005.

226 Yraida L. Guanipa, e-mail to the author, February 11, 2006.

227 Yraida L. Guanipa, e-mail to the author, November 9, 2005.

228 Juanita Diaz-Cotto, *Gender, Ethnicity and the State: Latina and Latino Prison Politics* (Albany, NY: State University of New York Press, 1996), 366–67.

229 Human Rights Watch Women's Project, *All Too Familiar: Sexual Abuse of Women in U.S. State Prisons* (Washington, DC: Human Rights Watch, 1996), 429.

230 Ibid.

231 Juanita Diaz-Cotto, *Gender, Ethnicity and the State: Latina and Latino Prison Politics* (Albany, NY: State University of New York Press, 1996), 347.

232 Stacy Barker, letter to the author, March 22, 2006.

233 *Overton v. Bazzetta*, 2002 FED App. 0118P (6th Cir). However, the U.S. Supreme Court overturned the appeal court's ruling: http://supreme.lp.findlaw.com/supreme_court/decisions/lower_court/01-1635.6th.html.

234 Stacy Barker, letter to the author. March 22, 2006.

235 Anonymous, "Another Day in Prison," *Clamor* 33 (July/August 2005): 28.

236 Human Rights Watch Women's Project, *All Too Familiar: Sexual Abuse of Women in U.S. State Prisons* (Washington, DC: Human Rights Watch, 1996), 236–37.

237 The *USA* case was settled in May 1999. MDOC agreed to provide more training on sexual misconduct to both staff and prisoners, to maintain a database of complaints of sexual misconduct, to require male officers to announce their presence when entering women's living quarters, and to suspend pat-down searches of female prisoners by male officers. The settlement failed to provide an independent oversight mechanism to monitor the reporting, investigating and prosecution of sexual abuse. It also permitted MDOC to issue major misconduct tickets to women whose claims of sexual abuse are deemed "unfounded," leaving open the possibility of institutionally sanctioned retaliation.

238 Human Rights Watch Women's Project, *All Too Familiar: Sexual Abuse of Women in U.S. State Prisons* (Washington, DC: Human Rights Watch, 1996), 6.

239 Barbara Bloom, Barbara Owen, and Stephanie Covington, *Gender-Responsive Strategies: Research, Practice, and Guiding Principles for Women Offenders* (National Institute of Corrections, 2003) 60, http://www.nicic.org/pubs/2003/018017.pdf.

240 Writing about incarcerated survivors in Canada, Jan Heney and Connie Kristiansen note that "just as 'the healthy, normal, emotionally resilient child will learn to accommodate to the reality of continuing sexual abuse,' an incarcerated survivor may try to adapt to the reassertion of these dynamics in prison using the coping skills she learned as a child." ["An Analysis of the Impact of Prison on Women Survivors of Childhood Sexual Abuse," *Women and Therapy* 20 (1997): 6]. The Vera Institute of Justice has stated, "Women with a history of being sexually assaulted are at higher risk of future sexual revictimization than women who have never been assaulted. Research suggests that psychological processes initiated by sexual revictimization may result in behaviors that can increase victims' exposure and vulnerability to potential offenders." [Robert Davis, Pamela Guthrie, Timothy Ross and Chris O'Sullivan, *Reducing Sexual Revictimization: A Field Test with an Urban Sample* (New York: Vera Institute of Justice, 2006), 1, http://www.vera.org/content/reducing-sexual-revictimization-field-test-urban-sample]

241 Jennifer Bagwell, "Barred from View: How Michigan Keeps the Lid on Allegations of Widespread Sexual Abuse Against Female Inmates," *Metro Times: Detroit's Alternative Weekly*, March 24, 1999.

242 Kari Lydersen, "Red Tape Lets Guards Rape Women Prisoners, Suit Argues," *New Standard*, January 6, 2006, http://newstandardnews.net/content/index.cfm/items/2730.

243 Bagwell, "Barred from View."

244 Melvin Claxton, Ronald J. Hansen and Norman Sinclair, "Guards Assault Female Inmates," *Detroit News*, May 22, 2005, http://detnews.com/2005/specialreport/0505/24/A01-189215.htm. Hook eventually pleaded guilty to criminal sexual conduct in the fourth degree. He was sentenced to four years in prison and served three years and four months before being "Discharged without Improvement." (MDOC Offender Tracking Information System, http://www.state.mi.us/mdoc/asp/otis2.html).

245 Christopher D. Cook and Christian Parenti, "Rape Camp USA: The Epidemic of Sexual Assault in Women's Prisons," *Disbarred: The Journal of the National Lawyers Guild Prison Law Project* 16, no. 1.

246 The Nevada Department of Prisons selected the Corrections Corporation of America (CCA) to design, build and operate a prison for women in Las Vegas. The prison opened in 1997 under CCA control. On October 1, 2004, the Nevada Department of Corrections assumed control of the prison. http://www.doc.nv.gov/snwcc/index.php.

247 Brenda V. Smith, "Rethinking Prison Sex: Self Expression and Safety," *Columbia Journal of Gender and Law* 15, no. 1 (January 31, 2006): 220. Nevada is one of three states that have enacted laws penalizing prisoners who "consent" to sex with staff. Arizona and Delaware are the other two states.

248 Associated Press, "Guard, Inmate Get Probation for Pregnancy," http://www.spr.org/en/news/2005/0420.asp. See also Carri Greer Thevenot, "Ex-Prison Guard Identified as Father of Inmate's Baby," *Las Vegas Review-Journal*, February 4, 2004, http://spr.igc.org/en/news/2005/0420.htm.

249 "Dee," letter to the author, September 28, 2001.

250 Jennifer Bagwell, "Barred from View: How Michigan Keeps the Lid on Allegations of Widespread Sexual Abuse Against Female Inmates," *Metro Times: Detroit's Alternative Weekly*, March 24, 1999.

251 Human Rights Watch, *Nowhere to Hide: Retaliation Against Women Incarcerated in Michigan State Prisons*, July 1998, http://www.hrw.org/reports98/women/Mich-04.htm.

252 Melvin Claxton, Ronald J. Hansen and Norman Sinclair, "Guards Assault Female Inmates," *The Detroit News*, May 22, 2005, http://detnews.com/2005/specialreport/0505/24/A01-189215.htm.

253 Jennifer Bagwell, "Barred from View: How Michigan Keeps the Lid on Allegations of Widespread Sexual Abuse Against Female Inmates," *Metro Times: Detroit's Alternative Weekly*, March 24, 1999.

254 Ironically, the Safe Prisons program, started after the federal Prison Rape Elimination Act was passed in 2003, is a peer education program to prevent sexual assault, bullying, manipulation, coercion and other forms of sexual abuse.

255 Dawn Reiser, letter to author, March 2008. The probability of severe punishment—both officially and informally—is not limited to Texas. When I sent her a draft of this chapter to read, "Dee" wrote back asking that I not use her real name when telling her story. "I'm afraid of someone here or somewhere reading it and all the rumors flying again. I've worked hard to keep it a secret at this [new] facility. It caused me a lot of problems."

256 Dawn Reiser, letter to author, May 31, 2008.

257 Dawn Amos, letter to the author, September 28, 2001.

258 Stop Prisoner Rape, *The Sexual Abuse of Female Inmates in Ohio* (Los Angeles, CA: Stop Prisoner Rape, 2003), 8, http://www.spr.org/pdf/sexabuseohio.pdf.

259 "Sexual Abuse of Female Inmates in Ohio," 6.

260 "Sexual Abuse of Female Inmates in Ohio," 8.

261 Human Rights Watch, *Nowhere to Hide: Retaliation Against Women Incarcerated in Michigan State Prisons,* July 1998.

262 At the time, Huron Valley was a 400-bed psychiatric hospital for prisoners. It is now a women's prison housing more than double the number of prisoners.

263 Human Rights Watch, *Nowhere to Hide: Retaliation Against Women Incarcerated in Michigan State Prisons,* July 1998.

264 Regan Ralph, letter to Attorney General Janet Reno, June 11, 1999, http://hrw.org/english/docs/1999/06/11/usdom4183.htm. (Ralph Regan is the Executive Director for Human Rights Watch's Women's Rights Division.)

265 Stacy Barker, letter to the author, March 22, 2006.

266 Anonymous prison employee, in discussion with the author, March 9, 2008.

267 *Brief of Amici Curiae, Center for Constitutional Rights et al. in opposition to defendant's motion for Summary Judgement: Amador et al. vs. Superintendents of DOCS*, U.S. District Court, Southern District of New York, 2005.

268 Kari Lydersen, "Watching You, Watching Me," *The New Standard,* January 6, 2006, http://newstandardnews.net/content/index.cfm/items/2730.

269 Alan Gustafson, "Halting Prison Sex Scandals Has Far-Reaching Effects," *Statesman Journal*, December 4, 2005. Reprinted at Stop Prisoner Rape website: http://spr.igc.org/en/news/2005/1204.htm.

270 "Prison Rape Elimination Act Becomes Federal Law," http://www.menstuff.org/issues/byissue/jailhouserock.html#federallaw.

271 Mark S. Fleischer, *Prison Rape Elimination Act—Appendix A: Rape and Coercive Sex in American Prisons*, Interim Findings and Interpretations on Preliminary Research, Mandel School of Applied Social Sciences, Case Western Reserve University.

272 Dawn Reiser, letter to the author. June 3, 2007.

273 Dawn Amos, letter to the author, June 12, 2005.

274 RJ, letter to the author, June 22, 2008.

275 Dawn Amos, letter to the author, March 23, 2008.

276 "Rape: Motive for Murder," *The Economist*, April 12, 1975, 71.

277 Jerrold K. Footlick, "Joan Little's Defense," *Newsweek*, February 24, 1975, 86.

278 Jerrold K. Footlick, "Defending Joan Little," *Newsweek*, July 28, 1975, 34.

279 "Joan Little's Story," *Time Magazine*, August 25, 1975, http://www.time.com/time/magazine/article/0,9171,913413,00.html?iid=chix-sphere.

280 Although the women's rights movement hailed the acquittal as a victory, Little herself was returned to prison to finish her seven-to-ten year sentence for breaking and entering. Two years later, the North Carolina parole board denied Little parole. She was released in 1979 on the condition that she stay out of North Carolina. See "little parole denied" in *off our backs* (Feb. 1977): 5, and Lee Lescaze, "Joan Little, Free in New York: 'It Feels Good to Be Out, '" *Washington Post,* June 1979.

281 Patricia Gagne, *Battered Women's Justice: The Movement for Clemency and the Politics of Self-Defense* (New York: Twayne Publishers, 1998), 185. Cites a 1992 interview with anonymous former prisoner.

282 Gagne, 185. Quotes from 1992 interview with anonymous former prisoner.

283 Barrilee Bannister, letter to the author, June 21, 2001.

284 Barrilee Bannister, "I Survived Conniving Corruption Corporation of America," *Tenacious: Writings from Women in Prison* 1 (Summer 2002): 20.

285 *Forts v. Ward,* Docket No. 79-2093, 79-2098, U.S. Court of Appeals, Second Circuit, http://bulk.resource.org/courts.gov/c/F2/621/621.F2d.1210.html.

286 Brenda V. Smith, "Watching Me, Watching You," *Yale Journal of Law and Feminism* 15, no. 225 (2003): 11. Reprinted at Stop Prisoner Rape website: http://www.spr.org/pdf/Watching%20You,%20Watching%20Me.pdf.

287 Human Rights Watch, *All Too Familiar.* See also, *Harris v. Garner: Statement of the Issues, Summary of the Argument* (21 October 1998), Project Diana: Online Human Rights Archive at Yale Law School, http://avalon.law.yale.edu/diana/110998-2.asp.

288 Jan Hoffman, "A Sexual Divide in Prison Searches," *New York Times,* April 9, 1993, http://query.nytimes.com/gst/fullpage.html?res=9F0CE3D81F3BF93 AA35757C0A965958260.

289 Human Rights Watch, *All Too Familiar.* In August 1996, the case was overturned by the DC Circuit Court. http://www.hrw.org/reports/1996/Us1.htm.

290 Nina Siegal, "Stopping Abuse in Women's Prison: Widespread Sexual Abuse of Women Prisoners," *The Progressive,* April 1999, http://findarticles.com/p/articles/mi_m1295/is_4_63/ai_54246113.

291 Barbara R. Levine, "Legislature Stops Prisoner Progress in Courts," *Prisons and Corrections Forum: A Publication of the State Bar of Michigan's Prisons and Corrections Section* 3, no.1 (Spring/Summer 2000): 24.

292 *Linda Nunn et. Al, Plaintiffs, v. Michigan Department of Corrections, et al. , Defendants.* U.S. District Court for the Eastern District of Michigan, Southern Division. 1997.

293 Ibid.

294 "Conditions at Women's Prisons: Litigation, Legislation, More Litigation," *Prisons and Corrections Forum: A Publication of the State Bar of Michigan's Prison and Corrections Section* 3, vol.1 (Spring/Summer 2000): 8.

295 Stacy Barker, letter to the author, March 22, 2006.

296 Caroline Wolf Harlow, *Educational and Correctional Populations,* special report to the Department of Justice, 2003.

297 Two notable exceptions are Michelle Fine's 2001 *Changing Minds: The Impact of College in a Maximum-Security Prison* and Johanna E. Foster's and Rebecca Sanford's "Does Gender Shape Women's Access to College Programs in U.S. State Prisons?" in *Equal Opportunities International* 25, no. 7 (2006).

298 Johanna E. Foster and Rebecca Sanford, "Does gender shape women's access to college programs in US state prisons?" *Equal Opportunities International* 25, no. 7 (2006): 590.

299 Foster and Sanford, 591.

300 The Santa Cruz Community Studies Department and the Extended Studies Department provided credit for the courses and registered prisoners as "mature students."

301 Karlene Faith, "The Santa Cruz Women's Prison Project, 1972–1976," in *Schooling in a Total Institution*, ed. Howard S. Davidson (Westport, CT: Bergin & Garvey, 1995), 180–181.

302 Ibid., 177–8.

303 Ibid., 177.

304 Faith had ended a letter to a prisoner with the word "Venceremos" (literally "we will conquer"), a colloquialism that many activists used to indicate overcoming all obstacles to freedom. However, the guard who read her letter assumed that Faith was connected with a group called "Venceremos," which had claimed credit for an escape from a neighboring men's prison. Faith—and the program—was allowed to return to the prison only after a thorough investigation of her background (Faith, "Women's Prison Project,"182–3).

305 Faith, "Women's Prison Project,"185. Faith does not go into detail about what had caused that particular break in the program or what the women had resolved to do in that instance.

306 Sarah B. Ames, "Protests Put Women's Prison in Spotlight," *The Oregonian*, October 31, 1988, B02.

307 Gretchen Schumacher, letter to the author, July 26, 2002.

308 Juanita Diaz-Cotto, *Gender, Ethnicity and the State: Latina and Latino Prison Politics* (Albany, NY: State University of New York Press, 1996), 351–2. The emphasis on bilingual and Spanish-language materials reflected the fact that Latinas were the fastest growing group within the prison population and had additional language needs.

309 Michelle Fine, Kathy Boudin, Iris Bowen, Judith Clark, Donna Hylton, Migdalia Martinez, "Missy," Rosemarie Roberts, Pamela Smart, Maria Torre and Debora Upegui, *Changing Minds: The Impact of College in a Maximum Security Prison*, 2001, http://web.gc.cuny.edu/che/changingminds.html.

310 Jerrye Broomhall, letter to the author, January 14, 2008.

311 Ibid.

312 Marcia Bunney, "One Life in Prison: Perception, Reflection and Empowerment," in *Harsh Punishment: International Experiences of Women's Imprisonment*, ed. Sandy Cook and Susanne Davies (Boston: Northeastern University Press, 1999), 24.

Notes

313 Ibid., 24.

314 Ibid., 26.

315 RJ, letter to the author, February 14, 2008.

316 U.S. Department of Education Office of Correctional Education, *Pell Grants and the Incarcerated*. Washington (DC: U.S. Department of Education, 1995).

317 Michelle Fine, Kathy Boudin, Iris Bowen, Judith Clark, Donna Hylton, Migdalia Martinez, "Missy," Rosemarie Roberts, Pamela Smart, Maria Torre and Debora Upegui, *Changing Minds: The Impact of College in a Maximum Security Prison*, 2001,http://web.gc.cuny.edu/che/changingminds.html.

318 Robert Worth. "Bringing College Back to Bedford Hills," *New York Times*, June 24, 2001. Reprinted at: http://prisonreader.org/BedfordNYT.html.

319 Michelle Fine and Maria Elena Torre, "The Impact of College Education on Inmates in the New York State Region," Testimony to the New York State Democratic Task Force on Criminal Justice Reform. Public Hearings, State Office Building, Brooklyn, New York, December 4, 2000.

320 Michelle Fine, Kathy Boudin, Iris Bowen, Judith Clark, Donna Hylton, Migdalia Martinez, "Missy," Rosemarie Roberts, Pamela Smart, Maria Torre and Debora Upegui, *Changing Minds: The Impact of College in a Maximum Security Prison*, 2001, http://web.gc.cuny.edu/che/changingminds.html.

321 Ibid.

322 Robert Worth. "Bringing College Back to Bedford Hills," *The New York Times*, June 24, 2001. Reprinted at: http://prisonreader.org/BedfordNYT.html.

323 One can see the disparity between Bedford Hills Correctional Facility and other women's prisons simply by looking across the street. The Taconic Correctional Facility, a medium-security women's prison, is located literally across Harris Road. Unlike Bedford Hills, Taconic receives virtually no attention or outside support. Taconic did not offer college programming until 2003, when Gina Shea, a long-time advocate for prisoner education, and Johanna E. Foster, a college professor, established College Connections: Higher Education for Women in Prison.

324 Marianne Brown, letter to the author, October 5, 2005.

325 Dawn Amos, letter to the author, July 15, 2001.

326 Dawn Amos, letter to the author, April 7, 2001.

327 Ibid.

328 Dawn Amos, letter to the author, July 15, 2001.

329 Michelle Fine, Kathy Boudin, Iris Bowen, Judith Clark, Donna Hylton, Migdalia Martinez, "Missy," Rosemarie Roberts, Pamela Smart, Maria Torre and Debora Upegui, *Changing Minds: The Impact of College in a Maximum Security Prison*, 2001,http://web.gc.cuny.edu/che/changingminds.html.

330 Jerrye Broomhall, letter to the author, January 14, 2008.

331 Michelle Fine and Maria Elena Torre, "Bar None: College Education in Prison," *Journal of Social Issues* 63, no. 3 (2005): 573.

332 Kathy Boudin, "Participatory Literacy Education Behind Bars: AIDS Opens the Door," *Harvard Educational Review* 63. no. 2 (Summer 1993): 212.

333 Ibid., 217.

334 Ibid., 218.

335 Ibid., 219. Juana's story, "Chocolate and Me," was later published by the PWA Coalition in *Surviving and Thriving with AIDS: Collective Wisdom*, vol. 1 (1988).

336 Ibid., 225.

337 Ibid.

338 Ibid.

339 Ibid.

340 Ibid., 228. Both changes in personnel and the political climate influenced the administration's withdrawal of support. The education supervisor, who had not only supported Boudin's program but also had been the link between the teacher and the prisoner peer educators, left the prison for another job. New York State cut its budget for education, laying off teachers and creating anxiety among those remaining about their own job security. This led to resistance to the idea of prisoners teaching or even actively participating in their own learning process. Finally, the political climate was becoming increasingly hostile towards prisoners, prisoner initiatives and program innovation.

341 Linda Caldwell, "A Prisoner's Literacy Experience," *Tenacious: Art and Writings from Women in Prison* 2 (2002): 24–5.

342 Ibid., 26.

343 Ibid., 26–7.

344 Prisoner at Ohio Reformatory for Women, letter to Books Through Bars— New York City, n.d. Although there are various programs that send free books to prisoners throughout the United States, only a few exist specifically for women. The other programs receive requests mostly from men, reinforcing the belief that women prisoners neither organize nor network.

345 Dawn Amos, letter to the author, April 7, 2001.

346 In April 2008, the Oregon Department of Corrections changed this restriction to allow books in from "recognized vendors" who are not book publishers.

347 Jerrye Broomhall, letter to the author. March 5, 2008.

348 Kebby Warner, letter to the author, February 27, 2008.

349 Dawn Amos, letter to the author, February 18, 2008.

350 A preliminary study by Johanna E. Foster, cofounder of two higher education initiatives in women's prisons in New York and New Jersey, found that in the 18 states that allow college courses in women's prisons, programs are not available at every facility. Thus, a woman enrolled in Bedford Hills' College Bound program can be transferred to Albion or Beacon, two women's prisons with no college opportunities. See Johanna E. Foster, "Bringing College Back to Prison: The State of Higher Education Programs for Incarcerated Women in the U.S.", 8th International Women's Policy Research Conference (June 2005).

351 RJ, "Untitled," *Tenacious: Art and Writings from Women in Prison* 14 (Spring 2008).

352 RJ, letter to the author, February 14, 2008.

353 RJ, letter to the author, March 12, 2008.

Notes

354 RJ, letter to the author, February 14, 2008.

355 Rhonda Leland, letter to the author, postmarked September 27, 2002.

356 Rhonda Leland, letter to the author, postmarked October 4, 2002.

357 Ibid.

358 Rhonda Leland, letter to the author, postmarked October 22, 2002.

359 Rhonda Leland, letter to the author, October 16, 2002.

360 Ibid.

361 Jerrye Broomhall, letter to the author, January 14, 2008.

362 Jerrye Broomhall, letter to the author, January 30, 2008.

363 Dawn Reiser, letter to the author, February 11, 2008.

364 Marcia Bunney, "One Life in Prison: Perception, Reflection and Empowerment," in *Harsh Punishment: International Experiences of Women's Imprisonment*, ed. Sandy Cook and Susanne Davies (Boston: Northeastern University Press, 1999), 28.

365 Ibid., 28–29.

366 Ibid., 29.

367 Kathy Boudin and Judith Clark, "A Community Of Women Organize Themselves To Cope With The AIDS Crisis: A Case Study From Bedford Hill Correctional Facility," *Columbia Journal of Gender and the Law* 1, no.1, Jan 31, 1991.

368 Kathy Boudin, "Participatory Literacy Education Behind Bars: AIDS Opens the Door," *Harvard Educational Review* 63. no. 2 (Summer 1993): 221.

369 Ibid., 223.

370 The formation of the AIDS Counseling and Education program was separate from Boudin's use of HIV/AIDS to promote critical thinking in the ABE class.

371 Kathy Boudin, "Participatory Literacy Education Behind Bars: AIDS Opens the Door," *Harvard Educational Review* 63. no. 2 (Summer 1993): 225.

372 Ibid., 226.

373 Marilyn Buck, "Women in Prison and Work," *Feminist Studies* 30 no. 2 (2004): 451–55.

374 In 1817, New York established the Auburn State Prison. Breaking from the Pennsylvania Quaker model that enforced 24-hour silence and isolation as a means of rehabilitating offenders, the Auburn system allowed its (male) prisoners to work together during the day but live in enforced silence and isolation at night. The Auburn system proved more profitable and became the dominant model for U.S. prisons. In 1825, Auburn began housing women prisoners in its attic. The women were put to work picking wool, knitting and spooling. They were not subject to the rule of silence.

375 The discrepancy in ages dates back to the start of the Auburn system. In the mid-1800s, women incarcerated at New York's Mount Pleasant Female Prison worked long hours sewing clothes for male prisoners as well as making buttons and trimming hats. Although their wages were not recorded, they were apparently paid much less than their male counterparts. Critics later used this fact against the prison's reform-minded matron Eliza Farnham, charging that

her attempts to rehabilitate women by providing time for religious observance, educational programs and reading prevented the prison from gaining more profit. Farnham responded with the point that women in the female prison were paid less than men. See Nicole Hahn Rafter, *Partial Justice: Women, Prisons, and Social Control* (New Brunswick: Transaction Publishers, 1990), 18–19.

376 Karen F. Lahm, "Equal or Equitable: An Exploration of Educational and Vocational Program Availability for Male and Female Offenders," *Federal Probation* 64, no. 2 (2000): 43.

377 D.S Young and R.F. Mattucci, "Enhancing the Vocational Skills of Incarcerated Women Through a Plumbing Maintenance Program," *Journal of Correctional Education* 57, no. 2 (2006): 130.

378 Barrilee Bannister, letter to the author, postmarked April 4, 2002.

379 Barrilee Bannister, letter to the author, no date.

380 Tim Reiterman and Jenifer Warren, "Prison Jobs Program Just Barely Working," *Los Angeles Times*. July 18, 2004. Reprinted at Prison Talk messageboard: http://www.prisontalk.com/forums/showthread. php?t=69244.

381 Woman at Central California Women's Facility, letter to the author, April 22, 2002.

382 Marianne Brown, letter to the author, September 20, 2005.

383 According to the UNICOR website, this new partnership offers "all the benefits of domestic outsourcing at offshore prices. It's the best-kept secret in outsourcing!" http://www.unicor.gov/services/contact_helpdesk.

384 Kirsten, former prisoner at FMC Carswell, e-mail to the author, February 28, 2008.

385 Tammi Ann Allowitz, e-mail to the author, March 4, 2008.

386 Kirsten, former prisoner at FMC Carswell, e-mail to the author, February 28, 2008.

387 Yraida L. Guanipa, e-mail to the author, December 18, 2005.

388 Woman at FMC Carswell, letter to the author, postmarked October 2, 2002.

389 Dawn Amos, letter to the author, July 15, 2001.

390 Dawn Amos, letter to the author, March 15, 2002.

391 Ibid.

392 Marianne Brown, letter to the author, October 5, 2005. Marianne Brown has been incarcerated since June 2001.

393 Dawn Amos, letter to the author, March 15, 2002.

394 Dawn Amos, letter to the author, October 23, 2005.

395 Dawn Amos, letter to the author, January 1, 2006.

396 Kebby Warner, letter to the author, April 29, 2002.

397 Kebby Warner, letter to the author, April 25, 2007. Relief porters sweep and mop the floors of their housing units. Warner would have earned $6.52 for the month she worked, but the prison deducted most of that amount to repay a previous indigent loan.

398 Woman at Dwight Correctional Center, letter to the author, March 20, 2002.

399 Woman at Dwight Correctional Center, letter to the author, March 20, 2002.

Notes

400 "Dedication to Yoland R.," *The Fire Inside* 20 (2002): 1, http://www. womenprisoners.org/fire/000168.html.

401 Cynthia Chandler, "Death and Dying in America: The Prison Industrial Complex's Impact on Women's Health," *Berkeley Women's Law Journal* 18 (January 31, 2003).

402 Ibid. Cites interviews with Michelle Andrews, CCWF prisoner, June 10 to August 24, 2001.

403 California Department of Corrections and Rehabilitation, *Weekly Report of Population*, July 14, 2008, http://www.cdcr.ca.gov/Reports_Research/ Offender_Information_Services_Branch/WeeklyWed/TPOP1A/ TPOP1Ad080709.pdf.

404 Marianne Brown, letter to the author, September 20, 2005.

405 Marianne Brown, letter to the author, postmarked February 11, 2008.

406 Kebby Warner, letter to the author, April 3, 2005. Warner later lost that job when she was sent to segregation or "the hole."

407 Linda Caldwell, "A Prisoner's Literacy Experience," *Tenacious: Art and Writings from Women in Prison* 2 (Fall 2002): 25.

408 Dawn Amos, letter to the author, October 19, 2004.

409 Dawn Amos, letter to the author, February 3, 2005.

410 Dawn Amos, letter to the author, August 19, 2005.

411 Buck, "Women in Prison and Work."

412 RJ, letter to the author, June 3, 2006.

413 Elisa Brehm, "Arizona Sheriff Introduces Female Chain Gangs," *World Socialist Web Site*, http://www.wsws.org/articles/2003/nov2003/gang-n19_.shtml.

414 Margie Wood, "DOC Pilot Program Working Well," *Pueblo Chieftain*, July 11, 2007. The farmers pay the Department of Corrections $9.60 per prisoner per hour, which covers not only the $4 daily wage but also the expenses of their supervisor/guard, meals and transportation.

415 Margie Wood, "Inmates Prefer Work in Fields to Kitchen Duty," *Pueblo Chieftain*, July 11, 2007.

416 Kebby Warner, letter to the author, July 24, 2002.

417 Barrilee Bannister, letter to the author, September 12, 2002.

418 Marianne Brown, letter to the author, October 5, 2005.

419 Yraida L. Gunaipa, e-mail to the author, November 29, 2005.

420 Yraida L. Gunaipa, e-mail to the author, December 18, 2005.

421 Ibid.

422 Nancy Kurshan, "Women and Imprisonment in the U.S.: History and Current Reality," http://prisonactivist.org/women/women-and-imprisonment.html.

423 Meryl LaTronica, "Prisoners Talk About Labor on the Inside," *Sojourner: The Women's Forum*, 15.

424 RJ, Letter to the author, June 4, 2008.

425 RJ, Letter to the author, June 22–23, 2008.

426 Ibid. On June 5, 2008, in response to the continued shortage of farm workers, Colorado governor Bill Ritter signed into law a program allowing migrants from Mexico to work on Colorado farms. The law uses the federal

H2A(agricultural worker) visa program. Although its impact has yet to be seen, RJ and others at La Vista wonder if it means an end—or a significant reduction—to the DOC's farm crew program. "It seems less of a hassle for the farm owners to deal with these workers rather than with DOC and CI [Colorado Industries] contracts plus the different bosses and changing faces of the women," she wrote on June 23, 2008. For more about the new law, see Naomi Zeveloff's "Colorado Scrambles to Secure Farm Labor Amid Anti-Immigrant Sentiment." *Colorado Independent*. June 16, 2008, http://coloradoindependent.com/view/colorado-scrambles.

427 Laura Maca, "I Had to Quit my Job," *Break the Chains!* 17 (2004): 12.

428 Nancy Kurshan, "Women and Imprisonment in the U.S.: History and Current Reality," http://prisonactivist.org/women/women-and-imprisonment.html.

429 *New York Times*, "Women Inmates Also Have Grievances," January 14, 1973.

430 According to an objection brief filed by Legal Services for Prisoners with Children, the settlement agreement failed to provide adequate standards for pregnancy-related care (according to the CDC, 7% of women incarcerated in California are pregnant); health assessments and follow-up treatments for breast and cervical cancer, gynecological problems, health conditions related to surviving sexual, physical or mental abuse; annual pap smears, especially for women with HIV; and testing for the virus linked to cervical cancer. http://www.prisonerswithchildren.org/pubs/plata.pdf.

431 Human Rights Watch Women's Project, *All Too Familiar: Sexual Abuse of Women in U.S. State Prisons* (Washington, DC: Human Rights Watch, 1996), 2.

432 Karlene Faith, *Unruly Women: The Politics and Confinement of Resistance* (Vancouver: Press Gang Publishers, 1993), 235.

433 Julie Sullivan, "Compromising Positions: Prison Staff Work Closely with Inmates, But When a Relationship Becomes Too Close, It's a Threat to Security," *Spokesman Review*, June 17, 1998, 7.

434 Human Rights Watch Women's Project, *All Too Familiar: Sexual Abuse of Women in U.S. State Prisons* (Washington, DC: Human Rights Watch, 1996), 256–7.

435 Ibid., 259. A letter from Kebby Warner, dated February 27, 2008, confirms that this is still the case.

436 Dawn Amos, letter to the author, May 14, 2001.

437 Ibid., 123.

438 "Elsie," letter to the author, March 20, 2002. In many states, a prisoner must go through and exhaust the prison's bureaucratic grievance system before going to the courts for intervention.

439 Marcie Monroe, "Unite and Write—Stop Whining!" *The Fire Inside* 15 (August 2000), http://www.womenprisoners.org/fire/000237.html.

440 Michigan attorney Sharon Dunn, who works with incarcerated women, stated that the number of grievances did not adequately reflect the women's complaints and concerns. "There was certainly a suppression of being able to file grievances in the weeks after the move," she told Detroit newspaper *Metro Times*. Many women had no access to grievance forms and thus were unable

to voice their complaints. See Joseph Kirschke, "Hard Time," *Metro Times: Detroit's Weekly Alternative*, March 2, 2005, 12.

441 *Metro Times: Detroit's Weekly Alternative*, "Hard Time, Long Time," January 25, 2006.

442 Yraida L. Guanipa, e-mail to the author, February 11, 2006.

443 Yraida L. Guanipa, e-mail to the author, November 9, 2005.

444 Dawn, letter to the author, February 11, 2008.

445 "Elsie," letter to the author, March 20, 2002.

446 Mariane Sadelmyer, letter to *Sojourner's: The Women's Forum* 24, no. 8.

447 Marcie Monroe, "Unite and Write—Stop Whining!" *The Fire Inside* 15 (August 2000), http://www.womenprisoners.org/fire/000237.html.

448 Arditi, Goldberg, Hartle and Phelps, "The Sexual Segregation of American Prisons," *Yale Law Journal* 82 (1973): 1242.

449 *Glover v Johnson*, 478 F. Supp. 1075 (E.D. Mich. 1979).

450 Ibid.

451 Women in Prison Project of the Correctional Association of New York, *Bedford Hills 2005*, 6. *Todaro* did not solve all of the prison's health care problems. The Correctional Association also found that women with abnormal test results often experienced delays in receiving consistent follow-up care. Some of the women also reported that, rather than provide care, nurses were advising those with yeast infections to buy yogurt from the prison commissary to treat themselves.

452 "Defend the Lives of Women in Prison," *Prison News Service* 51 (May/June 1995): 2.

453 Stacy Barker, letter to the author, March 22, 2006. The state settled *Barker v. MDOC* for $95,000.

454 Human Rights Watch, *All Too Familiar*, 232. According to the Michigan Court of Appeals database (as of February 21, 2008), the trial date for *Neal* is January 14, 2008.

455 American Civil Liberties Union, "Know Your Rights: The Prison Litigation Reform Act (PLRA)", http://www.aclu.org/images/asset_upload_file79_25805.pdf. Congressional sponsors of the PLRA submitted a list entitled "Top Ten Frivolous Inmate Lawsuits," including a $1,000,000 suit because a prisoner's ice cream had melted and another because a litigant had been served chunky instead of smooth peanut butter. By highlighting lawsuits such as these, the bill's sponsors drew media and public attention away from the very real issues that many prisoners seek to remedy through the courts.

456 Norman Sinclair, "Prisoner Complaints Unheeded," *Detroit News*, May 24, 2005, http://www.detnews.com/2005/specialreport/0505/24/A01-191652.htm.

457 Kari Lydersen, "Red Tape Lets Guards Rape Women Prisoners, Suit Argues," *The New Standard*, January 6, 2006, http://newstandardnews.net/content/index.cfm/items/2730.

458 Ginger Adams Otis, "Female Prisoners Sue State for Guards' Sex Abuse," http://www.womensenews.org/article.cfm/dyn/aid/1257/context/archive.

459 Women in Prison Project for the Correctional Association of New York, *Women in Prison Fact Sheet* (June 2006), 47, 51. Cites the New York Department of Correctional Services, *Hub system*.

460 Kari Lydersen, "Red Tape Lets Guards Rape Women Prisoners, Suit Argues," *The New Standard*, January 6, 2006, http://newstandardnews.net/content/index.cfm/items/2730.

461 Norman Sinclair, "Prisoner Complaints Unheeded," *The Detroit News*, May 24, 2005, http://www.detnews.com/2005/specialreport/0505/24/A01-191652.htm.

462 *New York Times*, "Attacking Prisoners' Rights," December 21, 1999.

463 "California Agrees to Settle Inmates' HIV Privacy Claims," *AIDS Policy and Law* 12, no.17 (September 19, 1997).

464 Legal Services for Prisoners with Children (LSPC), "Strategies for Change: Litigation," http://www.prisonerswithchildren.org/issues/litigation.htm.

465 Silja J.A. Talvi, "Critical Condition: The Deaths of Eight Inmates Renew Concerns About Medical Care Inside California's Prisons," *In These Times*, April 2, 2001. Reprinted on Talvi's website: http://www.well.com/~sisu/prisondeaths.html.

466 LSPC, "Strategies for Change: Litigation."

467 California Coalition for Women Prisoners, http://www.womenprisoners.org/about/000085.html.

468 Barbara Bloom, Barbara Owen, and Stephanie Covington, *Gender-Responsive Strategies: Research, Practice, and Guiding Principles for Women Offenders* (National Institute of Corrections, 2003) 124, http://www.nicic.org/pubs/2003/018017.pdf.

469 Adam Liptak, "Prisons Often Shackle Pregnant Inmates in Labor," *New York Times*, March 2, 2006. See also Kaiser Daily Women's Health Policy, "Arkansas Department of Corrections Changes Policy Requiring Pregnant Inmates to Wear Metal Shackles During Labor," April 19, 2004. Available Online at: http://www.kaisernetwork.org/daily_reports/rep_index.cfm?DR_ID=23247

470 Juanita Diaz-Cotto, *Chicana Lives and Criminal Justice: Voices from El Barrio* (Austin, TX: University of Texas Press, 2006), 206, 211. Men in the local jail system had daily outdoor recreation time.

471 Michigan Department of Corrections, "Nunn Case Dismissed," March 7, 2003. http://www.michigan.gov/corrections/0,1607,7-119--62843--,00.html.

472 "Conditions at Women's Prisons: Litigation, Legislation, More Litigation," *Prisons and Corrections Forum: A Publication of the State Bar of Michigan's Prisons and Corrections Section* 3, no.1 (Spring/Summer 2000): 8.

473 *Seattle Post-Intelligencer*, "Inmate Impregnated by Guard Settles for $150,000," February 12, 1999. Reprinted at: http://www.encyclopedia.com/doc/1G1-64091142.html.

474 Julie Sullivan, "Compromising Positions: Prison Staff Work Closely with Inmates, But When a Relationship Becomes Too Close, It's a Threat to Security," *Spokesman Review*, June 17, 1998, 7.

475 Ibid.

476 Laurence M. Cruz, "House Passes Bill Criminalizing Sex Between Prison Guards and Inmates," *The Associated Press State and Local Wire*, April 8,

Notes

1999. Washington State laws about custodial sexual misconduct can be found at: http://apps.leg.wa.gov/RCW/default.aspx?cite9A.44.170 and http://apps.leg.wa.gov/RCW/default.aspx?cite9A.44.160.

477 Rob Thaxton, "Red, White and Blue Fascism," *Chain Reaction* 5: 6–7.

478 Bruce Golding, "Law Criminalized Guard-Inmate Sex," *The Journal News: A Gannett-Suburban Webpaper*, July 1, 2001,

479 Gary Heinlein, "Prison Sex Could Draw Prison Term," *The Detroit News*, October 11, 1999.

480 Marjorie M. Van Ochten, "Media Access in the MDOC," *Prisons and Corrections Forum: A Publication of the State Bar of Michigan's Prisons and Correction* 3, no.1 (Spring/Summer 2000): 3.

481 Diana Block, "Punishment, Women and the Media," *Sojourner: The Women's Forum* 25, no. 4. (December 1999): 39. See also http://prisonerswithchildren.org/issues/media.htm.

482 Ellen M. Barry, "Bad Medicine: Health Care Inadequacies in Women's Prisons," *Criminal Justice Magazine* 15, no. 1 (Spring 2001).

483 Dan Pens, "Bag'm, Tag'm and Bury'm: Wisconsin Prisoners Dying for Health Care," *Prison Legal News* 12, no. 2 (2001): 1–2.

484 Ibid.

485 Pens, 7.

486 Dawn Amos, letter to the author, May 14, 2001.

487 Mary Glover, telephone interview with the author, October 12, 2008. Disciplinary tickets adversely affect a prisoner's chance of an early release.

488 Barrilee Bannister, letter to the author, June 21, 2001.

489 Mariane Sadelmyer, letter to Sojourner: *The Women's Forum* 24:8 (April 1999): 4.

490 Stacy Barker, letter to the author, March 22, 2006.

491 Glover, telephone interview, October 12, 2008.

492 "Dedication," *The Fire Inside*. 4. (May 1997) http://www.womenprisoners.org/fire/000482.html.

493 A. Clay Thompson, "Cancer in the Cells," *San Francisco Bay Guardian*, February 24, 1999. Ted Koppel and ABC spent nearly a year negotiating with the California Department of Corrections to film inside Valley State Prison for Women. While Koppel was finally granted almost full access to the housing units, solitary confinement cells, chow halls, medical facilities, main yards and receiving areas, he was not allowed to set up prearranged interviews with prisoners.

494 Jenifer Warren, "Attorneys Criticize Propose Limits on Legal Visits to Inmates," *The Los Angeles Times*, July 25, 2002.

495 Joseph Kirschke, "Hard Time," *Metro Times: Detroit's Weekly Alternative*, March 2, 2005, 15.

496 Yraida L. Guanipa, e-mail to the author, November 9, 2005.

497 Glover, telephone interview, October 12, 2008.

498 Ibid.

499 "Elsie," letter to the author, May 8, 2002.

500 Yraida L. Guanipa, "Media," (unpublished work, August 20, 2005).
501 Paige and Beck, *Prisoners in 2004*, http://www.ojp.usdoj.gov/bjs/pub/pdf/p04.pdf.
502 Guanipa, "Media."
503 Ericka Jones, "Inside/Outside 1999-2001 Project Report," prepared for *Sojourner: The Women's Forum* (Boston, MA).
504 Sydney Heizer Villa, "Prison Transports LGBTs to Pre-Stonewall Era," *Sojourner: The Women's Forum* 27, no. 3 (November 2001): 23.
505 Jamie Bowen, "Private Prisons—It's All About Money," *Sojourner: The Women's Forum* 27, no.1 (September 2001): 15.
506 Sydney Heizer Villa, "Prison Transports LGBTs to Pre-Stonewall Era," *Sojourner: The Women's Forum* 27, no. 3 (November 2001): 23.
507 Ericka Jones, "Unanswered Questions in Prisoner's Suicide in Ohio," *Sojourner: The Women's Forum* 26, no. 4 (December 2000): 45.
508 Ericka Jones, "Inside/Outside 1999-2001 Project Report," prepared for Sojourner: *The Women's Forum* (Boston, MA).
509 "Elsie," letter to the author, October 8, 2005.
510 Rebecca Smith, letter to *Sojourner: The Women's Forum* 25, no. 9 (May 2000): 49.
511 Rhonda Leland, "The Need for Prison Education," *off our backs* 33, no. 11–12 (November/December 2004): 48.
512 Rhonda Leland, letter to *off our backs* 34, no. 9-10 (September/October 2004): 61.
513 California Coalition for Women Prisoners, http://www.womenprisoners.org/fire.
514 "Editorial: The Power of Writing," *The Fire Inside* 25 (Summer 2003), http://www.womenprisoners.org/fire/000336.html.
515 Break the Chains! organizer, e-mail to the author, September 27, 2005.
516 Eleanor Novek, "The 'Devil's Bargain:' A Natural History of a Prison Newspaper," presented at a convention of the Association for Education in Journalism and Mass Communication, Kansas City, MO, August 2003.
517 Rebecca Sanford, e-mail to the author, December 2, 2004.
518 Rebecca Sanford, e-mail to the author, December 2, 2004.
519 Eleanor Novek, "The 'Devil's Bargain:' A Natural History of a Prison Newspaper," presented at a convention of the Association for Education in Journalism and Mass Communication, Kansas City, MO, August 2003.
520 Melvina McClain, "Education is the Key to Freedom and Power," *Perceptions* 3, no.3 (October 2002): 10. See also Jennifer Cebula's interview on the same page.
521 Marianne Brown, letter to the author, September 20, 2005.
522 Marianne Brown, letter to the author, December 22, 2006.
523 Yraida L. Guanipa, e-mail to the author, September 17, 2005.
524 Barrilee Bannister, "The Creation of *Tenacious: Writings from Women in Prison*," *Clamor* 31 (March/April 2005): 63.
525 Stephanie Walters, letter to the author, July 21, 2007.
526 Yraida L. Guanipa, e-mail to the author, July 12, 2005.
527 Yraida L. Guanipa, e-mail to the author, July 11, 2005.

Notes

528 Yraida L. Guanipa, e-mail to the author, July 10, 2005.

529 Steffi Lewis, e-mail to the author, July 12, 2006.

530 Yraida L. Guanipa, e-mail to the author, July 4, 2005.

531 Yraida L. Guanipa, e-mail to the author, December 10, 2005.

532 "Elsie," letter to the author, November 30, 2005.

533 Oregon Department of Corrections, *Mail Notice Violation*, April 5, 2004.

534 J.L., letter to *Sojourner: The Women's Forum* 25, no.11 (July/August 2001): 13.

535 Ericka Jones, "Unanswered Questions in Prisoner's Suicide in Ohio," *Sojourner: The Women's Forum* 26, no. 4 (December 2000): 45.

536 Yraida L. Guanipa, e-mail to the author, May 14, 2006

537 Yraida L. Guanipa, e-mail to the author, May 21, 2006.

538 Ibid.

539 Guanipa continued her e-mail series after her release in December 2006, renaming it "Prison Issues Talk." She chronicled the challenges and obstacles she faced as an ex-prisoner trying to readjust to the outside world.

540 Nicole Chaison, e-mail to the author, December 13, 2004.

541 Rebecca Sanford, e-mail to the author, December 2, 2004.

542 California Coalition for Women Prisoners, "About Us," http://www.womenprisoners.org/about/000082.html.

543 Diana Block, "Punishment, Women and the Media," *Sojourner: The Women's Forum* 25, no. 4. (December 1999): 39.

544 Yraida L. Guanipa, "Media," (unpublished work, August 20, 2005).

545 Barrilee Bannister, letter to the author, September 11, 2005.

546 On March 1, 2003, the INS (Immigration and Naturalization Service) was abolished and its functions transferred to the new Department of Homeland Security. The Bureau of Immigration and Customs Enforcement (ICE), part of Border and Transportation Security, a separate enforcement directorate, was set up to oversee the detention of asylum seekers.

547 In 2002, approximately half of the 202,000 immigrants detained by INS were from Mexico. Other substantially large populations detained by the INS were originally from Cuba, El Salvador, Guatemala, Honduras, China, Jamaica, Haiti and the Dominican Republic. See Office of Immigration Statistics, Department of Homeland Security, *2003 Statistical Yearbook of the Immigration and Naturalization Services*, 175.

548 G. Atchison, "The War at Home Targets Immigrants," *Sojourner: The Women's Forum* 27, no.6 (2002): 9. MassINC is a public-policy think tank promoting the growth and vitality of the middle class in Massachusetts through Economic Prosperity, Lifelong Learning, Safe Neighborhoods and Civic Renewal.

549 Steven A. Holmes, "Immigration Aids Strong Growth in Many U.S. Metropolitan Areas," *Laredo Morning Times*, May 11, 2000.

550 Diana Smith, "Poll Shows Security Important to U.S.," *Laredo Morning Times*, February 24, 2003.

551 M. G. Fuentes, "No a los ilegales," *Hoy*, Jan 4, 2005, 3.

552 E. E. Castillo, "Border Feared Vulnerable to Terrorists," *Laredo Morning Times*, October 8, 2004.

553 Rachel L. Swarns, "As Senators Debate Immigration Bill, Frist Offers His Own," *New York Times*, March 17, 2006.

554 In 2001, in *Zadvydas v. Davis*, the Supreme Court curtailed the INS's ability to detain deportees indefinitely.

555 Mark Dow, interview by Amy Goodman, *Democracy Now!*, May 4, 2006. Available Online at: http://www.democracynow.org/2006/5/4/two_immigrants_who_followed_the_path. For more on the Interior Enforcement Strategy, see Richard M. Stana, "Immigration Enforcement: Challenges to Implementing the INS Interior Enforcement Strategy," testimony before the Subcommittee on Immigration and Claims, Committee on the Judiciary, House of Representatives, June 19, 2002. Available online at http://www.gao.gov/cgi-bin/getrpt?GAO-02-861T.

556 "A Look Inside U.S. Immigration Prisons," *Democracy Now!*, May 4, 2006. Transcript at: http://www.democracynow.org/2006/5/4/a_look_inside_u_s_immigration.

557 Joseph Greene (Acting Deputy Executive Associate Commissioner for Field Operations) and Edward McElroy (District Director, New York, U.S. Immigration and Naturalization Service), statement before the House Committee on the Judiciary Subcommittee on Immigration and Claims regarding a Review of Department of Justice Immigration Detention Policies, December 19, 2001, http://www.ilw.com/immigdaily/News/2001,1228-Greene.pdf.

558 Office of Inspector General, Department of Homeland Security, *Detention and Removal of Illegal Aliens*, OIG-06-33, April 2006, 2. Available Online at: http://www.oig.dhs.gov/assets/Mgmt/OIG_06-33_Apr06.pdf. As of this writing (March 7, 2008), no follow-up data has been made publicly available.

559 Office of Immigration Statistics, Department of Homeland Security, *2003 Statistical Yearbook of the Immigration and Naturalization Services*, 177.

560 Kendra A. Wallace, e-mail to Tara Magner, Policy Director of the National Immigrant Justice Center, May 14, 2008.

561 Hamdiya/Yvonne Cooks, "Post Prison Detention," *The Fire Inside* 30 (Spring/Summer 2005), http://www.womenprisoners.org/fire/000554.html.

562 Human Rights Watch reports that since IIRIRA was passed, at least 1.6 million children and spouses have been separated from their relatives because of deportation. However, neither child welfare agencies nor INS gather information on the families of deportees or the citizenship of foster children's parents. Julianne Ong Hing and Seth Wessler, "When an Immigrant Mom Gets Arrested," *ColorLines* 45 (July/August 2008), http://www.colorlines.com/article.php?ID=379.

563 Nina Bernstein, "A Mother Deported, and a Child Left Behind," *The New York Times*, November 24, 2004, http://www.nytimes.com/2004/11/24/nyregion/24deport.html.

564 Peter Prengaman, "Immigration Activist Deported to Mexico," *Breitbart.com*, August 20, 2007, http://www.usatoday.com/news/nation/2007-08-20-2962407204_x.htm. See also Gretchen Ruethling, "Chicago Woman's Stand Stirs Immigration Debate," *New York Times*, August 19, 2006.

Notes

565 Cheryl Little and Joan Friedland, *Krome's Invisible Prisoners: Cycles of Abuse and Neglect* (Miami, FL: Florida Immigrant Advocacy Center, Inc., 1996), 3.

566 Human Rights Watch, *Locked Away: Immigration Detainees in Jail in the United States*, September 1998, www.hrw.org/reports98/us-immig/Ins989-05.htm.

567 Matthew Purdy and Celia W. Dugger, "Legacy of Immigrants' Uprising: New Jail Operator, Little Change," *New York Times*, July 7, 1996.

568 Cooks, "Post Prison Detention."

569 Ibid.

570 Women's Commission for Refugee Women and Children, *Innocents in Jail: INS Moves Refugee Women from Krome to Turner Guilford Knight Correctional Center, Miami* (New York: 2001), 13. http://womensrefugeecommission.org/docs/ins_tgk.pdf.

571 Women's Commission for Refugee Women and Children, *Behind Locked Doors: Abuse of Refugee Women at the Krome Detention Center* (New York: Women's Commission for Refugee Women and Children, 2000), 15.

572 Ibid., 4.

573 Ibid., 16.

574 Women's Commission for Refugee Women and Children, *Innocents in Jail: INS Moves Refugee Women from Krome to Turner Guilford Knight Correctional Center, Miami* (New York: 2001), 18. http://womensrefugeecommission.org/docs/ins_tgk.pdf.

575 Kazu Haga, "Alex Sanchez: Gang Violence Prevention Activist Released from INS!" *The Prison Book Project Newsletter* (Fall 2002): 5.

576 Women's Commission for Refugee Women and Children, *Innocents in Jail: INS Moves Refugee Women from Krome to Turner Guilford Knight Correctional Center, Miami* (New York: 2001), 19. http://womensrefugeecommission.org/docs/ins_tgk.pdf

577 Ibid.

578 Ibid., 15.

579 David Crary, "Critics Decry Immigrant Detention Push," *Washington Post*, June 24, 2006, http://www.washingtonpost.com/wp-dyn/content/article/2006/06/24/AR2006062400514.html. As of May 2008, 50% of all female detainees are held at ten facilities: Pearsall (TX), Broward (Pompano Beach, FL), Willacy (Raymondville, TX), Pinal County Jail (Florence, AZ), Hutto (Taylor, TX), Etowah County Jail (Gadsen, AL), San Diego (CA), Houston (TX), Tacoma (WA) and Port Isabel (Los Fresnos, TX). Kendra A. Wallace, e-mail to Tara Magner, May 14, 2008.

580 Jane Guskin and David Wilson, *The Politics of Immigration: Questions and Answers* (New York: Monthly Review Press, 2007), 127. Cites Detention Watch Network, *Immigration Detention—An Overview*. Available as Word document at: http://www.detentionwatchnetwork.org/educatecongress

581 Alisa Solomon, "Detainees Equal Dollars: The Rise in Immigrant Incarcerations Drive a Prison Boom," *The Village Voice*, August 14–20, 2002, http://villagevoice.com/news/0233,Solomon,37426,1.html.

582 Human Rights Watch, *Locked Away: Immigrant Detainees in Jails in the U.S.* (New York: Human Rights Watch, 1998), 63.

583 Sarah Daniel, letter to the author, May 25, 2006.

584 Women's Commission for Refugee Women and Children, *Innocents in Jail: INS Moves Refugee Women from Krome to Turner Guilford Knight Correctional Center, Miami* (New York: 2001), 3. http://womensrefugeecommission.org/docs/ins_tgk.pdf.

585 Women's Commission for Refugee Women and Children, *Liberty Denied: Women Seeking Asylum Imprisoned in the United States* (New York: 1997),17, http://womensrefugeecommission.org/docs/liberty.pdf.

586 Women's Commission for Refugee Women and Children, *A Cry for Help: Chinese Women in INS Detention* (New York: 1995), 8. The Women's Commission was unable to verify the exact number of female detainees housed at Orleans Parish Prison. Numbers provided by the INS and asylum advocates ranged from 10 to 13. The women had arrived on the *Golden Venture*, a ship smuggling over 300 Chinese from the Fujian Province that had run aground off Rockaway Beach, New York.

587 RJ, letter to the author, January 29, 2008.

588 Women's Commission for Refugee Women and Children, *Innocents in Jail: INS Moves Refugee Women from Krome to Turner Guilford Knight Correctional Center, Miami* (New York: 2001), 7. http://womensrefugeecommission.org/docs/ins_tgk.pdf.

589 Ibid.,10.

590 Women's Commission for Refugee Women and Children, Liberty Denied: Women Seeking Asylum Imprisoned in the United States (New York: 1997), 13.

591 The *Golden Venture* was a ship smuggling over 300 Chinese from the Fujian province to the U.S. It made headlines in 1993 when it ran aground off New York's Rockaway Beach. Ten passengers drowned while trying to swim to shore. The others were detained in INS centers, local jails and state prisons for years while their asylum claims were reviewed.

592 Women's Commission for Refugee Women and Children, *Liberty Denied: Women Seeking Asylum Imprisoned in the United States* (New York: 1997), 17.

593 Although these fans produced excessive noise, most detainees told Human Rights Watch observers that they preferred the noise to the extreme heat of non-circulating air. Human Rights Watch letter to INS Commissioner Doris Meissner, October 30, 2000, http://hrw.org/english/docs/2000/10/30/usdom649.htm.

594 Ibid.

595 Donna Gehrke and Karen Branch, "Sit-Down Strike Held at Krome," *Miami Herald*, August 27, 1991.

596 The INS has a "no-release" policy for Haitian asylum seekers. For Cuban asylum-seekers, the agency employs a "wet foot/dry foot" rule: Cubans intercepted at sea are returned to Cuba while those who make it to U.S. soil are allowed to stay. Both policies are still in effect today, although Brothers to the Rescue, an anti-Castro group that searches for Cuban refugees in the Florida Straits, insists that the INS often violates this rule, repatriating asylum seekers

who have landed on shore. "Briefing on Haitian Asylum Seekers and U.S. Immigration Policy," June 21, 2002, http://www.law.umaryland.edu/marshall/usccr/documents/civrightsbriefhaitianasylum.pdf.

597 Andres Viglucci and Harold Maass, "Hunger Strike Continues for Some," *Miami Herald*, January 9, 1993.

598 Andres Viglucci, "159 Stick to Hunger Strike: Meeting with INS Fails to End Krome Protest," *Miami Herald*, January 5, 1993.

599 Andres Viglucci, "More Haitians Being Freed from Krome," *Miami Herald*, July 10, 1993. The article does not specify the gender(s) of the released detainees.

600 Women's Commission for Refugee Women and Children, *A Cry for Help: Chinese Women in INS Detention* (New York: 1995), 9.

601 These 22 women, some of whom had also been held in New Orleans' OPP, included eight from the *Golden Venture*. See Kenneth B. Noble, "Golden Venture Refugees on Hunger Strike in California to Protest Detention," *New York Times*, December 2, 1995.

602 Candy Kit Har Chan, "Detained Refugees End Hunger Strike: Fate of Chinese Immigrants Still in Question," *Asianweek* 17, no.9 (January 5, 1996): 8.

603 Women's Commission for Refugee Women and Children, *Behind Locked Doors: Abuse of Refugee Women at the Krome Detention Center* (New York: Women's Commission for Refugee Women and Children, 2000), 14.

604 In November 2003, the federal government agreed to pay Madrazo $95,000 to satisfy "any and all claims." The payment, according to the settlement, does not imply that the government was liable for Smith's crime. See Alfonso Chardy, "$95,000 Paid in Sex Abuse Suit," *Miami Herald*, November 26, 2003.

605 Alisa Solomon, "Nightmare in Miami," *Village Voice*, March 20 to 26, 2002. Madrazo's assailant, Lemar Smith, originally charged with two felonies, was allowed to plead guilty to two misdemeanor counts. He was sentenced to eight months in prison and one year probation. The other officer, Clarence Parker, had lost his job at Krome during the investigation and was hired at a facility for juvenile offenders. A judge sentenced him to three years probation and ordered Parker to immediately resign from his new job.

606 Alisa Solomon, "Nightmare in Miami," *The Village Voice*, March 20 to 26, 2002. Krome continued to be used for male detainees, who allege that physical and sexual abuse have continued.

607 Women's Commission for Refugee Women and Children, *Innocents in Jail: INS Moves Refugee Women from Krome to Turner Guilford Knight Correctional Center, Miami* (New York: 2001), 6. http://womensrefugeecommission.org/docs/ins_tgk.pdf.

608 Ibid., 11.

609 A credible fear interview is a screening for those seeking asylum from persecution in their home countries. If the person passes the interview, he/she will be allowed to present a claim for asylum. If the asylum officer determines that there is no credible fear, the person is deported.

610 Women's Commission for Refugee Women and Children, *Behind Locked Doors: Abuse of Refugee Women at the Krome Detention Center* (New York: Women's Commission for Refugee Women and Children, 2000), 20.

611 Women's Commission for Refugee Women and Children, *Innocents in Jail: INS Moves Refugee Women from Krome to Turner Guilford Knight Correctional Center, Miami* (New York: 2001), 26. http://womensrefugeecommission.org/docs/ins_tgk.pdf.

612 Ibid., 10.

613 Women's Commission for Refugee Women and Children, *Behind Locked Doors: Abuse of Refugee Women at the Krome Detention Center* (New York: Women's Commission for Refugee Women and Children, 2000),15.

614 Ibid.

615 Ibid., 1.

616 Katherine Beckett and Theodore Sasson, *The Politics of Injustice: Crime and Punishment in America* (Thousand Oaks, CA: Sage Publications, 2004), 52.

617 Richard Milhous Nixon, "Message on Crime Control" (State of the Union Address, 1973). Full text available Online at: http://janda.org/politxts/state%20 of%20union%20addresses/1970-1974%20Nixon%20T/RMN73L.html.

618 Nicole Hahn Rafter, *Partial Justice: Women, Prisons, and Social Control* (New Brunswick: Transaction Publishers, 1990), 133.

619 Ibid., 143. From 1888 to 1922, black women constituted between 83 to 90% of women imprisoned in Tennessee.

620 Ibid.,141.

621 Mary Ellen Curtin, *Black Prisoners and Their World, Alabama, 1865–1900*, Carter G. Woodson Institute series in Black Studies (Charlottesville: University Press of Virginia, 2000), 6.

622 Nancy Kurshan, "Women and Imprisonment in the U.S.: History and Current Reality," http://prisonactivist.org/women/women-and-imprisonment.html.

623 Curtin, *Black Prisoners and Their World*, 6–7.

624 After instituting the county convict system, counties increasingly charged people with misdemeanors so as to keep them under local—rather than state—control. (Curtin, 7.)

625 Curtin, *Black Prisoners and Their World*, 109. Cites J.D. Douglass letter to W.D. Lee, July 11, 1888 (Letter Book, Feb–Sept 1888, DOC, Alabama Department of Archives and History).

626 Ibid.,126. Black women prisoners refused to comply with the rules of either the prison or the work camps, refusing to wear the prison garb assigned to them or to return directly to the prison once they had finished their work in the community, leading one inspector to fume, "The female convicts at this prison are a very unruly set and give a good deal of trouble."

627 Mary Ellen Curtin, "The 'Human World' of Black Women in Alabama Prisons, 1870–1900" in *Hidden Histories of Women in the New South,* ed. Virginia Bernhard, Betty Brandon, Elizabeth Fox-Genovese, Theda Perdue and Elizabeth Hayes Turner (Columbia, MO: University of Missouri Press, 1994), 20. Cites *Alabama General Assembly, Testimony Before the Joint*

Notes

Committee of the General Assembly, Appointed to Examine into the Convict System of Alabama, Session of 1888–89 (Montgomery: Brown Printing Co, 1889), 125.

628 Mary Ellen Curtin, *Black Prisoners and Their World*, Alabama, 1865–1900 (Carter G. Woodson Institute series in Black studies. Charlottesville: University Press of Virginia, 2000), 120. Cites Nicole Hahn Rafter, *Partial Justice: Women, Prisons, and Social Control* (New Brunswick: Transaction Publishers, 1990), chapter 6.

629 Nicole Hahn Rafter, *Partial Justice: Women, Prisons, and Social Control* (New Brunswick: Transaction Publishers, 1990), 141.

630 Ibid., 132.

631 Nancy Kurshan, "Women and Imprisonment in the U.S.: History and Current Reality," http://prisonactivist.org/women/women-and-imprisonment.html.

632 Nicole Hahn Rafter, *Partial Justice: Women, Prisons, and Social Control* (New Brunswick: Transaction Publishers, 1990), 25.

633 Joanne Belknap, *The Invisible Woman: Gender, Crime, and Justice* (Belmont, CA: Thomson/Wadsworth, 2007), 147.

634 Ibid., 147.

635 Estelle Freedman, *Their Sisters' Keepers: Women's Prison Reform in America*, 1830–1930 (Ann Arbor: University of Michigan Press, 1981), 16. Freedman asserts that virtually every account of prisons and jails during that time period mentions illegitimate births by women in custody.

636 Correctional Association of New York, *Inmates Under Custody: 1950–2003*, http://www.correctionalassociation.org/publications/factsheets.htm#WIPP

637 Drug Policy Alliance, *Race and the Drug War*, www.drugpolicy.org/communities/race.

638 Christian Parenti, *Lockdown America: Police and Prisons in the Age of Crisis* (London: Verso, 2001), 57. Cites *Sourcebook of Criminal Justice Statistics*, 1982, Table 4.7, BJS (Wash, DC: Government Printing Office, 1983), 400; *Sourcebook of Criminal Justice Statistics*, 1991, Table 4.7, BJS (Wash, DC: Government Printing Office, 1992), 444.

639 Anecdotal evidence suggests that the act resulted in a significant increase in women sent to federal prison, but I was unable to find any statistics or information on the number of women convicted of "conspiracy" under the Anti-Drug Abuse Act.

640 The total number of people in federal and state prison that year was 196,429. U.S. Department of Commerce, *Statistical Abstract of the United States, 1973*, 94th ed, www2.census.gov/prod2/statcomp/documents/1973-01.pdf.

641 Julia Sudbury, *Global Lockdown: Gender, Race and the Rise of the Prison Industrial Complex Around the World* (New York: Routledge, 2005).

642 Women in Prison Project of the Correctional Association of New York, *Women in Prison Fact Sheet*, http://www.correctionalassociation.org/publications/factsheets.htm#WIPP.

643 Between 1996 and 1999, over 96,000 women were subject to the welfare ban because of past drug convictions. However, researcher Patricia Allard points

out, "This [number] represents a very conservative estimate, because some reporting states provided limited data. For instance, some states only provided incarceration data and not probation data for felony drug convictions, leaving a potentially significant number of women unaccounted for in this estimate." Patricia Allard. "Crime, Punishment, and Economic Violence," in *Color of Violence: The Incite! Anthology* (Cambridge, MA: South End Press, 2006) 158, 293.

644 Lynne Haney, "Introduction: Gender, Welfare and States of Punishment," *Social Politics* 11, no. 3 (Fall 2004): 338.

645 Jill McCorkell, "Criminally Dependent? Gender, Punishment and the Rhetoric of Welfare Reform," Social Politics 11, no. 3 (Fall 2004):389.

646 Lynne Haney, "Introduction: Gender, Welfare and States of Punishment," *Social Politics* 11, no. 3 (Fall 2004): 342.

647 Christopher J. Mumola and Allen Beck, *Prisoners in 1996*, special report to the Department of Justice, July 21, 1997, 1, http://bjs.ojp.usdoj.gov/content/pub/pdf/p96.pdf.

648 Allen J. Beck and Paige M. Harrison, *Prisoners in 2000*, special report for the Department of Justice, August 2001, http://bjs.ojp.usdoj.gov/content/pub/pdf/p00.pdf.

649 Mary Ellen Curtin, "The 'Human World' of Black Women in Alabama Prisons, 1870–1900" in *Hidden Histories of Women in the New South*, ed. Virginia Bernhard, Betty Brandon, Elizabeth Fox-Genovese, Theda Perdue and Elizabeth Hayes Turner (Columbia, MO: University of Missouri Press, 1994), 21.

650 Mary Ellen Curtin, *Black Prisoners and Their World, Alabama*, 1865–1900 (Carter G. Woodson Institute series in Black studies. Charlottesville: University Press of Virginia, 2000), 12.

651 Bureau of Justice Statistics, *Census of State and Federal Correctional Facilities, 2000*, August 2003; Bureau of Justice Statistics. *Prison and Jail Inmates at Midyear 2004*, April 2005.

652 Linda Rocawich, "Lock 'Em Up: America's All-Purpose Cure for Crime," *The Progressive*, August 1987, 16.

653 Nancy Kurshan, "Women and Imprisonment in the U.S.: History and Current Reality," http://prisonactivist.org/women/women-and-imprisonment.html.

654 Dodge, " 'One Female Prisoner is of More Trouble than Twenty Males': Women Convicts in Illinois Prisons, 1836-1896," *Journal of Social History* (Summer 1999). Cites Freedman, 13.

655 Until the beginning of the twentieth century, there were two models of prisons for women: reformatories and custodial prisons. Reformatories housed women whose behavior had been deemed immoral; their objective was to recondition women to accept socially approved gender roles. Custodial prisons were designed solely to warehouse women. There was no pretense of rehabilitation or reform for prison inmates. No reformatories ever existed for men, regardless of how immoral or socially unacceptable their behavior. While Hudson was the first reformatory in New York State, it was not the first facility for women inmates. In 1835, a women's custodial prison for women was opened in Sing

Sing. During its 42 year existence, it experienced continual overcrowding and was finally closed in 1877.

656 "Albion Correctional Facility," http://www.correctionhistory.org/html/chronicl/docs2day/albion.html.

657 Clifford Young, *Women's Prisons: Past and Present and Other New York State Prison History* (Elmira Reformatory, NY: The Summary Press, 1932), 38.

658 State of New York Department of Correctional Services, *Hub System*, 3.

659 Real Cost of Prisons, "CA: New Prison Beds for Women Rejected by Legislative Committee," April 17, 2007, http://realcostofprisons.org/blog/archives/2007/04/ca_new_prison_b.html.

660 Linda Rocawich, "Lock 'Em Up: America's All-Purpose Cure for Crime," *The Progressive*, August 1987, 16.

661 UBUNTU is a women of color and survivor-led coalition in Durham, North Carolina, working to create a world free of sexual violence. They have started by creating small systems of community accountability while also holding film screenings, performances and workshops to raise awareness about the impact of gendered violence. In New York after the murder of two young women by the police, Sista II Sista, a collective of women of color fighting for social justice, established Sistas Liberated Ground, a zone in their neighborhood where crimes against women would not be tolerated. The group instituted an "action line" which women could call and not only inform the group as to what was happening, but also explore the options that they—and the group—could take to change the situation instead of simply calling the police. The group has also pushed the community to hold its members accountable for the harm they caused. In California, Generation Five is working to end childhood sexual abuse in five generations by addressing the root causes of violence rather than relying on incarcerating abusers.

662 Angela, Davis. *Are Prisons Obsolete?* (New York: Seven Stories Press, 2003), 103.

663 Alexander Lee, *"Changing Actions"* (lecture, the Scholar and Feminist Conference: Engendering Justice: Prisons, Activism and Change, Barnard College, New York. April 8, 2006).

664 Rachel Galindo, letter to the author, May 27, 2008.

INDEX

"Passim" (literally "scattered") indicates intermittent discussion of a topic over a cluster of pages.

Index

Index

Index

ACKNOWLEDGMENTS

Many thanks and much appreciation go to:

All of the women who courageously and patiently shared their stories with me. I am continually inspired by their fortitude.

Jessica Ross and Melissa Morrone, who allowed me to bounce ideas off them during countless Books Through Bars sessions and patiently read and critiqued draft after draft.

China Martens for her continual willingness to edit, listen to and encourage me.

Maria Muentes at Families for Freedom for her feedback on my chapter on immigrant women and for continuing to keep me updated about women in detention.

Jenna Freedman for material access and intellectual assistance.

The folks at ABC No Rio's computer center (particularly Daniel) for both tech support and their willingness to accommodate my mess.

Steven Englander for his no-nonsense advice and support through the book process.

Siu Loong for sleeping so soundly during those first years, scribbling all over my letters, charming the COs into letting us in when visiting hours were almost over, and forcing me to articulate my thoughts into easy-to-understand statements.

Jeanne Theoharis at Brooklyn College for helping me shape the early versions of this.

Jerome White-Bey, Eric of Austin-ABC and Anthony Rayson for pushing me not to keep this work hidden in a drawer.

Fly and Jessica Mills for putting me in contact with PM Press.

Chris Dodge for his eagle eyes and for going above and beyond what I thought an indexer usually does.

Jason Justice for his continued patience with my many changes.

Ramsey Kanaan, Romy Ruukel and Andrea Gibbons at PM Press for working with me to ensure that this book does justice to these women and their experiences.

Sex, Race, and Class—The Perspective of Winning: A Selection of Writings 1952-2011

ISBN: 978-1-60486-032-0
PM Press • $20.00 • 320 pages
By Selma James
Foreword by: Marcus Rediker
Introduction by: Nina López

In 1972 Selma James set out a new political perspective. Her starting point was the millions of unwaged women who, working in the home and on the land, were not seen as "workers" and their struggles viewed as outside of the class struggle. Based on her political training in the Johnson-Forest Tendency, founded by her late husband C.L.R. James, on movement experience South and North, and on a respectful study of Marx, she redefined the working class to include sectors previously dismissed as "marginal."

For James, the class struggle presents itself as the conflict between the reproduction and survival of the human race, and the domination of the market with its exploitation, wars, and ecological devastation. She sums up her strategy for change as "Invest in Caring not Killing."

This selection, spanning six decades, traces the development of this perspective in the course of building an international campaigning network. It includes the classic *The Power of Women and the Subversion of the Community* which launched the "domestic labor debate," the exciting *Hookers in the House of the Lord* which describes a church occupation by sex workers, an incisive review of the C.L.R. James masterpiece *The Black Jacobins*, a reappraisal of the novels of Jean Rhys and of the leadership of Julius Nyerere, the groundbreaking *Marx and Feminism*, and more published here for the first time.

The writing is lucid and without jargon. The ideas, never abstract, spring from the experience of organising, from trying to make sense of the successes and the setbacks, and from the need to find a way forward.

> "It's time to acknowledge James's path-breaking analysis: from 1972 she re-interpreted the capitalist economy to show that it rests on the usually invisible unwaged caring work of women."
> — Dr. Peggy Antrobus, feminist, author of *The Global Women's Movement: Origins, Issues and Strategies*

Don't Leave Your Friends Behind: Concrete Ways to Support Families in Social Justice Movements and Communities

ISBN: 978-1-60486-396-3
PM Press • $17.95 • 256 pages
Edited by Victoria Law and China Martens

Don't Leave Your Friends Behind is a collection of concrete tips, suggestions, and narratives on ways that non-parents can support parents, children, and caregivers in their communities, social movements, and collective processes. *Don't Leave Your Friends Behind* focuses on issues affecting children and caregivers within the larger framework of social justice, mutual aid, and collective liberation.

How do we create new, nonhierarchical structures of support and mutual aid, and include all ages in the struggle for social justice? There are many books on parenting, but few on being a good community member and a good ally to parents, caregivers, and children as we collectively build a strong all-ages culture of resistance. Any group of parents will tell you how hard their struggles are and how they are left out, but no book focuses on how allies can address issues of caretakers' and children's oppression. Many well-intentioned childless activists don't interact with young people on a regular basis and don't know how. *Don't Leave Your Friends Behind* provides them with the resources and support to get started.

Contributors include: The Bay Area Childcare Collective, Ramsey Beyer, Rozalinda Borcilă, Mariah Boone, Marianne Bullock, Lindsey Campbell, Briana Cavanaugh, CRAP! Collective, a de la maza pérez tamayo, Ingrid DeLeon, Clayton Dewey, David Gilbert, A.S. Givens, Jason Gonzales, Tiny (aka Lisa Gray-Garcia), Jessica Hoffman, Heather Jackson, Rahula Janowski, Sine Hwang Jensen, Agnes Johnson, Simon Knaphus, Victoria Law, London Pro-Feminist Men's Group, Amariah Love, Oluko Lumumba, mama raccoon, Mamas of Color Rising/Young Women United, China Martens, Noemi Martinez, Kathleen McIntyre, Stacey Milbern, Jessica Mills, Tomas Moniz, Coleen Murphy, Maegan 'la Mamita Mala' Ortiz, Traci Picard, Amanda Rich, Fabiola Sandoval, Cynthia Ann Schemmer, Mikaela Shafer, Mustafa Shakur, Kate Shapiro, Jennifer Silverman, Harriet Moon Smith, Mariahadessa Ekere Tallie, Darran White Tilghman, Jessica Trimbath, Max Ventura, and Mari Villaluna.

> "A powerful mixture of self-help and literature, putting 'family values' in a new light and on the agenda of social justice movements. And it's not just self-help for radicals who are parents, but food for everyone who seeks to become their better, more compassionate selves."
> —Roxanne Dunbar-Ortiz, activist, teacher, author of *Outlaw Woman: A Memoir of the War Years: 1960-1975*

Lucasville:
The Untold Story of a Prison Uprising, 2nd ed.

ISBN: 978-1-60486-224-9
PM Press • $20.00 • 256 pages
By Staughton Lynd
Preface by Mumia Abu-Jamal

Lucasville tells the story of one of the longest prison uprisings in United States history. At the maximum security Southern Ohio Correctional Facility in Lucasville, Ohio, prisoners seized a major area of the prison on Easter Sunday, 1993. More than 400 prisoners held L block for eleven days. Nine prisoners alleged to have been informants, or "snitches," and one hostage correctional officer, were murdered. There was a negotiated surrender. Thereafter, almost wholly on the basis of testimony by prisoner informants who received deals in exchange, five spokespersons or leaders were tried and sentenced to death, and more than a dozen others received long sentences.

Lucasville examines both the causes of the disturbance, what happened during the eleven days, and the fairness of the trials. Particular emphasis is placed on the inter-racial character of the action, as evidenced in the slogans that were found painted on walls after the surrender: "Black and White Together," "Convict Unity," and "Convict Race."

An eloquent Foreword by Mumia Abu-Jamal underlines these themes. He states, as does the book, that the men later sentenced to death "sought to minimize violence, and indeed, according to substantial evidence, saved the lives of several men, prisoner and guard alike." Of the five men, three black and two white, who were sentenced to death, Mumia declares: "They rose above their status as prisoners, and became, for a few days in April 1993, what rebels in Attica had demanded a generation before them: men. As such, they did not betray each other; they did not dishonor each other; they reached beyond their prison "tribes" to reach commonality."

> "*Lucasville* is one of the most powerful indictments of our 'justice system' I have ever read. What comes across is a litany of flaws deep in the system, and recognizably not unique to *Lucasville*. The detailed transcripts (yes, oral history!) give great power to the whole story."
> — Howard Zinn, author of *A People's History of the United States*

FRIENDS OF PM PRESS

These are indisputably momentous times—the financial system is melting down globally and the Empire is stumbling. Now more than ever there is a vital need for radical ideas.

In the four years since its founding—and on a mere shoestring—PM Press has risen to the formidable challenge of publishing and distributing knowledge and entertainment for the struggles ahead. With over 175 releases to date, we have published an impressive and stimulating array of literature, art, music, politics, and culture. Using every available medium, we've succeeded in connecting those hungry for ideas and information to those putting them into practice.

Friends of PM allows you to directly help impact, amplify, and revitalize the discourse and actions of radical writers, filmmakers, and artists. It provides us with a stable foundation from which we can build upon our early successes and provides a much-needed subsidy for the materials that can't necessarily pay their own way. You can help make that happen—and receive every new title automatically delivered to your door once a month—by joining as a Friend of PM Press. And, we'll throw in a free T-shirt when you sign up.

Here are your options:

- **$25 a month** Get all books and pamphlets plus 50% discount on all webstore purchases

- **$40 a month** Get all PM Press releases (including CDs and DVDs) plus 50% discount on all webstore purchases

- **$100 a month** Superstar—Everything plus PM merchandise, free downloads, and 50% discount on all webstore purchases

For those who can't afford $25 or more a month, we're introducing **Sustainer Rates** at $15, $10 and $5. Sustainers get a free PM Press T-shirt and a 50% discount on all purchases from our website.

Your Visa or Mastercard will be billed once a month, until you tell us to stop. Or until our efforts succeed in bringing the revolution around. Or the financial meltdown of Capital makes plastic redundant. Whichever comes first.

ABOUT PM PRESS

PM Press was founded at the end of 2007 by a small collection of folks with decades of publishing, media, and organizing experience. PM Press co-conspirators have published and distributed hundreds of books, pamphlets, CDs, and DVDs. Members of PM have founded enduring book fairs, spearheaded victorious tenant organizing campaigns, and worked closely with bookstores, academic conferences, and even rock bands to deliver political and challenging ideas to all walks of life. We're old enough to know what we're doing and young enough to know what's at stake.

We seek to create radical and stimulating fiction and non-fiction books, pamphlets, T-shirts, visual and audio materials to entertain, educate and inspire you. We aim to distribute these through every available channel with every available technology—whether that means you are seeing anarchist classics at our bookfair stalls; reading our latest vegan cookbook at the café; downloading geeky fiction e-books; or digging new music and timely videos from our website.

PM Press is always on the lookout for talented and skilled volunteers, artists, activists and writers to work with. If you have a great idea for a project or can contribute in some way, please get in touch.

PM Press
PO Box 23912
Oakland, CA 94623
www.pmpress.org